Ludwig M. Lachmann

SUBJECTIVISM AND ECONOMIC ANALYSIS

The extraordinary heterogeneity of the scholars interested in the work of Ludwig M. Lachmann – Austrians, Keynesians, Post Keynesians, New Institutional economists, Old Institutional economists and even some Sraffians – testifies to the importance of his ideas. Lachmann made important contributions to the defence and development of the modern Austrian school of economic thought. Few economists have rivalled his willingness to confront problems that appear to fall outside the grasp of the conventional tools of the discipline. His methodological insights in the area of radical subjectivism are particularly important and are the focus of this collection.

The contributions in this volume explore, from a variety of perspectives, the methodological issues raised by Lachmann's work. Leading scholars discuss such issues as:

- the connection of Lachmann's ideas to those of Max Weber
- the critique of equilibrium analysis
- the implications of radical subjectivism for policy activism
- the philosophical foundations of radical subjectivism

Subjectivism and Economic Analysis is a fitting tribute to a ground-breaking economist and makes a major contribution to an important field of research.

Roger Koppl is a Professor of Economics and Finance at Fairleigh Dickinson University, New Jersey, USA. He has published widely in the fields of political economy and economic history. **Gary Mongiovi** is an Associate Professor of Economics at St John's University, New York, USA and co-editor of *The Review of Political Economy*.

ROUTLEDGE FRONTIERS OF POLITICAL ECONOMY

SUBJECTIVISM AND ECONOMIC ANALYSIS

Essays in memory of
Ludwig M. Lachmann

*Edited by Roger Koppl and
Gary Mongiovi*

ROUTLEDGE

London and New York

First published 1998
by Routledge
11 New Fetter Lane, London EC4P 4EE

Simultaneously published in the USA and Canada
by Routledge
29 West 35th Street, New York, NY 10001

Typeset in Garamond by Routledge
Printed and bound in Great Britain by Biddles Ltd,
Guildford and King's Lynn

British Library Cataloguing in Publication Data
A catalogue record for this book is available from the British Library

Library of Congress Cataloging in Publication Data
Subjectivism and economic analysis: essays in memory of Ludwig M.
Lachmann/edited by Roger Koppl and Gary Mongiovi.
Included bibliographical references.
1. Lachmann, Ludwig M. 2. Economics. 3. Economics–methodology.
4. Economics–History–20th century. I. Lachmann, Ludwig M.
II. Koppl, Roger, 1957–   . III. Mongiovi, Gary.
HB107.L33S83   1998
330–dc21   98–7044
                                 CIP

ISBN 0–415–11058–0

CONTENTS

CONTENTS

CONTENTS

CONTENTS

CONTRIBUTORS

Jörg Bibow, University of Hamburg, Germany.

Peter J. Boettke, George Mason University, Fairfax, Virginia.

Maurizio Caserta, University of Catania, Italy.

Lásló Csontos[†], Central European University, Budapest, Hungary.

Steven Horwitz, St Lawrence University, Canton, New York, USA.

Roger Koppl, Fairleigh Dickinson University, Madison, New Jersey, USA.

Brian J. Loasby, University of Stirling, Scotland.

Gary Mongiovi, St John's University, New York, USA.

Stephen D. Parsons, DeMontfort University, Leicester, England.

Jochen Runde, Girton College, Cambridge, England.

Steven T. Sullivan, New York University, New York, USA.

Carlo Zappia, University of Siena, Italy.

1

INTRODUCTION

Roger Koppl and Gary Mongiovi

The extraordinary heterogeneity of the scholars interested in the work of Ludwig Lachmann testifies to the importance of his ideas. Lachmann gets serious attention from Austrians, Keynesians, Post Keynesians, New Institutional economists, Old Institutional economists, and even some Sraffians. Most of these schools are represented in this volume. Even the two editors of this volume are very far apart on issues of political economy, technical economic theory, and methodology. This unusual diversity suggests that what Lachmann had to say was significant. He was working at the foundations of our science, where depth of insight counts for more than technical prowess. And the problems Lachmann found at the foundations have been recognised as important by very diverse economists. The path leading to Lachmann's broad influence led him through four different countries on three different continents speaking two different languages, uniting one very long and distinguished career.

Lachmann's career as an economist began in his native Berlin during the years of the Weimar Republic. In 1924 he enrolled in the University of Berlin where Werner Sombart would become his dissertation advisor. As a member of the 'younger historical school', Sombart had a respect for the ideas of Max Weber and a distaste for the Austrian school. While a student in Berlin, Lachmann hired Emil Kauder as his tutor. Studying both Pareto and the Austrians, they came to view the subjective theory of value as essentially correct and the general equilibrium theory of Walras and Pareto as inadequate. Thus, Lachmann ended his studies in Germany an adherent of both the method of understanding (*Verstehen*) practised by German interpretive sociology and of the Austrian theory of marginal utility.

The intellectual position to which Lachmann was led by his

1

studies with Sombart and Kauder was hardly welcome or natural in German academic circles. The German historical school had always been hostile to the Austrians. Moreover, Lachmann was a liberal and, in his own words, 'support for, and understanding of, the market economy, never very strong in these circles, had almost vanished' by the late twenties (Lachmann 1981). Lachmann was to spend most of his professional life defending positions that were dismissed out of hand by academic orthodoxy.

Lachmann, twice damned as both Jew and liberal, left Hitler's Germany for England in 1933. There he studied under Hicks and Hayek at the London School of Economics. In London, he met another student of Hayek, George Shackle. But it was not Shackle who taught him the importance of expectations in economics. It was through his contacts with another refugee scholar, Paul Rosenstein-Rodan, that Lachmann learned the importance of expectations. Rosenstein-Rodan had been an assistant to Hans Mayer, who held Menger's chair in the University of Vienna. 'It was Rosenstein-Rodan', Lachmann once explained, 'who in discussing Austrian trade cycle theory with me said, "Ah yes, but whatever happens in the business cycle is in the first place determined by expectations"' (Lachmann 1978). The subjectivism of expectations was to become a peculiarly Lachmannian theme.

In the 1930s, Hayek's thought dominated discussion at the LSE. The Great Depression put an end to that. Keynes had the right medicine. Or so it seemed. Hayek and the Austrians were eclipsed. Hicks, Kaldor, Lerner, and Shackle were all carried along in the Keynesian tide. Even Robbins quietly distanced himself from his early indiscretion, the Mises–Hayek theory of the trade cycle. As Walter Grinder (1977) has put it, by the time the war began, 'the only consistent and thoroughgoing Hayekians left were Lachmann and Hayek himself'. Lachmann found himself in considerable intellectual isolation once again, just as in Berlin before.

After a fellowship which permitted him to visit many schools in the United States including the University of Chicago where he participated in Frank Knight's seminar, Lachmann taught at the University of London and then the University of Hull. In 1949, he was appointed to the chair in Economics and Economic History at the University of Wittwatersrand in South Africa. During these years he developed his radical subjectivist position with a constancy of purpose that never flagged in the face of mainstream indifference.

The renaissance of the Austrian school began in the 1970s and soon came to be centred at New York University. Under the direction of Israel Kirzner, a programme in Austrian economics was begun. At Kirzner's invitation, Lachmann was brought to NYU in 1975 as a Visiting Research Professor. Until 1987 when his health prevented it, Lachmann travelled each spring to NYU to participate in the Austrian Economics Colloquium and to give a seminar on 'Topics in Advanced Economic Theory'.

In these final years Lachmann's patient exposition of his radical subjectivist views finally received the sort of attention it deserved. Young Austrians were not the only students coming under his influence. Post Keynesians and other opponents of neoclassical orthodoxy also discovered him. By the time Lachmann died in December 1990 he had ensured a future for his ideas by leaving behind him a large and heterogeneous group of young scholars strongly influenced by his work.

The difficulty in classifying Lachmann according to schools of thought testifies to the originality of his thought. Lachmann is generally thought of as an Austrian economist. And yet the academics who most zealously claim that label generally repudiate Lachmann's views as 'nihilistic'. Lachmann's closest intellectual ally was probably G. L. S. Shackle, a scholar generally counted among the Keynesian or Post Keynesian ranks. Hayek once described Lachmann's *Capital and its Structure* (1956) as containing all that was of value in Hayek's own *Pure Theory of Capital*. Nevertheless, Lachmann was to reject his teacher's definition of economics as the study of the unintended consequences of human action (Lachmann 1986: 32–3). The influence of Sombart was to be reflected in Lachmann's book *The Legacy of Max Weber* (1971b). Sombart may even have been one of the influences encouraging Lachmann to take a sceptical view of the predictive powers of economic theory. As we have seen, however, Sombart's influence was not sufficient to keep Lachmann from identifying with the Austrian tradition of Menger, Mises, and Hayek.

The great variety of influences on Lachmann and the great variety of persons upon whom he had an influence are reflections of a marked openness of his thought and character. Lachmann was personally a very open-minded thinker. He was one of the few serious scholars, for instance, to give careful consideration to the anti-inflation proposal of Abba Lerner and David Colander. (For a time, their proposal was required reading for students in NYU's programme in Austrian Economics.)

Lachmann's attitude towards students was also that of openness. He was always available for discussions with graduate students. He made graduate students feel like equal participants in an ongoing and urgent discussion. He encouraged them to apply their own minds to the issues of economic theory. Lachmann taught his students what the leading problems of economics theory are. He pursued them with undeviating attention. Even when his dentures once fell out during class lecture, he was unperturbed. Wrapping the dentures in a handkerchief and stuffing them in his pocket, he continued to lecture as if nothing had happened. But the grin he could not suppress betrayed his amusement. Perhaps his aplomb on this occasion was a lesson. Let's get on with the business at hand and not be disturbed by such trifles as loose dentures.

Lachmann's openness of mind and spirit was frequently passed on, as if by osmosis, to the students who came under his influence. Lachmann charmed his students and held them, fascinated, in his grip. We believe the ultimate source of Lachmann's magic was a simple characteristic that has become increasingly rare in academe and out: intellectual honesty.

His undeviating pursuit of truth as he saw it led him to a methodological position whose central element is 'subjectivism'. Lachmann's subjectivism embraced three interrelated themes that run through his work: the explanatory primacy of subjective evaluations; the importance of expectations; and the inadequacy of equilibrium models of the market.

Lachmann viewed historical events as the outcome of purposeful human action that originates in the formation of plans. Since it is purposeful action that economists seek to understand, their principal task, according to Lachmann, is to elucidate the mental processes by which plans are formed. Subjectivism is the methodological doctrine that economic explanation must trace all causality to such mental acts, which differ from person to person. This subjectivist view of things is what Lachmann meant by methodological individualism.

Lachmann distinguished three 'levels' of subjectivism (1990). First, the subjectivism of wants recognises that different people have different tastes and pursue different ends. Second, the subjectivism of ends and means recognises that people may pursue similar ends in dissimilar ways. People have diverse, sometimes erroneous, ideas about the best ways to achieve any goal. Finally, the subjectivism of active minds recognises that in all aspects of action the active mind may produce interpretations and possibilities the observing economist cannot imagine in advance. 'The mental activity of ordering and formulating ends, allocating means to them, making and revising plans, determining when action has been successful, all these are its forms of expression' (Lachmann 1982: 37). This is 'radical subjectivism'.

The radical subjectivism to which Lachmann was committed went far beyond the specification of agents' preferences as part of the data which regulate prices, outputs, and distribution in a market economy. His notion of subjectivism derives instead from the fact that agents must form plans on the basis of their interpretation of events that take place in a changing world about which they have incomplete knowledge. The mental acts that precede action are therefore the products of human ingenuity – imaginative responses to the uncertainty of social existence; and they are based to a significant degree on agents' expectations about future states of nature.

As early as 1943 Lachmann insisted that 'it is the subjective nature of . . . beliefs which imparts indeterminateness to expectations as it is their mental nature which renders them capable of explanation' (Lachmann 1943: 72–3). In this essay Lachmann mapped out a position from which he never retreated. Because expectations are themselves shaped by the course of economic events, they cannot be regarded as parametric. Nor, according to Lachmann, can we connect them in any systematic way to observable phenomena: he denies the possibility of establishing any univocal link between events and the expectations to which they give rise. A given configuration of events, he argues, can generate any number of expectational responses. A price rise in a particular market, for example, could lead some agents to expect further price increases and others to expect a reduction in price, with corresponding consequences for their subsequent actions.

Thus expectations 'have to be regarded as economically indeterminate' (ibid.: 67). For underlying the price signals given off by the market, 'there lurks ultimately the problem of interpretation' (Lachmann 1956: 67). This reasoning, according to Lachmann, shatters the usefulness of equilibrium analysis as a device for understanding market-level phenomena (though he allowed a limited heuristic role for equilibrium at the level of the individual economic actor). The problem is that the system has no way of getting into equilibrium, because the market process itself entails continuous revision of the expectations that would presumably be required to sustain such a position. Accordingly, he rejects the notion that theoretical models are capable of predicting what will happen in a particular set of circumstances, because no model can anticipate agents' expectational responses to those circumstances.

Lachmann's radical subjectivism led him to oppose 'late classical formalism' and what he called the 'Neo-Ricardian counterrevolution.' Lachmann coined the term 'late classical formalism' in 1971 to characterise neoclassical economists who had 'adopted an arid formalism as their style of thought, an approach which requires them to treat the manifestations of the human mind in household and market as purely formal entities, on par with material resources' (Lachmann 1971a: 181). This formalism, Lachmann argued, had drained the theory of any value. The theory 'has nothing to say' when 'confronted with real problems' (ibid.: 182). He quotes Mises's diagnosis that the theory is 'A superficial analogy … spun out too long, that is all' (ibid.: 182). Lachmann's summing up is scathing: 'From Walras to Samuelson we find the same manner of reasoning, the same arbitrary assumptions, the same unwarranted conclusions' (ibid.: 189).

Lachmann's radical subjectivism led him to criticise the 'Neo-Ricardian counterrevolution'. As Lachmann used the term, 'Neo-Ricardianism' identified the Cambridge followers of Piero Sraffa and Joan Robinson, the UK side of the Cambridge–Cambridge controversy. Lachmann did not carefully distinguish Keynesian Cambridge economists from Sraffian Cambridge economists, a curious lapse in view of the important methodological differences that distinguish the two traditions. His criticisms relate, in any case, mainly to the Sraffian branch, and were directed at what he regarded as its excessive formalism, at its attachment to the concept of equilibrium, and at its emphatic rejection of subjectivism: 'A style of economic thinking in which there is no place for human preferences, let alone time preferences, is hardly acceptable to the heirs of Menger' (Lachmann 1977: 29). Nevertheless, he did recognise some points of common ground between Austrian and Sraffian criticisms of orthodoxy, in particular concerning the inadequacy of the neoclassical treatment of capital as a value-aggregate; but of course he differed with the Sraffians on how economic theory might be reconstructed to avoid capital-theoretic problems.

For Lachmann 'it is intelligibility and not determinateness that social science should strive to achieve' (Lachmann 1943: 68). We must take account not only of the 'subjectivism of wants' (that is, preferences), but also the 'subjectivism of interpretation'. The proper aim of economic theory, then, is to make events *intelligible* by showing why, in a given episode, a set of facts were interpreted by agents in a particular way.

As the language of Lachmann's 1943 essay shows, the problems of 'interpretation' were central to his understanding of expectations and radical subjectivism. In *The Legacy of Max Weber* (1971b), Lachmann identifies the 'method of interpretation' or, what is the same thing, the 'method of *Verstehen*' as the proper method of the social sciences. This was the same method espoused by Max Weber. Lachmann denied that the method was peculiarly related to the philosophical idealism of the German Historical School from which Weber emerged. It is 'much older than German idealism and the Historical School which, partly, sprang from it. . . . It is nothing less than the traditional method of classical scholarship' (1971b: 18). The method of *Verstehen* is simply the traditional method of interpreting texts, but applied to human action. From about 1980, Lachmann began to use the word 'hermeneutics' to describe this method. Originally hermeneutics was the science (*Wissenschaft*) of interpreting the Christian Bible. But as the term is employed today, it is the same method of classical scholarship that Lachmann extolled.

From Weber, Lachmann also drew insight into the role of institutions. The traditional method of economic analysis explains the co-ordinating function of markets in terms of a process of gravitation towards some well-defined equilibrium position. Lachmann's scepticism towards the notion of equilibrium led him to look elsewhere for the source of social order. He found it in the prevailing institutional framework. Institutions are rules that limit the range of actions individuals are likely to take in a particular situation, as for example, when two cars meet at an intersection. Such rules simplify the formulation of plans by creating a setting within which many sorts of behaviour are governed by convention and can therefore be anticipated with some degree of confidence. In this way a network of social institutions contributes to the co-ordination of the plans of atomistic agents.

An important task of social science, then, is to explain how particular institutions emerged and how they perform their co-ordinating functions. Lachmann's approach to this task involves a more-or-less straightforward application of his subjectivist method. He contends that institutions originate as unintended by-products of purposeful human action (Lachmann 1971b: 67–8). A successful innovative practice, discovered by individuals in the pursuit of their own interests, will be imitated by other individuals who recognise its utility, until it crystallises into standard practice: 'Successful plans thus gradually crystallize into institutions' (ibid.: 68). A systematic statement of Lachmann's views on institutions can be

ROGER KOPPL AND GARY MONGIOVI

found in his book on Max Weber, but he appears to have recognised the important co-ordinating function of institutions much earlier (see Lachmann 1937).

Throughout his long and fruitful career Lachmann embraced problems that fall outside the reach of the conventional tools of economics. His enthusiasm for his subject never waned, though he could not have been unaware that his words were often cast before an indifferent, sometimes hostile, audience. The enduring relevance of his message is evident in the work of Austrian and Post Keynesian scholars who continue to grapple with, and cast new light upon, those same problems.

The characteristic themes and problems of Lachmann's methodological thought have been taken up in various ways by the authors of this volume.

In Chapter 2, Brian Loasby draws on his correspondence with Lachmann to compose an intellectual portrait of him as 'an optimist without illusions.' Loasby shows how several elements of Lachmann's personal and intellectual life fit together. Lachmann's personal openness is related to both his methodological pluralism and his political pluralism. Lachmann eschewed grandiose claims for open societies. In Loasby's interpretation this reflects, in part, Lachmann's own treatment at the hands of powers who thought themselves uniquely competent to judge the truth. Loasby shows himself to share Lachmann's intellectual honesty and humility when he describes his portrait as 'an interpretation' which is 'defensible' but 'certainly not definitive'.

Stephen Parsons in Chapter 3 views Lachmann's notion of 'a Plan' from, e.g., *The Legacy of Max Weber* as both development and criticism of Mises's praxeological theory of action. Lachmann's emphasis on institutions and his later emphasis on 'the context of intersubjective meaning' call into question Mises's claims regarding the role of deduction in understanding human action. They may also induce us to question the 'privileging' of the Cartesian subject characterising Mises's theory of action.

In Chapter 4, Koppl attempts to examine the 'problem of expectations' as Lachmann represented it. Koppl relates the problem to the ideas of Keynes and Mises whose systems are found unable to resolve the problems Lachmann posed. Drawing on Hayek and Schutz, he adumbrates a theory of expectations that satisfies Lachmann's call for a subjectivism of active minds.

The gifted Hungarian economist László Csontos died tragically of congenital heart failure at the age of 43. His work was notable for its deep insight and meticulous argument. Trained in both sociology and economics, Csontos had an extraordinary grasp of the complex relationship between Weber and the Austrians. In the essay posthumously published as Chapter 5 of this volume, Csontos used his rich understanding of Weber's writings on the method of ideal types to argue for a weaker version of methodological dualism than that adopted by Lachmann. Because Lachmann neglected Weber's distinction between subjectively and objectively rational ideal types, Csontos argued, he wrongly imagined his notion of 'Plan' to be a departure from Weber's ideal type. The notion of 'intentional explanation' covers all these cases and brings Lachmann's notion of Plan back under the umbrella of cause and effect. The logical structure of explanation is just about the same in the natural and social sciences.

Drawing on his earlier work with Victoria Chick, Maurizio Caserta in Chapter 6 develops the idea of 'provisional equilibrium' (Chick and Caserta 1994). This concept is an attempt to address the problem of novelty. 'As soon as we permit time to elapse we must permit knowledge to change,' Lachmann argued, 'and knowledge cannot be regarded as a function of anything else' (Lachmann 1959: 92). In Lachmann's system the flow of time and novelty implied that market equilibrium is at best fleeting. Through the device of partial specification, however, provisional equilibria can be defined. These equilibria are provisional because they may be upset by factors that are internal, but not fully specified. Caserta illustrates with an open-economy macroeconomic model.

In Chapter 7, Carlo Zappia uses Karen Vaughn's recent survey of Austrian economics as a springboard for a critical assessment of trends within the school. Vaughn's book, *Austrian Economics in America: The Migration of a Tradition*, is an internal history of the American revival of the Austrian school told by one of its most important leaders. Vaughn concludes her survey with an endorsement of Lachmann's 'clarion call' to build from a more radical subjectivism of real time and incomplete knowledge. Zappia ranges beyond the self-imposed limits of Vaughn's survey to encourage Austrians to incorporate the ideas of such figures as Bowles and Gintis. Unlike most Austrians, who distinguish 'information' from 'knowledge' (see, for example, Thomsen 1992), Zappia argues that a careful consideration of the economics of information greatly weakens Austrian arguments against equilibrium models.

Steven Horwitz in Chapter 8 unites Lachmann's two most important book-length essays: *Capital and Its Structure* (1956) and *The Legacy of Max Weber* (1971b). Horwitz draws on the Austrian theory of capital to criticise lingering elements of objectivism in Lachmann's account of institutions. We often recognise a kind of hierarchy among institutions that puts some in the background as higher-order and unchanging and others in the foreground as lower-order and subject to change. This hierarchy, however, is entirely 'subjective'. Which institutions are background depends on the problem at hand and the perspective adopted. No one 'true' hierarchy exists. Horwitz illustrates with the history of banking. Institutional changes have come about through a kind of dialectic between legal and market institutions. During this dialectic, each set of institutions has been background to the other. The whole institutional structure is characterised by the kind of complementarities and multispecificity discussed in the Austrian theory of capital.

Lachmann has sometimes been called an 'Austro-Keynesian'. In Chapter 9, Peter Boettke and Steven Sullivan ask if such a position can be maintained consistently. Can one advocate radical subjectivism in economic method and Keynesian interventions in economic policy? Drawing, in part, on Lachmann's 1935 MSc thesis, 'Capital Structure and Depression', they show that such a position was adopted by Lachmann. They argue, however, that a non-interventionist policy preference is more consistent with radical subjectivism.

In Chapter 10, Jochen Runde and Jörg Bibow enrich Lachmann's analysis of the influence of expectations on share prices. Lachmann's theory, as developed in Chapter 2 of his *Capital and Its Structure* (1956), concerns the role of divergent or convergent expectations about the value of a financial asset. Drawing on J. M. Keynes and E. M. Miller, Runde and Bibow distinguish between the expectation of a share's future price and the appraisal of its 'correct' value. Liquidity, carrying costs, risk aversion and estimates of the risk aversion of others are just some of the complicating factors driving this distinction.

Each chapter responds to Lachmann's work in a different and challenging way. We submit them to the reader in the hope that he or she will share our enthusiasm for them. We hope the reader will also share our continually enriched appreciation of the ideas of one of the most impressive scholars we have been privileged to know, Ludwig Lachmann.

Acknowledgements

The editors wish to express their gratitude to Don Lavoie, who provided the photograph of Professor Lachmann, which appears in the frontispiece to this volume, and The Mises Institute, for permission to utilise in this Introduction material that has previously appeared in *The Austrian Economics Newsletter*.

References

Chick, V. and Caserta, M. (1994) 'Provisional equilibrium and macroeconomic theory', discussion paper, University College, London.

Grinder, W. (1977) 'In pursuit of the subjective paradigm', Introduction to L. Lachmann, *Capital, Expectations and the Market Process*, Kansas City: Sheed, Andrews and McMeel (1977 edn).

Lachmann, L. (1937) 'Uncertainty and liquidity preference', *Economica* N.S., 4: 295–308.

—— (1943) 'The role of expectations in economics as a social science', in *Capital, Expectations and the Market Process*, Kansas City: Sheed, Andrews and McMeel, pp. 65–80 (1977 edn).

—— (1956) *Capital and Its Structure*, London: Bell and Sons, Ltd.

—— (1959) 'Professor Shackle on the economic significance of time', in *Capital, Expectations and the Market Process*, Kansas City: Sheed, Andrews and McMeel (1977 edn).

—— (1971a) 'Ludwig von Mises and the market process', in *Capital, Expectations and the Market Process*, Kansas City: Sheed, Andrews and McMeel, pp.181–93 (1977 edn).

—— (1971b) *The Legacy of Max Weber*, Berkeley: The Glendessary Press.

—— (1977) 'Austrian economics and the present crisis of economic thought,' in *Capital, Expectations, and the Market Process*, Kansas City: Sheed, Andrews and McMeel, pp. 25–41.

—— (1978) 'An interview with Ludwig Lachmann', *Austrian Economics Newsletter*, 1: 1–15.

—— (1981) 'Foreword', in L. von Mises, *Epistemological Problems of Economics*, New York: New York University Press.

—— (1982) 'Ludwig von Mises and the extension of subjectivism', in I. M. Kirzner (ed.) *Method, Process and Austrian Economics: Essays in Honor of Ludwig von Mises*, Lexington, MA: D. C. Heath.

—— (1986) *The Market as an Economic Process*, Oxford: Basil Blackwell.

—— (1990) 'G. L. S. Shackle's place in the history of subjectivist thought', in S. F. Frowen (ed.) *Unknowledge and Choice: Proceedings of a Conference in Honour of G. L. S. Shackle*, New York: St Martin's Press.

Thomsen, E. (1992) *Prices and Knowledge: A Market Process Perspective*, New York: Routledge.

2

LUDWIG M. LACHMANN

Subjectivism in economics and the economy

Brian J. Loasby

I never met Ludwig Lachmann. I did not even begin corresponding with him until the last years of his life. That was my fault, for I repeatedly delayed taking the opportunity on the insidious excuse that I would have something more interesting to say in a few months' time. I should have been more aware, because of what I had already learned from his work, that he had many interesting things to say at any time. This was immediately demonstrated when I did write, as was the courtesy and intellectual curiosity that impressed so many who knew him and his work much better than I did. Since his objective was to make what contribution he could – and that was not small – to our common understanding of economic questions, and of the ways in which we might best improve that understanding, it seems appropriate in this chapter to outline the themes that I have taken from his publications and from his correspondence with me. (I shall cite his final book, which offers an admirable conspectus of his vision.) As he would be the first to point out, what follows is an interpretation; but since it is based on some shared points of reference – for example, admiration for the work of George Shackle and George Richardson, similar ideas about the compatibility of some of Keynes's major ideas with an Austrian view, the need to enquire into what happens in markets – and since parts of this interpretation were tested in our correspondence, I am reasonably confident that, though certainly not definitive, it is defensible.

Methodology

Ludwig Lachman was a radical subjectivist – too radical for many of his fellow Austrians, for he did not believe it possible to demonstrate that market processes were necessarily always superior to any alternative. There could be serious failures of co-ordination (as will be noted later); and since the market process had no end, no definitive judgement was possible. His advocacy of market systems, which did not preclude specific criticisms, was based on a reasoned faith. Like Sir Karl Popper's advocacy of an open society, which Popper knows is not capable of empirical proof, it reflected both the unreliability of human benevolence and the inadequacy of human knowledge, which were also the grounds of Adam Smith's reasoning. Assume these human limitations away, and it is easy to reach the apparent conclusion of the planning debate, that a planned economy can equal the best that a market system can do, and surpass it in coping with externalities, public goods and the distribution of income. That this conclusion was so widely accepted among economists followed naturally from the use of the very same assumptions in the planning model as underlay the formal analysis of market systems: though these assumptions denied the existence of the fundamental difficulties that face us, they were necessary to arrive at a determinate solution to the twin problems of efficient allocation, as defined by Jevons, and efficient co-ordination, as defined by Walras.

Yet many economists still appear to believe that we do not need to worry about methodology. In fact such economists normally have a strong methodological commitment to the use of formal models, and to the use of whatever false assumptions (such as given tastes, rational expectations and common knowledge) may seem necessary in order to yield a determinate, if sometimes multiple, answer. That false assumptions can lead, not only to false theories, but – more dangerously – to false policies, does not seem to be a possibility that most economists take seriously. Ludwig Lachmann did. Like many Europeans in the 1930s, the course of his life was changed by such a false policy. Moreover, it was not merely false notions of planning that he criticised. Planning in Eastern Europe had been unable to prevent massive malinvestment; but in a letter of 29 April 1990 – a time, it may now be hard to recall, of widespread optimism – he foresaw that 'getting market economies started in Eastern Europe, after half a century, will give rise to a host of problems hardly as yet appreciated'; and on 22 July 1990 wrote: 'The more I think about

Russia the more pessimistic I become. How can this end well? Of course market institutions cannot be introduced by political fiat.' Formal theories of market co-ordination are no less dangerous than formal models of planning.

One should never underrate the ability of very clever people to be very silly, even to the public peril. It was, perhaps, above all as a defence against illusions that Lachmann insisted on maintaining the subjectivist perspective. The economic problem is not to allocate known resources to clearly defined ends, but to make the best of the knowledge that each person has, and of the opportunities that that person can envisage, and also, significantly, to find ways of increasing that knowledge and discovering new opportunities. As Mises above all insisted, it is a problem of human initiative, conditioned by the perception of human circumstances, not of programmed response to objective data. Human activity is problem-solving. This is Popper's view also; and, like Popper, Lachmann saw that problems had to be defined before they could be solved, and moreover, that the way in which they were defined often had a major influence on the solution that was chosen. 'Information' must be interpreted, and interpretation is problematic. All this is true both of the individual agent, and of the observer who is trying to make sense of the individual's actions; my exploration of this perspective in *Equilibrium and Evolution* (1991) owed something to Lachmann, and I greatly regret that I was unable to discuss it with him.

Lachmann was the most resolute advocate of subjectivism as the means of investigating the consequences of individual purposes, understanding and expectations, all of which differ between people, and change with time and experience. He was also the most resolute critic of formalism, in which all these elements are transformed into data supposedly available to the analyst, and usually to the agent as well. It is sometimes asserted that it is important to work out the properties of an equilibrium based on this data, either because, if people eventually learn the true facts, this equilibrium may be interpreted as the destination of a process that is itself too difficult to handle directly or, more ambitiously, that identifying the destination is a useful prelude to investigating such a process. The latter argument, which Walras took very seriously, is rarely heard nowadays, since the algorithms of rational choice, which are supposed to guide, or at least predict, action at all times, are defined only for situations in which everyone other than the chooser is already pursuing an optimal strategy. But since rational choice is believed to be indispensable, the discovery that it requires equilibrium has been used to justify the claim that all situations must necessarily be rational choice equilibria.

Now Lachmann recognised the necessity of abstraction, for every interpretation is an abstraction. Economists and economic agents, all human beings, use models. But the choice of model is not innocuous: 'It does matter which features of reality we accentuate in our schemes, and which we abstract from' (Lachmann 1986: 42). It matters for the management of General Motors just as much as for a monetary theorist; indeed it is characteristic of Lachmann's perspective that the central issues of economic method are the central issues of human action. In neither is there any sure route to success; in both there are many opportunities for failure. One common principle is that the single-minded pursuit of any model, or family of models, will eventually lead one astray. The art is knowing when to stop. This, I suggested in a letter to him, is the central issue in appraising Marshall, who was acutely conscious of the problem; and we can now see, in counterpoint to the standard complaint that Marshall failed to pursue the logic of his models, the occasional suggestion that he pursued that logic too far, and should have given much more emphasis to evolutionary concepts.

Marshall and equilibrium

Lachmann was very sympathetic to Marshall, and to my interpretation of Marshall. In a letter of 22 July 1990 he commented that:

> I know less about Marshall than I should. Moreover some of what I did learn in 62 years has turned out to be wrong. E.g. I learned from Schumpeter that there is no real difference between him and Pareto. This is surely wrong. On the other hand, Schumpeter used to praise Marshall's Book V as the seeds of everything worth studying in economics. The validity of this view now seems to turn on how important equilibrium was to Marshall.

He had earlier (Lachmann 1986: 142–3) praised Marshall's partial equilibrium analysis as 'a model within the framework of which equilibrium and interaction between (a somewhat limited number of) individuals can be reconciled'. If equilibrium entails consistency – because otherwise there is the possibility of changing something for the better – then its extension from a single plan to a set of interacting plans must be problematic, and if this set is expanded into a general equilibrium, especially so. This is why the model of central planning, in which, by definition, there is only a single plan, looks so plausible in comparison with a general equilibrium of independently formulated plans, which seems only too likely to be frustrated by the 'wastes of competition'. But Marshall offers 'a restricted environment as regards time and space' in which an approximate compatibility of plans might be achievable – especially when we pay due attention to Marshall's concern for the pattern of continuing relationships within which the criticism and testing of plans takes place.

In his letter of 22 July 1990, Lachmann went on to agree with me that Marshall:

> was nearer to Menger than to Jevons. This is what has impressed me for some time. Why, then, did he stress equilibrium? I think there is this to consider. An economist espousing equilibrium need not do so because he believes that in the real world equilibrating forces are overwhelming. Few people hold this view. But if we are concerned with 'wealth' and feel we must be able to 'measure' it we will sooner or later find out, as Wicksell did, that such measurement is possible only in equilibrium, hence the latter's importance. Could it be that here we have the real reason why Marshall espoused equilibrium, as he undoubtedly did?

It seems to me that in this paragraph Lachmann illustrates a major theme in the development of economic theory. Adam Smith's initial thesis in the *Wealth of Nations* was that wealth could most effectively be increased through the division of labour, because this led to the continuing development of specialised capabilities. But if we contrast individual self-sufficiency with specialisation, we can immediately identify two problems. Our first thoughts nowadays go to the question of co-ordination; but we may also be concerned how to add up the outputs of all these specialists, in order to see whether the total really is greater than that achievable by self-sufficiency, or indeed by a different degree or pattern of specialisation. Much the best solution to this problem of evaluation is an unvarying measure – if it can be found; and, as we know, Adam Smith and his successors tried hard to find one in costs of production. That an unvarying measure of value could also provide an anchor for the price system, and thus help to co-ordinate specialised activities, was extremely convenient; but we should not forget that the signals on which Smith relied to stimulate movement in the direction of co-ordination through a competitive process which should not be confused with perfect competition, were market prices that were out of line with natural prices. Smith thus had what we would now call both a theory of equilibrium and a theory of equilibration, a combination that has proved beyond the grasp of neoclassical economists.

The logical flaw in Smith's value system is that the process that generates increasing wealth does so by changing the costs of production by which this increase is to be measured. But this difficulty is relatively minor compared with that of basing any kind of natural value in an evolving system upon marginal utility, for economic progress extends consumption to lower-rated uses. The eventual solution was found by postulating a general equilibrium in which price measured not only the marginal utility of every commodity but also its marginal cost, which was itself a precise measure of the marginal utility forgone by not diverting an increment of resources to the best alternative use. It will be observed that this precise measure requires not only general equilibrium, but perfect competition, together with such other well-known conditions as the absence of public goods.

This was not good enough for Marshall, who saw that welfare depended on what happened inside the margin; so he adapted Ricardo's concept of rent to devise a general measure of both producers' and consumers' surplus. In principle, such measures could provide rankings which might be very different from those based on equilibrium values alone, but their validity depended on equilibrium. Although Marshall did not expect that his measures would be adequate for anything more than estimates of the magnitude of changes in welfare as a result of changes within particular industries, even that proved to be an extravagant hope; but it is noteworthy that the measurements employed in cost–benefit analysis rely on Marshall's ideas, and on the conception of equilibrium that underlies them. If the validity of such incremental measurement is doubtful, what are we to make of measures of national income that depend on a set of assumptions that are always violated, and often grossly violated, by the economies to which those measures are applied?

It is easy to understand why some economists are not satisfied with such a basis of valuation, but it is not so easy to agree that

Neo-Ricardian valuation is an adequate alternative. Joan Robinson did not accept it. As Lachmann agreed, in a letter of 17 August 1989, she was never quite a Sraffian. If we do not know how to measure something that we would like to measure, then, as Lord Kelvin remarked, our knowledge may be of a meagre and unsatisfactory kind; but if we insist on fictitious measurement then our knowledge, if apparently less meagre, will be much more unsatisfactory – for it will be false.

Catallactics

Lachmann shared the common perception that in the last quarter of the nineteenth century the focus of economic analysis turned from plutology – the science of wealth – to catallactics – the theory of exchange. Yet catallactics proved to contain a deep internal contradiction. For Lachmann, its essential feature is the exploration of purposeful action: that implies an orientation towards the future, which is unknown, but not unimaginable. Uncertainty – or, as Lachmann's kindred spirit, George Shackle, came to call it, unknowledge – does not imply chaos (Lachmann 1986: 139); reason and experience allow us to create intelligent, if fallible, expectations. But such expectations do have to be created; they cannot be mechanically formed. We may, if we choose, rely on some formal procedure to convert data into forecasts, but the choice is our choice, and any procedure that we choose must itself be a human creation. Even if it were to be, in some sense, a 'correct model', it would nevertheless be a human invention, as is every scientific theory, and its correctness would remain forever open to doubt. Lachmann understood Popper's arguments. But, like many natural scientists, he also understood their liberating potential: predictive failure is an opportunity to improve our knowledge, for we learn as a consequence of our mistakes, and the improvement of our knowledge depends on our ability to make conjectures which go well beyond the evidence (ibid.: 152). That the key to human progress is imagination, and that imagination is inconceivable without 'unknowledge', is a theme that belongs uniquely to George Shackle; but no one was more aware of its significance than Ludwig Lachmann.

Yet such modes of thought are incompatible with modern formalism. Lachmann (1986: 25) endorsed Joan Robinson's complaint that:

> Economic analysis, serving for two centuries to win an understanding of the Nature and Causes of the Wealth of Nations, has been fobbed off with another bride – a Theory of Value . . . economists for the last hundred years have sacrificed dynamic theory in order to discuss relative prices.
>
> (Robinson 1956: v)

We have already seen why the rejection of cost-of-production theories should apparently evoke an urgent need to invent some alternative basis of value, and why utility-based measures should be inadequate unless anchored in a perfectly competitive general equilibrium. We might now observe also that the centre of gravitation provided by 'natural values' had to be replaced by some other principle of co-ordination if economists were to offer a formal solution to the allocation problem in a decentralised economy. Unfortunately the chosen solution to these twin requirements entailed a very high opportunity cost, as Joan Robinson (eventually) and Lachmann clearly realised.

One of the first to recognise the problem was Alfred Marshall; and he was prepared to tolerate a good deal of ambiguity in order to exploit the advantages of mechanical metaphors in the (intendedly) first volume of his *Principles* while maintaining that, even in its foundations, the theme of economics must be 'living force and movement'. Moreover, Marshall believed that he saw an eventual prospect of combining a theory of growth with a theory of co-ordination: co-ordination is achieved, imperfectly and with cyclical lapses, by a combination of organisation and competitive selection, and this combination also provides both incentives and opportunities for the generation of new ideas.

Lachmann became increasingly conscious of his affinity with Marshall: his own account (Lachmann 1986: 16–17) of the intra-market processes of innovative variation and imitation, that transform both products and technology by continuous competitive improvement, is thoroughly Marshallian, with Chamberlinian touches. In a letter of 29 April 1990, he wrote: 'The Firm is very much Marshall's child. Neither Walras/Pareto nor the Austrians know it. Why? What did Marshall need it for?' The prime reason, I suggest, is that firms were the principal agents of the intra-market processes to which Lachmann drew attention – in the British economy, which Marshall knew from his factory visits no less than in the pages of the *Principles*. A second major reason is that his conception of the firm as a source of variation allowed him to construct an industry equilibrium that incorporated ceaseless change. We should never forget that the long-run equilibrium model of the firm, which has become a familiar textbook tradition, though often attributed to Marshall, is actually a rejection of Marshall's theory, for it depicts the extinction of enterprise, and the end of hope.

We should not accuse either Jevons or Walras of a lack of interest in the analysis of economic progress. Jevons died young, with a great potential unrealised, and Walras declared that his eventual objective was to construct a theory of change. But when Walras tried, as an important step towards that theory, to move from equilibration in exchange to equilibration in production, and to do so by means of a theory of entrepreneurial action, he found that disequilibrium production entailed path-dependency, in which equilibria derived from the original data were of doubtful relevance. He was unable to resolve this difficulty, and therefore fell back on a prior co-ordination of pledges to ensure that only equilibrium quantities were ever produced. But, as Lachmann (1986: 118) pointed out, this is a false production economy, and it excludes the means of progress that Walras had himself introduced: entrepreneurial conjectures. Marshall understood that general equilibrium analysis would not allow him to handle creativity and turned in the opposite direction from Walras, in order to preserve the link with the classical tradition. In doing so he implicitly aligned himself with Menger, who had no desire to construct a general equilibrium, preferring the freedom to discuss knowledge, uncertainty and the unintended consequences of purposeful action. An affinity between Marshall and Lachmann, who is perhaps the most Mengerian of Austrian economists, is thus perfectly natural: for this most radical of subjectivists was no less anxious than Marshall to conserve the wisdom of Adam Smith.

Human action

Lachmann shared Marshall's conception of 'the fundamental characteristics of modern industrial life. . . . They are . . . a certain independence and habit of choosing one's own course for oneself . . . a habit of forecasting the future and of shaping one's course with reference to distant aims' (Marshall 1920: 5). Action depends on the knowledge that the actor possesses at the time of action, and the way in which it is used. Even if, as in neoclassical practice, this action is triggered by some exogenous impulse, the actor's knowledge is crucial. It has long seemed to me extraordinary that economists subject the agents in their models to shocks, which by definition are events for which no provision has already been made, and assume that these agents nevertheless know immediately what is the optimal response. Within the logic of a neoclassical model, a shock is a refutation of the agent's interpretative system and requires a reconstruction of the procedure for making optimal decisions. But the recognition that something is wrong is not sufficient to demonstrate precisely what is wrong, let alone how to put it right. Learning from experience, as Lachmann (1986: 46) pointed out, is a problem-solving activity; and we cannot know what people will learn. That it will be 'the correct model' is a presumption that closes the model by closing it against common observation, and begs the question of effective co-ordination, which was once supposed to require analysis.

Lachmann emphasised three aspects of knowledge that receive little attention in mainstream economics: its heterogeneity and the consequent need to impose our personal order upon it; the complementarity of different kinds of knowledge in developing understanding and in formulating a sensible plan of action; and the entanglement of knowledge with time. Because the past is knowable, though not definitively, in a way that the future is not, the flow of time creates knowledge, and simultaneously destroys part of the stock. For none of us is knowledge 'given': it has to be acquired, and outdated knowledge has to be replaced. The economics of information seeks to grasp some of the shadows cast by this process; but it allows only for the progressive elimination of possibilities as they come nearer, not for the continuous creation of possibilities hitherto unthought of. New ideas, even the possibility that there might be new ideas, are outside the scope of formal economics, for how can we model what has not yet been thought of?

Lachmann's view of human knowledge is orthogonal to formal conventions, of game theory no less than general equilibrium. He summarised his criticism in a letter of 13 August 1989:

> In their irrational zeal to imitate the style of classical mechanics neoclassical formalists use the words 'rationality' and 'choice' in such a fashion as to pervert their meaning. For them reason has come to mean the maximisation of GIVEN functions! Choice has come to designate situations in which it cannot exist! With a 'given' preference set, what choice do we have? It is clear that those who have

perpetrated these confusions are confusing human action with mere reaction to changing circumstances. Our mind is in continuous motion, making and ordering experience. The formalists confuse this activity with its momentary product, which is an order, but not one that could last.

When people try to work out what to do they break problems up into manageable units; and if we wish to understand human action so must we. I do not know what Lachmann thought of the ways in which Herbert Simon used his concepts of decomposability and bounded rationality, but he certainly made effective use of similar ideas. Instead of general theorising about 'the market process', it was necessary to get down to the detail of particular markets, and subsequently to explore inter-market relationships. Lachmann's emphasis can be clearly differentiated from that of both Schumpeter and Kirzner: unlike Schumpeter, he believed that most progress resulted from a multitude of specific changes within particular markets, and unlike Kirzner, he believed that people were creative and not merely alert – the ten-dollar bill had to be imagined before it could be brought within one's grasp.

These differences arise from a more fundamental distinction: Lachmann insisted not only that all action, and all thought, relies on rules and conventions, but that these rules and conventions are likely to vary between markets in ways that significantly affect the course of history. In a letter of 2 July 1989 he wrote:

> I entirely agree with you when you exhort us Austrians to pay more attention to institutions and organisations. . . . In fact my Chapter 6 is at bottom an attempt to explain fixprice markets of our world in terms of their institutional and organisational peculiarities, with salesmen and the hierarchies to which they belong rather than merchants.

In that chapter (Lachmann 1986: 103–38), Lachmann explores the causes and consequences of the different ranges of action envisaged by different classes of agent, noting (ibid.: 120–1) that in Keynes's *General Theory* entrepreneurs have a much wider range than workers. Realising the potential gains from the division of labour requires a standardisation of tasks and, to a substantial extent, of the products that result from those tasks. And so markets in which production costs are falling are likely to be markets in which customers are not only price-takers but product-takers, dependent for their range of choice on the ways in which entrepreneurs exploit their own broader scope for initiative. The large organisations that deliver these standardised products must also restrict the range of action of their employees – notably of their salesmen, for the advantages of efficient production must not be frittered away in the costs of negotiating prices and conditions with every customer. Whether the need for conformity in large organisations can be reconciled with the encouragement of initiative through 'empowerment' is a question currently being explored in many companies. If it is to be achieved, it will clearly require new institutions, probably in some variety to suit different specific situations.

Industrial markets in which there are few customers each placing large orders operate with different conventions, and there are other kinds of markets with their own particular patterns of behaviour, and variations between classes of participants in the degree and kind of discretion. All these patterns are open to challenge, and many are challenged, sometimes successfully. The process of institution building has no determinate conclusion. Here is scope for a major Austrian programme of empirical research, of a kind without precedent in economics. It would be much more like business history than econometrics, but if, as Lachmann agreed with Hicks, economics is on the edge of history, why not?

In any study of particular markets, we should not forget the obvious point, on which Mises insisted, that goods are exchanged for money. The analysis of a barter economy is not sufficient for an economy that runs on money and credit. Credit in particular, as Lachmann (1986: 85) reminds us, is endogenous: its creation requires agreement between lender and borrower, and thus a perceived convergence between their purposes and between their interpretations of the appropriate ways of achieving them. So much is obvious from any reasonably diligent observation of financial markets. Convergence does not mean identity: in some transactions, for example where there is a pooling of risk, something very close to identity is required, but a banker making a secured loan is much less interested in the profitability of the business than in the prospective value of the hypothecated assets in the best alternative use to which they could be put should that business fail; and in speculative markets it is the conflict of expectations that motivates agreement on a specific transaction. Financial markets cannot be properly understood by postulating a representative market, any more than interaction between individuals can be understood by postulating a representative agent.

Financial assets provide purchasing power; but they also provide the power to delay purchases, in the hope of seizing future opportunities, to allow speedy response to future threats against which no satisfactory insurance can be purchased, or simply while attempting to assess the significance of some development. The implications of such delays for the co-ordination of economic activities will be considered shortly, but first we should give due credit to Lachmann's recognition that people may also develop the power of future action by the accumulation of physical assets. Indeed, the durability of physical assets impels their owner to look to the future, which cannot be known. No one has given more emphasis than Lachmann to the importance of capital combinations, which enable complementarities to be exploited for specific purposes, but at some inevitable cost in flexibility.

Capital and capabilities

Economists who have little sympathy for Austrian conceptions have paid attention to capital combinations only as part of the conditions of equilibrium, either in neoclassical terms or as an implication of the gravitational principle of a uniform rate of profit; but the practical question for those who have charge of capital is how to shape their own particular combinations to suit their own particular purposes in the light of their own particular knowledge and expectations. As Menger taught us, there are no goods without knowledge, and what good is constituted by a particular assemblage of capital is determined by those who are contemplating its use. This good changes as knowledge changes, even if there is no change in the capital instruments. Capital combinations must be understood in terms of their orientation. The need to review the orientation of a firm's capital, and to reshape it accordingly, as knowledge, expectations and innovative ideas change, implies a particular concern for the problems of capital maintenance. Lachmann (1986: 68–70) reminded us that the preservation of a constant income stream can hardly ever be secured by the direct replacement of particular items as they wear out, or even by the purchase of improved equipment sufficient to maintain production of unchanged products at an unchanged rate. Keynes's (1936: 69–70) user cost, which influences the entrepreneur's choice between conserving or using up his equipment, depends on 'the expected sacrifice of future benefit', and this expectation is likely to differ between firms, and to change over time.

Since, as Lachmann insisted, the plans of individuals, or of organisations, rest on complementary assemblages of knowledge and of other kinds of capital, the productive capacity of an economy depends upon complementarities, which are partly crafted, but also partly the unintended consequences of human action which was directed towards other purposes. People learn by doing, by using (Rosenberg 1982: Chapter 6) and by choosing (Woo 1992: Chapters 5 and 6); but neither they nor we, as analysts or observers, can foresee what they will learn. Here Lachmann's perspective comes very close to that of Penrose (1959), and it comes even closer in his emphasis on the orientation of each particular capital combination, which is equivalent to the 'productive opportunity' available to those in charge of a Penrosian firm. This productive opportunity, like Lachmann's orientation, is subjective, but not arbitrary.

Lachmann's treatment of capital combinations, and particularly their relationship with complementary structures of knowledge and the overriding importance of orientation, give him a substantial claim to be recognised as a founder of the modern capability-based theory of the firm. He recognised that complementarity often dominates relationships between particular pairs or groups of firms, and that when it does it may need to be managed by working agreements, as has been argued by Richardson (1960, 1972), whom Lachmann admired (letter of 2 July 1989). Relationships between the capital combination that is embodied in a particular firm and those who buy and sell the shares that are its financial counterpart may not be so easy to manage because stock exchanges are merchants' markets, in which participants can be either buyers or sellers, switching rapidly between the two, and entering and leaving the market at will, whereas the managers of the firm are committed to their side of the markets in which they operate, and to the capital structures that they have built up. This particular kind of intermarket relationship deserves particular attention.

I would much like to have heard Lachmann's comments on Alfred Chandler's (1992) argument that some of the major problems of the American economy have resulted from the attempt by many business leaders to behave as merchants, buying and selling companies or divisions of companies, at the expense of their traditional role of shaping the capabilities of their businesses to match their changing long-term visions of the markets in which those capabilities are to be used. A portfolio of businesses can be swiftly rebalanced, but the capabilities that constitute the productive assets within that portfolio cannot. Nor can the relationships between those capabilities. This seems to be precisely the type of analysis for which Lachmann argued, and it exposes the limitations of contemporary theories of corporate governance.

Co-ordination

The analysis of economic processes operating within and between markets offers a distinctive perspective on the co-ordination of economic activities. The economic problem is the continual creation of order on the basis of continually changing knowledge, which is widely dispersed and always imperfect. It is a problem that is never perfectly solved, and that Lachmann, unlike most Austrian economists, insisted could sometimes prove too difficult for a market system, because the requisite knowledge was not available or not effectively communicated. If the division of labour promises greater productivity but imposes greater demands for co-ordination, the division of knowledge promises an increase of local knowledge but threatens to prevent the effective communication, and in particular the shared interpretation of communication, that effective co-ordination requires.

Each person tries to construct a plan that is internally consistent, for there are always gains from eliminating inconsistency. Moreover, one can learn more from the failure of a plan, as from the failure of a scientific hypothesis, if it is internally consistent and the failure of plans, as of scientific hypotheses, is a necessary, though not sufficient, condition of progress. That a perfectly co-ordinated economy is an economy in which progress has ceased is a thought that might disturb some orthodox economists; it is a thought that impelled Schumpeter, despite his great admiration for Walras's achievement, to go outside Walras's theory for an explanation of economic development.

Because agents' plans are based on different knowledge and different expectations about an unknowable future, there is no reason to believe that they will be entirely compatible, even within a single market. Will they be adjusted towards compatibility? They may be, but the process may be impeded by differences in interpretation – Why did customers refuse to buy? Why do our competitors seem to have lower costs? – by divergent expectations, and by unexpected changes. Learning by doing, using or choosing may lead different people in different directions, as Penrose (1959) observed, although the institutions of a particular market, like the institutions of a scientific community, may inhibit conjectures. Often there will be no wish to make plans compatible. As we have previously noted, speculation depends on a conflict of expectations, that must lead to the frustration of some plans. In his letter of 17 September 1989, Lachmann commented that Hayek was never interested in speculation, and that Mises, who was, failed to see its significance for the analysis of co-ordination. And so it was left to Shackle to point out that a speculative equilibrium must necessarily be based on incompatible plans. But speculation is by no means the only problem, as Lachmann (1986: 5) knew very well. Even the simple act of arbitrage with which Kirzner (1973) introduces his concept of entrepreneurship is designed to invalidate the plans of high-price sellers and low-price buyers: and the process of competition – in contrast to the myth of perfect competition – entails the deliberate collision of plans. That the competitive ideal should have become a model of perfect co-ordination exemplifies the ability of economists to exclude from their analysis the problems that they set out to solve.

Inter-market co-ordination is also problematic. Walras recognised that the attainment of a general equilibrium could be assured only by simultaneous contracting. Where this does not happen, the sequence in which markets operate may be important. Changes that improve co-ordination in one market are likely to disrupt plans in other markets; and the chain of responses – which are based, let us not forget, on human interpretation of what has happened, and human forecasts of what will happen next – may move the economy away from, rather than towards, general equilibrium. This is particularly likely if people are unsure of their interpretations, lack confidence in any forecast they can make and, as noted earlier, decide to delay commitment to any new plan until prospects appear clearer.

The importance of business confidence in maintaining high levels of activity was clearly recognised by both Marshall and Keynes; and Keynes incorporated it into the simplest possible kind of inter-market analysis with his division between investment (much of which could not, Keynes insisted, be based on probability judgements) and consumption goods, in which equilibrium within the former market set the conditions for the latter. Lachmann, like all Austrians, was not happy with such a level of aggregation, but he emphasised the importance of complementarity. In a world full of substitutes, nothing actually matters very much: as Fogel (1964) demonstrated, the United States could have managed very well without the railways, and in such a world each of us could manage very well without any particular item of consumption or any particular job, because a slight adjustment of aspirations would immediately produce an acceptable alternative. But that is not our world and the dangers of complementarity are the obverse of the opportunities that it brings.

'Every market of course tends to eliminate excess demand or supply, but may do so by quantity, not price adjustment, and thus engender multiplier effects' Lachmann wrote on 17 September 1989. However, these effects are not adequately represented by a mechanical sequence. Lachmann echoed Ohlin's (1937: 239) criticism of Keynes's formulation, which was based on the Swedish conception of subjective expectations: consumption decisions, like production and investment decisions, depend on assessments of future prospects, and though these assessments are influenced by the past they are not determined by it. Consumption, like investment, can change without any change in the data; and it does. In this, as in other respects, Lachmann was a constructive as well as a sympathetic critic of Keynes, and believed that the quarrel between Keynes and the Austrians was quite unnecessary: 'This is a view I have held for a long time' wrote Lachmann on 13 August 1989. He recognised Keynes as a major, if not always consistent, proponent of subjectivist ideas, and the Austrians had no explanation of general unemployment.

Conclusion

Lachmann was a thoroughgoing subjectivist. Subjectivism is an epistemological stance that does not imply the rejection of a substantive reality; it certainly does not imply that 'thinking makes it so'. But it does imply that thinking depends on interpretative frameworks, that no framework can be comprehensive and that logical argument, though necessary for consistency, is insufficient for truth. The future is unknowable. But though mistakes are therefore inevitable, creativity is thereby made possible.

Lachmann was consistent in the application of his scheme of thought to the economy and to the practice of economists. There were no determinate equilibria, and no proofs of any persistently dominant tendencies to co-ordination – not by the exercise of rational choice, nor by reason of gravitational principles, nor by evolutionary selection, nor even by unimpeded market processes; nor was there any uniquely correct way of doing economics. The discipline of economics, the economy and the polity were therefore best ordered as open and pluralist societies. This was a practical appraisal, but also a moral judgement, for Ludwig Lachmann had experienced the consequences of a belief by the powerful that they had access to the truth, and was rightly disturbed by the evidence of such belief among some of the most powerful within the profession of economics. He was correspondingly ready to acknowledge (in his letter of 2 July 1989) that Frank Hahn 'is really much too intelligent and sensible a man, and too good an observer of the academic scene, to be happy with neoclassical formalism'.

Economic agents and economists are human, with human powers, human propensities and human limitations. By assembling complementary capabilities in pursuit of a well-ordered plan, they can achieve a great deal, but by attempting to assemble all the capabilities of a society within a single plan they forgo many possibilities. Moreover, those people who believe themselves capable of directing such a plan are almost certainly unfit for the task, both intellectually and morally; and if they are not unfit when they undertake it, they can hardly fail to become so. Co-ordinating a multitude of plans is very costly, never completely successful, and continually needs to be redone; and the process is marked by some spectacular failures, the penalties for which are distributed without much regard for merit. To make strong claims for pluralistic, open societies is to court disappointment; but it is reasonable to believe that they are less bad than any alternative. This, on my interpretation, was Lachmann's view. He was an optimist without illusions.

References

Chandler, A. D. (1992) 'Corporate strategy, structure and control methods in the United States during the 20th century', *Industrial and Corporate Change*, 1: 263–84.

Fogel, R. W. (1964) *Railroads and American Economic Growth: Essays in Econometric History*, Baltimore: Johns Hopkins University Press.

Keynes, J. M. (1936) *The General Theory of Employment, Interest and Money*, London: Macmillan.

Kirzner, I. M. (1973) *Competition and Entrepreneurship*, Chicago: University of Chicago Press.

Lachmann, L. M. (1986) *The Market as an Economic Process*, Oxford: Basil Blackwell.

Loasby, B. J. (1991) *Equilibrium and Evolution*, Manchester: Manchester University Press.

Marshall, A. (1920) *Principles of Economics*, 8th edn, London: Macmillan.

Ohlin, B. (1937) 'Some notes on the Stockholm Theory of Savings and Investment, Part II', *Economic Journal*, 47: 221–40.

Penrose, E. T. (1959) *The Theory of the Growth of the Firm*, Oxford: Oxford University Press.

Richardson, G. B. (1960) *Information and Investment*, Oxford: Oxford University Press.

—— (1972) 'The organisation of industry', *Economic Journal*, 82: 883–6.

Robinson, J. (1956) *The Accumulation of Capital*, Cambridge: Cambridge University Press.

Rosenberg, N. (1982) *Inside the Black Box*, Cambridge: Cambridge University Press.

Woo, H. K. H. (1992) *Cognition, Value and Price*, Ann Arbor: University of Michigan Press.

3

MISES AND LACHMANN
ON HUMAN ACTION

Stephen D. Parsons

In his book on Weber, Lachmann sets out a framework for investigating human action, which he retained in his final works (e.g. Lachmann 1990). Lachmann's analysis is interesting for a number of reasons. First, from the perspective of the history of Austrian economics, Lachmann must have been aware of the extent to which his approach would be controversial. Lachmann claims to 'carry forward Weber's ideas in the circumstances of today' (Lachmann 1971: 1), although recognising that Weber, as a student of Schmoller, 'remained very much the heir of the German Historical School all his life' (ibid.: 17). This, of course, was the very school that Menger had subjected to a rather vitriolic attack. Further, Weber was a friend of, and influenced by, Rickert, whom Mises had similarly accused of being 'bound to historicism' (Mises 1981: 5).[1] There thus arises the suspicion that, in drawing his analysis of human action from the one provided by Weber, Lachmann may be adopting a perspective that earlier Austrians had specifically rejected.

Second, although Lachmann's analysis was published in 1971, it anticipates, in significant ways, some of the arguments recently advanced in the philosophy of action (e.g. Bratman 1987). Third, once this perspective on Lachmann's argument is appreciated, his analysis can be read as an implicit critique of the rational choice theory that underpins conventional neoclassical economics.[2] Fourth, given the above, it is somewhat surprising that Lachmann's analysis appears not to have been taken up by economists sympathetic to the Austrian tradition.[3]

It will be argued that Lachmann's theory of human action, rather than signifying some betrayal of the Austrian tradition, can be

31

interpreted as an attempt to develop a more coherent understanding of human action than that prevalent in the work of Mises. This is because Mises's account is deficient both in terms of his understanding as to how human action is to be investigated and in his understanding as to what human action consists of. In fact, these two problems are interrelated: it is precisely because of his methodological approach that Mises encounters problems in explaining human action. Lachmann's theory can thus be understood as a criticism of and an attempt to resolve difficulties in both Mises's and rational choice theories of human action. These theories can be classified together in this respect because Lachmann is implicitly drawing attention to a problem they both share: explaining future intentions.

Mises and Lachmann on history and economics

Initially, it seems quite clear that Mises and Lachmann are in direct opposition concerning the subject matter of economics. Mises defined economics as an a priori universally valid science of human action:

> The science of human action that strives for universally valid knowledge is the theoretical system whose hitherto best elaborated branch is economics. In all its branches this science is a priori, not empirical . . . it is not derived from experience; it is prior to experience.
>
> (Mises 1981: 12–13)

The science of human action, or praxeology, was concerned with establishing certain universal categories, which are necessary with reference to human action: 'The cognition of praxeology is conceptual cognition. It refers to what is necessary in human action. It is a cognition of universals and categories' (Mises 1949: 51).

The 'necessity' referred to here is meant in a dual sense: the a priori categories of human action are required both in order to act and in order to comprehend the actions of others. As praxeology was a 'cognition of universals', then it could not comprehend the individual and unique. Because the unique could not be brought under universal categories, it was 'irrational', and thus the concern of history, not economics: 'Individuality is given to the historian, it is exactly what cannot be exhaustively explained or traced back to other entities. In this sense individuality is irrational' (Mises 1990: 12).

Mises is not making some ontological claim to the effect that reality is 'irrational'. Rather, he is advancing and claiming that any explanation of individuality cannot claim to be either 'exhaustive or unique' (ibid.: 13). It is impossible to indicate what would count as an exhaustive or unique explanation of individuality, as 'history can be written from different points of view' (ibid.: 12). In this Mises follows Rickert,[4] for whom 'reality is irrational in the sense that there is no criterion that can specify what would constitute a complete description of its aspects' (Oakes 1986: xvii).[5]

For Mises, as history, but not economics, was concerned with the individual, it attempts to understand the meaning of action: 'Understanding of the meaning of action is the specific method of historical research' (Mises 1990: 12).

In direct contrast to Mises, Lachmann attempts to develop a theory of action relevant to economics that commences from 'the Weberian notion that action derives its meaning from the mind of the actor' (Lachmann 1971: 9), or from the individuality that, for Mises, was the concern of the historical method. According to Lachmann, the emphasis on individual meaning signified 'a "positive" method of the German Historical School which Weber took over and adapted to his purpose' (ibid.: 10). The differences seem quite clear: from Mises's perspective, Lachmann is interested in the methods of history, not those of economics.[6]

Lachmann's implicit rejection of Mises's framework is quite understandable if it can be argued that Mises's attempt to derive certain a priori categories of human action is both futile and sterile. An argument along these lines would certainly be sympathetically received by Coddington:

> If subjectivist logic is followed to the point of becoming convinced that there is nothing for economists to do but to understand certain (praxeological) concepts, then the only problem that remains is that of subjugating one's conscience long enough to draw one's salary in exchange for imparting this piece of wisdom.
>
> (Coddington 1983: 61)

In contrast to this dismissal, it is quite plausible to argue that certain aspects of Mises's appeal to the a priori can be defended. However, such an argument does not signify that Lachmann's analysis must thus be rejected. This is because a modified notion of the a priori, although possibly necessary in order to grasp human action, is insufficient in elucidating the nature of human action. Consequently, rather than viewing Lachmann as rejecting Mises's account, it is quite plausible to argue that Lachmann's account is supplementary to that of Mises. However, not surprisingly, this argument does require the rejection of Mises's strict demarcation between economics and history.

Mises and the a priori

Mises and Lachmann are both strongly anti-naturalistic in their understanding of economics, believing that there is a sharp demarcation between the methods of economics and the natural sciences. With Lachmann, this anti-naturalism constitutes both a reason why Weber's work maintains significance and serves to distinguish Austrian and neoclassical economics:

> Weber espoused the method of interpretation (*Verstehen*) for the social sciences. In economics today the prevailing style of thought is a neoclassical formalism which is quite untouched by Weber's methodology and inclined to take it for granted that the methods of the natural sciences are the only scientific methods known to man. We shall try to show why in our view this is a field in which the dissemination of Weberian ideas promises to yield a rich harvest.
>
> (Lachmann 1971: 2)

In contrast, Mises rejects the relevance of a Weberian-inspired *Verstehen* for the reasons already indicated. As individuality is irrational, it is not possible to provide any unique interpretation: 'The experience with which the social sciences have to deal is always the experience of complex phenomena. They are open to various interpretations' (Mises 1990: 18).

It is precisely because experiences are open to various interpretations that economics must proceed deductively. Consequently, economics cannot appeal to experience in order to validate its theorems. This is because the striving for universally valid knowledge cannot be threatened by experiences open to a multiplicity of interpretations: 'The social sciences can never use experience to verify their statements. Every fact and every experience with which they have to deal is open to various interpretations' (ibid.: 5).

Given Mises's explicit rejection of the relevance of the historical method for economics, it may initially appear puzzling that he also, like Lachmann, indicates the significance of meaning for the social sciences: 'What makes natural science possible is the power to experiment; what makes social science possible is the power to grasp or to comprehend the meaning of human action' (ibid.: 9).

However, by 'comprehending the meaning of action' in economics, Mises does not refer to the Weberian notion of understanding meaning. Mises distinguishes the comprehension of meaning into two kinds: conceiving the meaning of an action, which is the concern of economics; and understanding the meaning of action, which is the concern of history. The distinction between conceiving meaning and understanding meaning is both important yet not immediately obvious. According to Mises:

> We conceive the meaning of action, that is to say, we take an action *to be such*. We see in the action the endeavour to reach a goal by the use of means. In conceiving the meaning of an action we consider it as a purposeful endeavour to reach some goal, but we do not regard the quality of the ends proposed and the means applied. We conceive activity as such, its logical (praxeological) qualities and categories.
>
> (Mises 1990: 9, emphasis added)

This statement is amenable to a number of interpretations. First, Mises could be arguing that we require certain a priori concepts in order to identify anything *as* human action, where human action is necessarily means/ends orientated. Second, Mises could be arguing that we must be in possession of concepts applicable to types of action, in order to comprehend any individual instances, or tokens, of any type of action. For example, we must be in possession of the concept of 'means' in order to comprehend any specific action as 'means/ends orientated'. Third, Mises could be arguing that every action can only be comprehended if we can apply the whole range of praxeological concepts to each action. Unfortunately, each of these interpretations receives textual support from Mises's own writings.

To appreciate some of the ambiguities in Mises's position, take the following argument:

> Economics therefore is not based on or derived (abstracted) from experience. It is a deductive system, starting from the insight into the principles of human reason and conduct. As a matter of fact all our experience in the field of human

action is based on and conditioned by the circumstances that we have this insight in our mind. Without this a priori knowledge and the theorems derived from it we could not at all realize what is going on in human activity. Our experience of human action and social life is predicated on praxeology and economic theory.

(Mises 1990: 9)

Ambiguities arise because Mises appears to:

1 conflate phenomenological and epistemological concerns. He refers both to our ability to experience something as human action and our specific knowledge concerning human action;
2 distinguish between a priori knowledge and theorems derived from it, yet argue that both are somehow necessary in order to 'realize what is going on in human activity';
3 distinguish between praxeology and economic theory, yet again argue that both are necessary in order to experience human action.

The weakest, yet most readily defensible, claim advanced by Mises can be interpreted in the following manner: in order to identify or recognise any movement as a human action, then we are a priori committed to ascribing certain concepts to this action. This could be termed the 'Davidsonian argument': 'If we are intelligibly to attribute attitudes and beliefs, or usefully to describe motions as behaviour, then we are committed to finding, in the pattern of behaviour, belief and desire, a large degree of rationality and consistency' (Davidson 1980: 237).

Davidson further argues that this a priori commitment to viewing behaviour as goal-orientated rational behaviour distinguishes the social sciences from the natural sciences:

Since psychological phenomena do not constitute a closed system, this amounts to saying they are not, even in theory, amenable to precise prediction or subsumption under deterministic laws. The limit thus placed on the social sciences is set not by nature, but by us when we decide to view men as rational agents with goals and purposes.

(Davidson 1980: 239)

Arguments similar to these can be readily extracted from Mises's work. For example, Mises argues that we can only differentiate intentional action from reactive behaviour if we assume that all intentional action is rational:

> Praxeology does not employ the term *rational*. It deals with purposive behaviour, i.e., human action. The opposite of action is not *irrational behaviour*, but a reactive response to stimuli on the part of the bodily organs and of the instincts, which cannot be controlled by volition. If we were to assign a definite meaning to the term *rational* as applied to behaviour, we could not find another meaning than: the attitude of men intent on bringing about effects.
>
> (Mises 1990: 23)

Consequently, it could be argued, from Mises's position, that we are a priori committed to discerning rationality in purposive behaviour. In other words, the concept of rationality is 'a priori' in so far as it must be employed *prior to* identifying anything *as* action. As action is assumed, a priori, to be rational, then a certain 'principle of charity' is in operation: we must assume that, from the perspective of individual actors themselves, they are acting rationally:

> In speaking of human action, we have in mind conduct that, in the opinion of the actor, is best fitted to attain an end he wants to attain, whether or not his opinion is also held by a better informed spectator or historian.
>
> (Mises 1990: 45)

The problem Mises is addressing can be formulated thus: we do not first identify an action, and then work out whether or not it is rational. Rather, in identifying anything as a human action, we already assume, or assume 'a priori', that this action is rational. Consequently, Mises is appealing to a much broader conception of rationality than that operating in rational choice theories:

> Economics does not deal with an imaginary *homo economicus* as ineradicable fables reproach it with doing, but with *homo agens* as he really is, often weak, stupid, inconsiderate, and badly instructed. . . . Its theorems are valid for all actions. . . . It is the scope of history and not of praxeology

to investigate what ends people aim at and what means they apply for the realization of their plans.

(ibid.: 24)

Whereas rational choice theory is normative, in the sense that it stipulates how individuals ought to behave if their behaviour is to be characterised as 'rational', Mises's theory assumes a priori that all human action is rational, and thus economics 'does not deal with the ought, but with the is' (ibid.: 23). Consequently, on this interpretation, Mises is arguing that we are a priori committed to viewing human behaviour as rational and purposive, and we must make this commitment a priori to identifying ('comprehending') anything as an action.

Given this, as economics is concerned with human actions that can only be recognised as such through certain constitutive principles, then economics is logically prior to the historical concern with the individual. As noted earlier, history is concerned to 'grasp the meaning of individuality' (ibid.: 12). However, in order that the meaning of any individual action can be understood, this individual action must have already been identified as an action. Consequently, praxeology is not only distinct from historical investigations, but historical investigations presuppose praxeology: 'The radical empiricism of the historicists went astray in ignoring this fact. No report about any man's conduct can do without reference to the praxeological a priori' (ibid.: 49).

From this perspective, it can be argued that praxeology is concerned to establish the most basic concepts relevant to identifying motions as actions. Unfortunately, as noted, Mises's writings also appear to vindicate alternative interpretations. For example, Mises argues that:

If we had not in our mind the schemes provided by praxeological reasoning, we should never be in a position to discern or grasp any action. We would perceive motions, but neither buying nor selling, nor prices, wage rates, interest rates, and so on.

(Mises 1949: 40)

If this is taken as arguing that we must be a priori committed to applying certain concepts to motions in order to render them intelligible as human actions, then the 'Davidsonian argument' finds additional support. However, if Mises is also attempting to establish that the various 'theorems' of marginal analysis that have been deductively arrived at are also necessary to comprehend human action, then this is a substantially stronger claim. In other words, why exactly are the concepts of 'buying', 'selling', etc., being introduced in connection with 'praxeological reasoning'?

One way of reconstructing the argument is as follows. Mises does recognise that, in order to 'have' a concept, we must both be able to think coherently with it and to recognise things in the world to which it applies. Consequently, Mises could be taken as arguing that, unless we know how to use the concept of, say, 'buying', we would discern only unintelligible motions. We must be capable of applying the type concept 'buying' to any individual actions that fall under this type. Further, presumably if we are to construct an economic theory concerned with the activity of buying, then we must be able to locate this concept, and thus use it in thinking, within a system of other concepts.

However, if Mises's argument is reconstructed in this form, then a number of problems surface. First, it is not clear why such concepts can claim an a priori status: they may just be learned, say, through socialisation. Second, the a priori categories Mises is concerned with must be both necessary and universal. This could mean either that all concepts are required in order to comprehend all possible human actions, or that all are required in order to comprehend each individual action. The former is considerably weaker than the latter, and would seem to run foul of the problem discussed in more detail below. It would seem to require that we know which concepts to apply to which actions, although it is only through these concepts that we can comprehend any actions at all.

This leaves the third possible interpretation of Mises's argument, which appears relevant to statements such as:

> No report about any man's conduct can do without reference to the praxeological a priori. There is no human action that can be dealt with without reference to the categorical concepts of ends and means, of success and failure, of costs, profit or loss.
>
> (Mises 1990: 49)

This implies that, in order to conceive the meaning of any action whatsoever, we must be able to apply concepts such as 'costs' and 'loss' to it. This suggests that Mises is attempting to establish that conceiving the meaning of *any* action requires *all* the concepts relevant to a marginal analysis. It is extremely difficult to appreciate how such an extravagant claim could be defended.

This problem is compounded by a related issue. Mises subscribes to the Cartesian assumption that it is the content of our own consciousness that can be most reliably known, and this forms the background to the attempt to indicate how various a priori concepts can be determined. Consequently, his 'natural' assumption is that, as these concepts are necessary in order to grasp the meaning of any action, and as 'we' act, they can be arrived at through an examination of our own consciousness:

> To the obvious question, how a purely logical deduction from aprioristic principles can tell us anything about reality, we have to reply that both human thought and human action stem from the same root in that they are both products of the human mind.
>
> (Mises 1990: 11)

The various problems indicated earlier cannot be avoided. Mises moves from the phenomenological concern with experiencing action to the epistemological concern with our knowledge of action, from a priori concepts to the concepts of marginal analysis, from praxeology to economic theory. At one level, Mises can be interpreted as starting from the premise that we must assume and ascribe rationality to individual actors in order to identify their 'movements' as actions in the first place. This indicates that we cannot identify human action independently of the a priori concepts that permit this identification in the first place. However, this argument becomes confused with that of establishing the 'truths' of marginal analysis. Further, given the lack of discrimination between phenomenological and epistemological concerns, Mises thinks he is justified in adopting a 'first person' approach. Consequently, given the argument that thought and action spring from 'the same root', Mises thinks that we can arrive at deriving the concepts of marginal analysis solely from analysing thought:

> However, what we know about our action under given conditions is derived not from experience, but from reason. What we know about the fundamental categories of action . . . is not derived from experience. We conceive all this from within.
>
> (Mises 1981: 13–14)

However, action and thought are quite distinct: because 'the mind' is necessary to identify action does not mean we can 'read off' certain truths about action directly from it. Mind might be necessary for identification, but it is not sufficient: we also require the actions themselves. Mises thus obliterates the differences between comprehending human action and performing valid deductions from the axioms of marginal analysis, between establishing the necessary conditions for comprehending action and establishing certain a priori 'truths'.

In summarising the above, two points are worth emphasising. First, certain of the concepts Mises defines as 'a priori' appear more basic, in the sense of possibly being universal, than others with regard to human action. Concepts such as 'rationality' and 'purposive' are significantly more general than concepts such as 'buying' or 'profits'. The less generalised concepts appear in the analysis because Mises confuses *comprehending* action with *explaining* action with the assistance of marginal theory. Second, we cannot, solely from an investigation into the contents of consciousness, recognise things in the world to which concepts apply. In order to justify our 'having' a concept, it is not sufficient to indicate how it coherently integrates with other concepts.

Expanding on the first of these points: the question of the universality of a priori concepts raises problems for Mises's analysis. As noted, Mises lists the concepts of ends and means as a priori praxeological categories. He also refers to the concept of causality as 'a category or an a priori of thinking and acting' (1962: 20), yet admits that the concepts of means and ends presuppose the category of causality (1958: 92). This suggests that Mises acknowledges some form of hierarchy within the various a priori categories. Now it may be plausible to defend the category of causality as a priori, as Kant himself argued.[7] However, as Mises himself recognises (1958: 92), the category of causality is also applicable in the natural sciences. Consequently, within the hierarchy of a priori categories, some, like causality, are universally applicable, whilst others, such as means and ends, are only applicable to human action. However, this implies that we must already know, prior to using any a priori categories of human action, that we *are* applying them to human action, and not to natural events. Yet it seems that it is only *because of* the a priori categories that we can comprehend anything *as* human action. Thus we must have comprehended certain movements as human actions, and not natural events, prior to the possibility of us being capable of so comprehending them.

Given these various problems with Mises's account, it is fruitful to make the transition to Lachmann's explanation of human action. Earlier it was suggested that Mises's sharp demarcation between the methods of economics and the methods of history cannot be sustained. It has been argued that Mises's defence of an a priori economics is not sustainable, although it may be possible to defend the weaker claim that comprehending human action requires some form of a priori concepts or principles.[8] However, in so far as only this weaker claim seems capable of defence, then Mises's claim that we can somehow 'deduce' truths about human action a priori must be rejected. Consequently, although we may now know how human action is to be approached (through constitutive concepts or principles), we do not know of what such action consists. Indeed, because Mises is committed to an a priori approach, his analysis of human action is deficient, and requires supplementing with Lachmann's account. In appreciating how, their different understandings as to what human action consists in must be investigated.

The problem of future intentions

Ebeling outlines Mises's theory of human action as follows. Purposeful behaviour is characterised by:

> Dissatisfaction with existing or expected conditions or circumstances; and imagined preferred state of affairs; and beliefs that methods were or could be available to bring about the desired change. 'Action' was a relationship between chosen ends, selected means and conduct or conscious behaviour to achieve the ends preferred with the means available.
>
> (Ebeling 1994: 87)

Consequently, we have a desire or preference, beliefs and conscious behaviour. In contrast, Lachmann suggests that conscious behaviour can only be understood in the context of 'a plan'. Consequently, Lachmann argues that the historian: 'Has to ascertain "The Plan", the coherent design behind the observable action in which the various purposes as well as the means employed are bound together' (Lachmann 1971: 20).

The argument that purposive or intentional behaviour can only be understood in the context of a plan is reiterated by Lachmann in a later work: 'Phenomena of human action . . . display an *intrinsic* order we dare not ignore: that which the human actors assigned to them in the making and carrying out of their plans' (Lachmann 1990: 136, emphasis in original). Lachmann can thus be perceived as raising two objections to Mises's analysis. First, purposive or intentional behaviour can only be adequately comprehended in the context of plans. Second, this necessitates a focus on the individual. Through detailing problems with Mises's account of human nature, it will be argued that Lachmann is correct on the first point, although the second point requires some modification.

Mises's emphasis on desires or preferences and beliefs, but not plans, suggests that his account of human action can be identified in terms of drawing a conclusion from an Aristotelian practical syllogism.[9] Consequently, we have, for example:

Major premise: I desire to eat something sweet;

Minor premise: I believe that the eating of this cake is the eating of something sweet;

Conclusion: Therefore, I eat this cake.

This is also the understanding of action underlying modern rational choice theory (Sugden 1991). However, there is a major problem with this understanding of human action. Say I desire to avoid pain and believe that going to the dentist will lead to my incurring pain, then I conclude that I should avoid going to the dentist. However, I also desire that my broken tooth no longer disfigures my appearance, and believe that going to the dentist will lead to my broken tooth being repaired, and thus conclude that I should go to the dentist. Consequently, my desires and beliefs lead to contradictory conclusions. The problem here is that we may want to reflect upon our desires and beliefs, and modify them. However, there is no component with the Aristotelian practical syllogism that allows for such reflection.

This immediately raises a problem for Mises's argument. According to Mises: 'Praxeology . . . does not enter into a discussion of the motives determining choice. . . . It deals with the choosing as such, with the categorical elements of choice and action' (1990: 20–1).

However, if it is *intrinsic to* the nature of choice that acting individuals reflect upon the 'motives determining choice', then any theory attempting to encompass the nature of choice must include this act of reflection as one of the 'categorical elements of choice'. Certain elements Mises wishes to exclude from praxeological consideration appear not to be capable of omission. Thus, according to Mises: 'The ultimate judgements of value and ultimate ends of human action are given for any kind of scientific inquiry; they are not open to further analysis' (1949: 21).

However, if these ends are not merely 'given' to the actor, but arrived at through reflection, and thus they are subject to further analysis by the actor, how can praxeology ignore this feature of human action, yet claim to grasp 'the categorical essence of choice and action as such' (Mises 1990: 21)? If it is part of the 'essence of choice' that ends are reflected upon, this must form part of the praxeological concern. Lachmann himself saw problems with Mises's account here, arguing that 'since ends lie in the unknowable future, how can they be "given" to us?' (Lachmann 1982: 38).

The severity of this problem for Mises can be appreciated if an attempt is made to modify his account to accommodate this problem. It could be argued that human action must be taken as corresponding to an 'unconditional' or 'all out' evaluative proposition that an action is desirable.[10] Thus, in the case of the visit to the dentist, after weighing various considerations, I would arrive at an 'all out' judgement that going to the dentist was desirable. As Bratman (1985) points out, this indicates that evaluative conclusions are both implicitly comparative and concern particular actions, not types of actions: for example, certain ways of doing things may be undesirable.

Yet if evaluative conclusions concern particular actions, not types of action, then they would appear not to be of any concern for praxeology, for whom the particular is the concern of history. However, if human action necessarily entails evaluative conclusions, yet these refer to particular actions, not types of actions, then we have a universal feature of human action that can only be made sense of in connection with particular actions. Mises's claim that praxeology, as a priori, is concerned with 'the pure elements of setting aims and applying means' (1990: 21) becomes highly suspect, as the 'purity' of these elements is directly threatened: the 'elements of setting aims' only appear comprehensible in the context of specific actions.

Mises desires to establish the investigation of human action on an a priori basis. However, if individuals do have incompatible ends, then any 'setting' of aims must refer to the actual context within which an action occurs. Further, if an individual is indifferent between alternative means to satisfy a particular end (say, there are two possible keyboard keys that can produce the same sign), then, again, any relationship between ends and means cannot be deduced a priori:

> If the antecedent situation contains the agent's having a desire for each of two or more incompatible ends or her being indifferent between alternative means to an intended end, then it has the potential to explain in the reasons way whichever of the alternative actions occurs.
>
> (Ginet 1990: 147)

However, being capable of reconstructing the reasons for an action from an antecedent situation is emphatically not the same as deducing everything about action from reason.[11] In taking this further, it is necessary to supplement Ebeling's initial account through reference to Mises's notion of 'setting aims'. According to Mises:

> Praxeology does not deal with technological problems, but with the categorical essence of choice and action as such, with the pure element of setting aims and applying means. . . . Praxeology deals with choice and action and with their outcome.
>
> (Mises 1990: 21)

The reference to 'setting aims', and the acknowledgement that action is purposive, allows the idea of intentionality to be introduced. Thus, according to Mises, action consists in desiring some preferred state of affairs to those pertaining at present, believing that certain actions would lead to this preferred state of affairs, aiming (or intending) to bring about this state of affairs, and consequently performing the required action.[12] Mises's theory thus shares the following assumptions with many theories of action, including rational choice theories (Bratman 1987):

1   the methodological priority of intention in action;
2   the desire–belief theory of intention in action. That is, the assumption that we understand intentional action, and action done with an intention, in terms of an agent's desires and beliefs, where actions stand in appropriate relations to those desires and beliefs;
3   the strategy of extension. The assumption that once we have an adequate account of acting intentionally and acting with an

intention we have all the necessary materials for a satisfactory treatment of future-directed intentions;

4   combining 2 and 3 above: the reduction of future-directed intentions to appropriate desires and beliefs.

It has been argued above that assumption 2 raises problems for Mises's own theory. However, assumptions 3 and 4 also raise problems, a possible resolution of which leads directly into Lachmann's theory of human action.

According to Bratman (1987), the attempt to extend an intentional account of action to deal with future-directed cases results in two problems. The first problem is analogous to the problem encountered by Buridan's ass. Bratman argues that rational intentions should be agglomerate. That is, if at one and the same time I rationally intend, or aim, to A and rationally intend, or aim, to B then it should be both possible and rational for me, at the same time, to intend or aim to A and to B. Thus, if two actions are known to be compatible, I can have the intention or aim to perform both, as well as the separate intention or aim to perform each. Also, if two actions are known to be incompatible, I cannot have the intention or aim to perform both. However, suppose, on my way back from work one evening, I can stop at either of two book shops, but not at both, and that both options are attractive. That is, I form an all-out judgement that stopping at one is as desirable as stopping at the other. In this case, do I have both intentions or aims, or do I have neither intention nor aim?

The second problem can be illustrated as follows. Suppose I want to buy copies of two books, and I know I will be in a certain bookstore. Further, I know that the bookstore will have one of the books, but not both, and do not know which one. In this case, although I intend or have an aim to buy both books, I believe I cannot. However, as I cannot intend or aim to do what I do not believe, then I cannot have the required intention or aim.

Bratman argues the problems with theories sharing the above assumptions is that they do not recognise that we form future intentions as parts of larger *plans* whose role is to aid the co-ordination of activities over time. Consequently, Bratman argues that the desire/belief/reason model can only have relevance if it is situated within the context of plans. Practical reason thus has two levels. On one level there are prior intentions and plans, which both pose problems and provide filters on options as potential solutions. On another level are desires, beliefs and reasons, which enter as considerations to be weighed in deliberating between relevant and admissible options.

If future intentions are necessary and sufficient conditions of intentional action, yet such intentions are only intelligible within the context of plans, then there would appear to be good reasons as to why Lachmann's account of human action appears preferable to that offered by Mises. In defence of this, it seems quite plausible to argue that correctly following a future intention is a sufficient condition of intentional action, in the sense that if someone has a future intention and correctly follows it in behaving, then this behaviour is an intentional action of theirs (Moya 1990). However, establishing future intentions as a necessary condition of fully intentional action is more difficult. The problem here concerns whether there are intentional actions which are not intended. If there are such actions, then future intentions are not necessary conditions of intentional action.

The following example, again drawn from Bratman, reveals the problem. Suppose during a war a commander encounters a village that is full of both enemy soldiers and civilians. The commander weighs his options, and considers that bombing the village in order to kill the enemy soldiers is a viable option, even though it will involve the killing of innocent civilians, which the commander very much regrets. If the bombing takes place, it is intentional under three descriptions – (i) bombing the village; (ii) killing enemy soldiers; (iii) killing many innocent civilians. However, although the action is intentional under these three descriptions, it is only intended under the first two. It is necessary to make this distinction to differentiate this act from one where the commander may want to kill the civilians, and thus, in bombing the village, intends to do just that. However, if the action of killing civilians is intentional, although not intended, then a future intention is not a necessary condition of fully intentional action.

However, two points are relevant. First, it has been argued that this problem is not as intractable as it may initially appear (see Moya 1990). Second, it would also appear to raise problems for Mises's account of human action. This is because, to adopt Mises's preferred terminology, the action detailed above is describable as purposive under three descriptions, yet only as aim-directed under the first two. However, it would seem that Mises regards all purposive behaviour as aim-directed, or as orientated towards ends. Therefore, if there are intentional actions that are not intended, or purposive actions that are not orientated towards ends, these raise at least as many problems for Mises's account as for Bratman's. Consequently, a defence of Mises could not appeal to such action in order to rebut Bratman's argument that an adequate account of human action must take account of individual plans. Given this, Lachmann's own account of human action requires investigating in more detail.

Lachmann on human action

Lachmann's notion of a plan allows him to bring the relationship between the method of understanding, action and meaning together as follows:

> All human action, if it is to be successful, requires a plan to guide it. To understand an action means to understand the plan which is being carried out here and now . . . all action derives its meaning from the plan which guides it.
> (Lachmann 1971: 12)

The plans that actions derive their meaning from have several characteristics. First, as Mises also recognised, individuals may desire to pursue a number of incompatible ends. Lachmann's argument here is that it is precisely through a plan that agents are able to establish some priority amongst these ends: 'In fact, "plan" is but a generalization of purpose. In reality actors, individuals as well as groups, pursue many purposes simultaneously and have to establish an order of priority amongst them' (Lachmann 1971: 33).

This is strongly reminiscent of Bratman's argument, noted earlier, that plans act as 'filters'. For Lachmann, in so far as plans allow purposes to be ordered, they also enable a 'comprehensive survey of means' (Lachmann 1971: 30) to be undertaken, and thus allow a coherent arrangement of means and ends to be formulated. It is the task of the social scientist to understand this coherence. Therefore, as noted previously, the historian:

> Must ask how far the variety of purposes pursued by the individual whose action he studies . . . 'fitted together'. He has to ascertain 'The Plan', the coherent design behind the observable action in which the various purposes as well as the means employed are bound together.
> (ibid.: 20)

As situating means and ends within a coherent whole, plans introduce a certain stability into human action:

> Human action is not determinate, but neither is it arbitrary. It is bounded . . . by the circumstances that, while men are free to choose ends they pursue, once they have made their choice they must adhere to it if consistent action with a chance of success is to be possible at all.
>
> (ibid.: 37)

Plans thus do not merely arrange means and ends coherently, they entail a certain commitment. Once an individual is committed to a certain plan, then this plan is adhered to. Consequently, with his notion of a plan, Lachmann can explain how future-directed intentions play a role in the period between the initial formation of any plan and its eventual execution:

> The fact . . . that human action exists in the form of plans, i.e. mental design, before it is carried out in time and space, permits us to study the relationship between human action and the plans which guide it.
>
> (ibid.: 30)

Of course, the commitment entailed in following a plan does not mean that plans cannot be modified or even abandoned. As plans may require revision in the light of new knowledge, they must be flexible:

> Every plan of course has to be flexible to succeed. The need for flexibility partly stems from the fact that some of the knowledge relevant to the action will only be acquired *in agendo*, i.e. after the plan has been drawn up and the course of action started.
>
> (ibid.: 40)

Plans thus enable the provision of coherence amongst actions, entail commitment, incorporate the significance of future intentions and require flexibility. Lachmann thus argues that his analysis of the significance of plans allows human action to be investigated in the spirit of Weber's analysis:

> In social theory our main task is to explain observable social phenomena by reducing them to the individual plans (their elements, their shape and design) that typically give rise to them. This is what Weber meant by the explanation

of action 'in terms of the meaning attached to it by the actor'.

(Lachmann 1971: 31)

Lachmann takes this Weberian legacy seriously: the notion of a plan provides 'a firmer and more convenient starting point for the methodology of the social sciences than the controversial notion of the Ideal Type' (ibid.: 33). Lachmann thus appears to accept Schutz's (1972) criticism of Weber's 'ideal type'. For Weber, the 'ideal types' were both methodological constructs that permitted the social scientist to investigate social life and yet were themselves generated in social life. However, as Schutz noted, if 'ideal types' were generated in everyday social life, then the social scientist had no privileged access to them. Lachmann also intends his 'plan' to signify a phenomenon generated by individual actors themselves (Lachmann 1971: 29).

However, although Lachmann's explanation of human action can consequently be read as an advance upon, and improvement of, Mises's own account, it generates certain problems of its own. In attempting to extend Weber's own analysis, Lachmann acknowledges that Weber identified purposes as causes of action. Lachmann situates this concern for a causal explanation within his exploration of the significance of plans as follows:

> It is readily seen (with the benefit of hindsight) that this conception of the nature of causal explanation of human action in terms of purposes would have provided a firmer and more convenient starting point for the methodology of the social sciences than the controversial notion of the Ideal Type. It is also easy to see how it is naturally linked to our concept of Plan. In fact, 'plan' is but a generalization of purpose.

(Lachmann 1971: 33)

However, Lachmann appears to be unaware of the extent to which his incorporation of the 'plan' into the investigation seriously disrupts the possibility of introducing causal explanation in the required form. Lachmann argues that the coherence of any plan can be tested on two levels:

1 whether the purposes he ascribes are in fact consistent with one another and fit into the framework of a general plan, the execution of which would account for the known facts;

2   whether the design and execution of such a plan are in fact
    consistent with whatever else is known about the intentions,
    circumstances, etc. of the individual whose action is the subject
    under study (ibid.: 20).

However, Lachmann does not appear to acknowledge the difference
between following a plan and acting according to a plan (Brand
1984). An individual may have a consistent plan, and the execution
of this plan may 'account for the known facts', but this does not
entail that the individual is following the plan correctly. For
example, an individual may be presented with a complicated mathematical puzzle, may indicate what plan they will pursue in
attempting to arrive at a solution, may arrive at the correct solution,
yet may not have followed the plan correctly. That is, the individual
may have made mistakes, yet arrived at the correct conclusion.
Consequently, even if we know what an individual's plan is, and
know that this is coherent, and can explain the 'known facts' with
this plan, we cannot conclude that, therefore, there is some form of
causal relationship between the plan and the 'known facts'. We need
to know that the plan has been followed correctly, and this
inevitably introduces a normative element into the investigation:
we need to establish how the individual ought to have acted, not
just how he or she did act.

The question of the relationship between Lachmann's own analysis and that provided by Weber raises further problems for the
former's account. In connection with the question of meaning,
Lachmann notes that 'natural phenomena have no "meaning"', and
thus sides with Weber against Menger: there are no 'exact laws'
governing economic conduct analogous to those found in nature.[13]
As the study of economic conduct requires the understanding of
meaning, then it is committed to the 'method of *Verstehen*'.
Lachmann consequently describes his own theory of action as
'inspired by the Weberian notion that action derives its meaning
from the mind of the actor' (Lachmann 1971: 9).

However, from Weber's perspective, there is a problem with this
argument. For Weber, reference to the individual mind is neither
necessary nor sufficient for understanding meaning:

The 'conscious motives' may well, even to the actor
himself, conceal the various 'motives' and 'repressions'
which constitute the real driving force of his action. Thus
in such cases even subjectively honest self-analysis has

only a relative value. Then it is the task of the sociologist to be aware of this motivational situation and to describe and analyse it, even though it has not actually been concretely part of the conscious intention of the actor.

(Weber 1978: 9–10)

Weber's reference to the 'motivational situation' does not appear to be recognised in Lachmann's account. In Weber's analysis, understanding the subjective, or intended meaning of any action requires a reference to the context, which Weber calls *Sinnzusammenhang*. This is usually translated as 'meaning complex' or 'context of meaning'. For example, Weber argues that 'we understand the motive of a person aiming a gun if we know that he has been commanded to shoot as a member of a firing squad, that he is fighting against an enemy, or that he is doing it for revenge' (Weber 1978: 9). We may know the meaning of any action when we know the intention it was performed with, but this does not reduce meaning to a solely mental product:

> For a science which is concerned with the subjective meaning of action, explanation requires a grasp of the complex of meaning in which an actual course of understandable action thus interpreted belongs. In all such cases, even where the processes are largely affectual, the subjective meaning of the action, including that also of the relevant meaning complexes (*Sinnzusammenhang*), will be called the intended meaning.
>
> (ibid.)

Lachmann's interpretation of Weber is perhaps understandable, given the argument that Weber's methodological pronouncements tend to reduce the emphasis on 'meaning complexes': 'Weber paid considerable attention to the way individual motivation was embedded in larger complexes of meaning and it was only that his vital methodological statements appeared to give less weight to this vital element in his work' (Albrow 1990: 127).

However, even if Lachmann's interpretation of Weber is understandable, it is unfortunate. In attending solely to the interpretation of meaning in terms of the 'mind of the actor', Lachmann invites the following comparison with textual analysis:

> Whenever one is in doubt about the meaning of a passage
> one tries to establish what the author 'meant by it', i.e. to
> what ideas he attempted to give expression when he wrote
> it. . . . It is evidently possible to extend this classical
> method of scholarship to human acts other than writings.
>
> (Lachmann 1971: 10)

Lachmann's explorations of the understanding of meaning thus
bear a strong psychological imprint – it is a matter of discovering
what lies in the mind of the other. However, as Gadamer notes,
psychological understandings of the act of interpretation 'presuppose that only a mind on the same level can understand another
mind' (Gadamer 1979: 466). Lachmann's account of understanding
meaning has unfortunate consequences for his understanding of the
relevance of plans.

Lachmann wants to continue what he identifies as the Austrian
tradition's emphasis on subjectivism. Consequently, according to
Lachmann, even given the same 'objective' situation, different individuals will respond differently because they regard the situation
with 'different eyes' (1971: 11). In line with the possibility of incor-
porating future intentions within his analysis, Lachmann gives this
observation a temporal slant: any attempt to understand human
action must take account of differences in perceptions of the future,
and thus 'to understand it (human action) we have to understand
what image of the future the actors are bearing in their minds'
(ibid.).

However, in fleshing out this observation about the relevance of
images in terms of plans, Lachmann also acknowledges that plans
can only be formulated in the context of what he terms 'institutions':

> Human action in society is interaction. Each plan must
> take account of, among many other facts, favourable and
> unfavourable, the plans of other actors. But these cannot be
> known to the planner. Institutions serve as orientation
> maps concerning future actions of the anonymous mass of
> actors.
>
> (Lachmann 1971: 12–13)

However, if institutions serve as 'orientation maps', then unless
any individual is conscious, at the time of formulating plans, of the
complete institutional context within which these plans are formu-

lated, then the meaning of action cannot be deduced solely from the contents of consciousness. Lachmann's problem here surfaces in an ambiguity concerning the notion of 'orientation'. In the above, institutions serve as 'orientation maps' which, presumably, must be taken account of by any individual when formulating a plan. However, Lachmann also argues that: 'Orientation entails plan. A plan has to contain a comprehensive account of ends, means, and obstacles to which a course of action is orientated' (ibid.: 38).

This appears to suggest that orientation is only possible through, and because of, the formation of a plan. 'Planning' thus allows orientation to ends, means and obstacles to occur:

> What we may hope to accomplish here is to be able to show to what ends, means, and obstacles human action is orientated. *Orientation* thus emerges as a concept as fundamental to praxeological study as determinateness to natural science.
>
> (ibid.: 37)

However, if a plan provides a form of horizon that enables an orientation to means, ends and obstacles, how do we first become aware of, and thus orientate ourselves towards, certain possible ends, means, and obstacles? Lachmann appears to neglect the consideration of the context within which plans are formulated. Again, this can be contrasted to Weber:

> Weber differentiates the concept of practical rationality from the three perspectives of *employing means, setting ends, and being orientated to values*. The instrumental rationality of an action is measured by effective planning of the application of means for given ends; the rationality of choice of an action is measured by the correctness of the calculation of ends in the light of precisely conceived values, available means, and boundary conditions; and the normative rationality of an action is measured by the unifying, systematizing power and penetration of the value standards and the principles that underlie action preferences.
>
> (Habermas 1984: 172)

It is some understanding of what is here referred to as the 'orientation to values' that appears missing from Lachmann's account. Consequently, a hiatus between the individual actor and the institutional context within which plans are formulated appears. This is significant in terms of the history of Austrian theory, because Lachmann is consequently unable to link the methods of the historian with those of the social scientist, including the economist. At one level, Lachmann attempts to forge this link by arguing that plans are 'observable':

> To understand an action means to understand the plan which is being carried out here and now. A phenomenon of human action is an observable event; so, in principle, is the making of plans. . . . Plans, strategic, economic or otherwise, are observable events.
>
> (Lachmann 1971: 12)

However, even if individual actions are observable events, the making of individual plans is not necessarily so. Further, given the distinction between following a plan and acting according to a plan, we cannot deduce the nature of a plan being followed from resultant actions. Consequently, Lachmann is forced to admit there exists an apparently unbridgeable gulf between the respective methods of the historian and the social scientist:

> There seems to be no reason why a method which is useful in the explanation of individual action should be less so in the explanation of classes of such actions. . . . It is true that in explaining recurrent patterns of action, the essential subject-matter of all social sciences, we cannot provide such explanation in terms of purposes, as elements of plans, because the purposes pursued by millions of people are of course numbered in millions. But often we are none the less able to provide explanations in terms of the elements common to all these plans, such as norms, institutions, and sometimes institutionalized behaviour. . . . As long as we are able to account for the recurrence of patterns of action in terms of such elements of plans, we are successfully employing the classical method of interpretation.
>
> (Lachmann 1971: 22–3)

Although Lachmann commences his argument by stating that the methods of the historian are equally applicable to the social scientist, he is forced to admit that the social scientist is interested not in individual plans as such, but in the 'elements common to all these plans'. Because Lachmann has not incorporated norms, from the start, in the context of the setting of individual plans, we are left with a gulf between the methods of the historian and the social scientist, between the individual actor and the institutions of society. Lachmann starts from the individual, in keeping with his desire to maintain the Austrian emphasis on subjectivism, and then attempts to incorporate institutions within an account that is conceived, from the start, individualistically.

In his later work, Lachmann modifies his analysis to take account of the context within which human action occurs:

> Most economic phenomena are observable, but our observations need an interpretation of their context if they are to make sense and add to our knowledge. Only meaningful utterances of a mind lend themselves to interpretation. Furthermore, all human action takes place within a context of 'intersubjectivity'; our common everyday world (the Schutzian 'life-world') in which the meanings we ascribe to our own acts and those of others are typically not in doubt and taken for granted.
>
> (Lachmann 1990: 138)

However, if interpretations are 'context dependent', and yet these contexts are 'taken for granted', then they are not necessarily accessible to individual consciousness. Consequently, in situating 'meanings' within a context which may simply be 'taken for granted' by the author, and in engaging in acts of interpretation from within our own 'taken for grantedness', any act of interpretation necessarily transcends the self-understanding of the author.[14]

Conclusion

Lachmann's analysis of the relevance of 'a Plan' in understanding human action allows for a resolution of some of the problems facing Mises's account of human action. In his later work, Lachmann acknowledges that these plans are formulated within a 'context of intersubjective meanings' (Lachmann 1990: 139). If this is the case, then the institutional context within which plans are formulated is relevant on two levels. First, it must be taken into account, even if only implicitly, by individual actors. Second, it must be taken into account in interpreting human action.

However, this argument raises a number of problems for

Austrian economics. If human actions can only be understood within a context, then any claim that certain truths concerning human action can be arrived at deductively is simply wrong. Further, if emphasis is now placed on the intersubjective context within which any human action occurs, then the much vaunted 'subjectivism' of Austrian economics would seem to be compromised. The Cartesian privileging of 'the subject' fits rather uneasily, if at all, within intellectual traditions stressing intersubjectivity.[15] These are major issues that clearly warrant more detailed examination. However, it is difficult to appreciate how 'Austrian economics' can avoid confronting them. Unless the difficulties in Mises's project can be resolved in an alternative manner, then, despite the possibility of defending a weak notion of 'the a priori', Lachmann's analysis would seem to form a viable starting point for any Austrian discussion of human action.

Notes

1 As Ebeling observes 'but Mises believed that Weber had remained too much the child of the German Historical School, with its theoretical relativism' (Ebeling 1994: 86).

2 Lachmann himself does not explore how his theory differs from rational choice theory.

3 In a recent collection of essays devoted to Austrian economics (Boettke and Prychitko 1994), several authors refer to 'plans'. However, there does not appear to be any awareness that this emphasis raises questions for rational choice theories.

4 Rickert was a leading Neo-Kantian philosopher. For a more detailed discussion of Mises's relationship to Rickert, see Parsons (1990).

5 Rickert's reference to the irrationality of reality was meant phenomenologically: it referred to our experience of reality. As noted below, Mises tends to confuse phenomenological and epistemological questions.

6 According to Mises, historical concepts are type concepts, or 'ideal-types', which organise data into classes. As such, they are 'inexact' in the sense that, as mental constructs, they simplify reality. To use Mises's own example, the type concept 'entrepreneur' refers to a class of individuals engaged in business who, in other regards, differ greatly. In contrast, in economics, the concept 'entrepreneur' refers to a 'specific function, that is the provision for an uncertain future. In this respect everybody is an entrepreneur . . . it is not the task of this classification in economic theory to distinguish men, but to distinguish functions' (Mises 1990: 14). Again, as economics is not concerned with individuality, it does not matter that all individuals are not only entrepreneurs, or that they perform this function in different ways.

7 For a defence of Mises's argument concerning the a priori status of the category of causality along Kantian lines, see Parsons (1997).

8 Boettke and Prychitko argue that a formal, deductive theory is one of the defining characteristics of Austrian theory, stating that praxeology is:

> a strictly formal, logically deductive approach that starts from allegedly self-evident axioms (such as the claim that individuals act purposively), and attempts to derive apodictically certain (logically irrefutable) conclusions . . . a praxeological economic theory which is grounded upon an absolutely true axiom (or set of axioms) generates absolutely true conclusions.
>
> (Boettke and Prychitko 1994: 288–9)

I have argued that a distinction must be made between any a priori concepts relevant to comprehending human action and the axioms of marginal analysis. If a formal deductive approach is a defining characteristic of Austrian theory, then this approach requires considerably more defence.

9 This is also the view espoused by Bhaskar: 'Aristotle was correct: the conclusion of a practical syllogism is an action' (Bhaskar 1979: 122).

10 This discussion of the problem with the Aristotelian syllogism and subsequent attempt at modification reflect the problems that Davidson (1980) came to recognise with his own account of human action. Initially, Davidson characterised intentional action as action explicable, in appropriate ways, by appealing to the agents' reasons for acting, where these reasons are appropriate pairs of agents' desires and beliefs. Consequently, in acting for a reason, there is an appropriate desire–belief pair that causes the action – hence, the practical syllogism. For an attempt to introduce a causal theory of action into Austrian concerns, see Mäki (1990). Unfortunately, and somewhat surprisingly, Mäki does not discuss Davidson.

11 At issue here is not only Mises's claim that 'what we know about our action under given conditions is derived not from experience, but from reason' (Mises 1981: 13–14), but also his claim that 'economics too can make predictions in the sense in which this ability is attributed to the natural sciences' (ibid.: 118). If desires or preferences are incompatible, or there is indifference between means, then predictions are not possible.

12 The introduction of intentionality does not remove the problems discussed above.

13 Weber denied Menger's contention that the 'laws' governing economic conduct (among which was Menger's own creation, the law of marginal utility) are 'exact laws' in the same sense as those found in nature. . . . In fact, abstract economic theory consisted essentially of rational schemes in which the conditions of successful action were defined in such a way as to require certain kinds of action. This is something very

different from the way in which natural events are 'determined' by their causes.

(Lachmann 1971: 25–6)

14 This is the argument advanced by Gadamer (1979). To put this argument in Lachmann's terms: any act of interpretation makes us aware of elements of both our own 'taken for grantedness' and that of the author.
15 Husserl encountered severe problems in attempting to retain a Cartesian subject and yet emphasise the importance of 'the lifeworld'. If the notion of intersubjectivity is and the context of meaning is fleshed out in either Wittgensteinian or Heideggerian terms, then any 'subjectivism' is seriously curtailed.

References

Albrow, M. (1990) *Max Weber's Construction of Social Theory*, Basingstoke: Macmillan.

Bhaskar, R. (1979) *The Possibility of Naturalism*, Brighton: Harvester.

Boettke, P. J. and Prychitko, D. L. (1994) 'The future of Austrian economics', in P. J. Boettke and D. L. Prychitko (eds) *The Market Process: Essays in Contemporary Austrian Economics*, Aldershot: Edward Elgar.

Brand, M. (1984) *Intending and Acting: A Naturalized Action Theory*, Cambridge, MA: MIT Press.

Bratman, M. E. (1985) 'Davidson's theory of intention', in B. Vermazen and M. B. Hintikka (eds) *Essays on Davidson: Actions and Events*, Oxford: Clarendon Press.

—— (1987) *Intention, Plans, and Practical Reason*, Cambridge, MA: Harvard University Press.

Coddington, A. (1983) *Keynesian Economics: The Search for First Principles*, London: George Allen and Unwin.

Davidson, D. (1980) *Essays on Actions and Events*, Oxford: Clarendon Press.

Ebeling, R. M. (1994) 'Expectations and expectation formation in Mises's theory of the market process', in P. J. Boettke and D. L. Prychitko (eds) *The Market Process: Essays in Contemporary Austrian Economics*, Aldershot: Edward Elgar.

Gadamer, H.-G. (1979) *Truth and Method*, 2nd edn, London: Sheed and Ward.

Ginet, C. (1990) *On Action*, Cambridge: Cambridge University Press.

Habermas, J. (1984) *The Theory of Communicative Action: Volume 1: Reason and the Rationalization of Society*, London: Heinemann.

Lachmann, L. M. (1971) *The Legacy of Max Weber*, Berkeley: Glendessary Press.

Lachmann, L. M. (1982) 'Ludwig von Mises and the extension of subjectivism', in I. M. Kirzner (ed.) *Method, Process and Austrian Economics: Essays in Honor of Ludwig von Mises*, Lexington, MA: Lexington Books.

—— (1990) 'Austrian economics: a hermeneutic approach', in D. Lavoie (ed.) *Economics and Hermeneutics*, London: Routledge.

Mäki, U. (1990) 'Practical syllogism, entrepreneurship, and the invisible hand', in D. Lavoie (ed.) *Economics and Hermeneutics*, London: Routledge.

Mises, L. von (1949) *Human Action: A Treatise on Economics*, London: Hodge.

—— (1958) *Theory and History*, London: Cape.

—— (1962) *The Ultimate Foundations of Economic Science*, Princeton: Van Nostrand.

—— (1981) *Epistemological Problems in Economics*, New York: New York University Press.

—— (1990) *Money, Method and Market Process: Essays by Ludwig von Mises*, Norwell, Mass: Kluwer.

Moya, C. J. (1990) *The Philosophy of Action*, Cambridge: Polity Press.

Oakes, G. (ed.) (1986) 'Introduction: Rickert's theory of historical knowledge', in H. Rickert *The Limits of Concept Formation in Natural Science*, Cambridge: Cambridge University Press.

Parsons, S. (1990) 'The philosophical roots of modern Austrian economics: past problems and future prospects', *History of Political Economy*, 22 (2): 295–320.

—— (1997) 'Mises, the a priori and the foundations of economics: a qualified defence', *Economics and Philosophy*, 13: 175–96.

Schutz, A. (1972) *The Phenomenology of the Social World*, London: Heinemann.

Sugden, R. (1991) 'Rational choice: a survey of contributions from economics and philosophy', *Economic Journal*, 101: 751–85.

Weber, M. (1978) *Economy and Society: Volume 1* (G. Roth and C. Wittich (eds)), Berkeley: University of California Press.

4

LACHMANN ON THE SUBJECTIVISM OF ACTIVE MINDS

Roger Koppl

Introduction

Ludwig Lachmann cast a spell. Almost, as it were, against your will, this modest and amiable man would induce you to change your thinking radically. He carried an unpalatable message that most of us, at first, wanted to reject. But for many of us the message came through in the end. When Lachmann first came to participate in the Austrian revival of the 1970s, few Austrians found his message hospitable. But when he left this group with his much grieved death, many of its most creative thinkers, most perhaps, were won over to the general contours of his position (Vaughn 1994).

What produced this great personal achievement of Lachmann? It was not, I think, his *solution* to any economic problem, but his *identification* of one. The problem Lachmann drew our attention to was the need for a theory of expectations in which each person's actions are animated by the spontaneous activity of a free human mind. I will call the problem of building a radically subjectivist theory of expectations, the 'Lachmann problem'.

It is not obvious how such a thing is to be done. How can I let the agents of my model be free and still predict anything – even within the model! If we take seriously the 'subjectivism of active minds', we seem to fall into the horrible pit of open possibility with no ladder upon which to get out. This, we have been told, is nihilism.

I think there is a way out. We can combine the radical subjectivist attention to human thoughts with a more 'objective' understanding of the evolution of rule-governed action. Doing so may permit us to correlate observable market conditions with certain properties of economic expectations. It may help us learn when economic expectations will be more prescient and when less. It may help us learn when markets are driven mostly by fundamentals and when they are more subject to fads and fashion. To anticipate, my proposal for solving the Lachmann problem puts Schutz and Hayek together. (Alfred Schutz was a sociologist notable for his use of Husserl's phenomenology. F. A. Hayek, of course, was one of the leading figures of Austrian economics.)

I will argue for an integration of Schutz and Hayek in the penultimate section. First though, I wish to review some of Lachmann's radical subjectivist ideas about expectations and to explain the 'Lachmann problem'. Lachmann drew on Keynes and Mises. It may be of some interest, then, to briefly indicate why neither Keynes nor Mises is likely to lead us to a solution of the Lachmann problem. After making that argument, I will turn to my proposed integration of Schutz and Hayek. The integration of Schutz and Hayek, I will argue, may let us solve the Lachmann problem. To make my case I will need to distinguish between two meanings of 'expectations'. On the one hand, economic 'expectations' are what the word most naturally suggests, namely, ideas about the future. These are the sorts of 'expectations' radical subjectivists have generally been talking about. On the other hand, the 'expectations' of many economic models are really dispositions or propensities to act in certain ways. I 'expect' inflation if I raise my output price. I will call expectations in the first sense 'psychological expectations'. I will call expectations in the second sense 'dispositional expectations'. If the argument of the latter part of this chapter is right, integrating Schutz and Hayek to solve the Lachmann problem means explaining both psychological and dispositional expectations and correlating the two explanations.

The Lachmann problem

In his 1943 essay 'The role of expectations in economics as a social science' ([1943] 1977), Lachmann mapped out a position from which he never deviated. It is this same position, for instance, that he adopted in an important essay for the *Journal of Economic Literature*, 'From Mises to Shackle: an essay on Austrian economics and the Kaleidic Society' (Lachmann 1976). Lachmann calls for a theory of expectations that goes beyond the efforts proposed by mainstream economists.

The 'modern theory' of the 1930s had brought the 'introduction of expectations' into economics (ibid.: 65). Some, Keynes among them, had treated expectations as 'data' (ibid.). Others had proposed to treat them as 'variables it is our task to explain' (Schumpeter 1939, vol. I: 55 as quoted in Lachmann 1943: 66). Lachmann rejected both ways of treating expectations.

We cannot regard expectations as mere 'data' given to us but must ask 'why they are what they are' (Lachmann 1943: 65). We are, indeed, 'compelled' to seek out a 'causal explanation' of economic expectations (ibid.: 65). Expectations, after all, are on a 'somewhat different plane' (ibid.: 66) from the distribution of mineral deposits or the public's preference between movie directors. The distribution of expectations, unlike that of mineral deposits, is 'largely the result of the experience of economic processes' (ibid.).

But neither can we regard expectations as variables to be inferred from the 'business situation'. Different interpreting minds will draw different inferences from the same 'objective' data. Thus, 'there will be as many "business situations" as there are different interpretations of the same facts, and they will all exist alongside each other' (ibid.: 67).

Here we come to the dark heart of Lachmann's ideas on expectations. Expectations are not constant, or even changing, data impinging, as it were, from outside the economic process; they are interpretations. But interpretations differ in ways that defy prediction: 'The absence of a uniform relationship between a set of observable events which might be described as a *situation* on the one hand, and expectations on the other hand, is thus seen to be the crux of the whole matter' (ibid.: 67). We are thus obliged to view expectations as 'economically indeterminate' (ibid.). For Lachmann, 'it cannot be emphasised too strongly' that attempts to test empirical hypotheses with historical data will be 'quite useless' if they are 'confined to the study of [the] relations between objective facts and expectations' (ibid.: 68). The best we can do is to render expectations 'intelligible' by seeing in them a plan based on an interpretation of the facts of experience (ibid.: 68–73).

For Lachmann, 'it is by reducing "action" to "plan" that we "understand" the actions of individuals' (ibid.: 69). He infers from this that 'it is the *subjective* nature of beliefs which imparts indeterminateness to expectations' but 'it is their *mental* nature which renders them capable of explanation' (ibid.: 73). He draws the further conclusion that economists must (in 1943), expand beyond 'the subjectivism of wants' to embrace 'the subjectivism of interpretation' (ibid.). I take this to be the same position expressed in 1976 as the invitation to 'extend' subjectivism from Mises to Shackle, from the subjectivism of 'tastes' to the subjectivism of 'expectations' (Lachmann 1976: 58). The theory of expectations whose absence Lachmann calls our attention to must embrace the 'subjectivism of interpretation' (ibid.: 69).

Lachmann has put a hard task indeed to economics. Expectations are to be neither data nor variables. They are to be endogenous, but not functionally related to observable facts. Rather than functional relations, we are to see in expectations subjective interpretations of facts whose meaning for future action is always more or less obscure.

A theory that satisfies Lachmann's call for a subjectivism of interpretations must satisfy three criteria. First, it must give expectations a place within economic theory. Second, the theory must be subjectivist in a strong sense: Expectations are produced by active minds, each of which is more or less unique. Finally, expectations must be endogenous to the market process.

The hard thing is to satisfy the second and third criteria simultaneously. Expectations may be right or wrong. Market efficiency depends crucially on the accuracy of economic expectations. If one doubts that markets tend to co-ordinate action, one may be inclined to think that expectations are formed through an essentially psychological process as in Keynes's Chapter 12. Greater faith in the market may incline one to think that expectations are indeed 'rational' in a sense close to that of Lucas and Muth. Both the New Classical and old Keynesian approaches to expectations, unfortunately, require one to choose in advance one's modelling strategy. One must decide a priori whether to represent expectations as 'rational' and co-ordinative or as 'psychological' and disequilibrating. The trick, I think, is to represent endogenously formed expectations in a way that skirts the unsatisfactory choice between *faith* and *doubt* in the co-ordinative prowess of markets. If we are stuck with an a priori choice between faith and doubt, an essential question of our discipline is not empirical or logical, but purely ideological.[1] If the Lachmann problem can be solved, perhaps we can avoid this ideologically charged choice.

Ludwig von Mises and the Lachmann problem

Lachmann claimed that Mises never extended his subjectivism from tastes to expectations. This may seem an odd claim to make of an author who emphasised uncertainty as strongly as did Mises. Mises showed a real appreciation for the subjectivism of expectations when he argued that the:

> farmer who in earlier ages tried to increase his crop by resorting to magic rites acted no less rationally than the modern farmer who applies fertilizer. He did what according to his – erroneous – opinion was appropriate to his purpose.
>
> (Mises 1957: 268)

And what are subjective expectations but opinions that might prove erroneous? An action based on failed expectations is 'contrary to purpose', but it is not irrational (Mises 1963: 20). And yet Lachmann's claim was a fair one. In spite of the very great role of subjective expectations in Mises's economics, Mises never let the subjectivism of expectation and interpretation enter into the structures of his pure economic theory.

The response of Mises to Lachmann's 1943 essay is informative (Mises 1943). Lachmann drew from his general considerations regarding expectations the specific inference, quoted by Mises, that 'Without fairly elastic expectations there can therefore be no crisis of the Austro-Wicksellian type' (ibid.: 79). With this claim, minor terminological points aside, Mises could 'fully agree' (ibid.: 251). Indeed, Mises reports, he had said as much in his *Nationaloekonomie* of 1940. He then produces a quote from it saying the 'teachings of the monetary theory of the trade cycle' may have spread widely enough that in the next credit expansion businessmen will replace the 'naive optimism' of the past with a 'greater scepticism' though it is 'too early to make a positive statement' (ibid.).

Mises develops the point. As long as a businessman is 'a businessman only and does not view things with the eye of an economist', the cycle story applies. But if a businessman wears the hat of an 'economist' too, then he may 'look askance at the low level of interest rates brought about by the credit expansion' (ibid.). The 'businessman' must be an 'economist' in order to see that today's credit conditions are false and temporary manifestations of excessive money growth.

Mises insists on viewing the more sophisticated actor as somehow more than a businessman; he is also an 'economist'. Thus, if expectations behave differently than we predict, it is because some outside element has entered the story. This is the rhetorical trope Imre Lakatos deftly labelled 'monster-barring' (Lakatos 1976: 14).

A businessman who knows the monetary theory of the trade cycle is like a man with two heads: He is a monster and ruled out of court.

A monster is a counterexample to your theory. When you call the counterexample a monster, you deny that it counts as a counterexample. This is how Mises handled Lachmann's comment on the elasticity of expectations. The case Lachmann mentions, according to Mises, is the one in which the businessman is also an economist. Mises takes his 'pure a priori' theory to discuss the behaviour of businessmen and not economists. Thus, Lachmann's example brings in something that doesn't pertain to the theory. The monster is barred, no mention of him may be made in future discussions of the subject.

Such monster-barring might seem so *ad hoc* that Mises would have been forced to confront the subjectivism of expectations. But Mises's epistemological views led him to see the problems of subjective interpretation as radically divorced from economic theory and the canons of scientific reason.

In an essay published originally in 1933, Mises distinguished between 'Conception and Understanding' (Mises 1933a). Conception is rational; it is 'discursive reasoning'. Understanding is the English translation of the German word '*Verstehen*'. 'Understanding seeks the meaning of action in empathic intuition of the whole' (ibid.: 133). When both apply, conception 'takes precedence over understanding in every respect' (ibid.: 133). But understanding can penetrate to something conception cannot reach: 'the apprehension of the quality of values' (ibid.: 134). It is when understanding enters that 'subjectivity begins' (ibid.: 134). For Mises, '[c]onception is reasoning; understanding is beholding' (ibid.). Mises would later call understanding 'the specific understanding of the historical sciences of human action' (Mises 1957: 264).

The 'understanding' Mises distinguishes from 'conception' is historical, he thought, not scientific. Economic theory is scientific, not historical. Thus, any knowledge we might have about the 'subjectivity' of others is historical, not theoretical. (Mises's distinction and its relation to the problem of expectations is discussed by Butos 1997 and Koppl 1997.)

It is very significant that Mises equates understanding with the subjective. It relegated the issue raised by Lachmann to the extra-theoretical categories of 'historical understanding' and 'intuition of the whole'. It neatly immunised economic *theory* from the issue that so occupied Lachmann. It is thus with good reason that Lachmann would say Shackle, not Mises, had 'extended the scope of subjectivism from tastes to expectations' (Lachmann 1976: 58). Lachmann claims that 'Mises hardly ever mentions expectations' (ibid.: 58). And a look at the index of Mises's magnum opus, *Human Action* (1963), shows no entry under 'expectations'. Though Mises was a subjectivist, his system of thought does not permit the development of a subjectivist theory of expectations.

J. M. Keynes and the Lachmann problem

Lachmann gave Keynes a mixed review. He clearly disliked the 'diatribe against the Stock Exchange' to be found in Chapter 12 of Keynes's *General Theory* (Lachmann [1969] 1977: 142). But he quotes G. L. S. Shackle favourably to the effect that the 'whole spirit' of Keynes's 1936 book was subjectivist and laudable (ibid.: 159). This is a more positive view of J. M. Keynes than many other Austrians take today. It is striking when put in its context: The article originally appeared in a 1969 *festschrift* for F. A. Hayek! In this same essay Lachmann credits Keynes with introducing expectations to 'Anglo-Saxon economics' in 1930 (ibid.: 157–8).

The subjectivism of Keynes has inspired more than one author to propose a synthesis of the ideas of Keynes and the Austrians (see Butos and Koppl 1997). But Butos and I have argued against that, at least for the Hayekian strand of Austrian economics. The philosophical differences separating the thought of Keynes and Hayek make any synthesis of them difficult (Butos and Koppl 1997). The basic philosophical ideas of Keynes drove him to view expectations as disconnected from any aspect of the market process except the self-referencing process of mass psychology that creates objectively baseless waves of optimism and pessimism.

Butos and I argue, in agreement with O'Donnell and others, that Keynes was a rationalist. Keynes believed that knowledge properly speaking was philosophically grounded and epistemologically certain. But he also believed that the conditions that permit induction and, therefore, knowledge of the future do not apply to the social world. As Butos and I put it, 'Keynes was a Cartesian rationalist who saw about him a non-Cartesian social world.' The impossibility of applying philosophical reason to the practical problems of investment and business forecasting led Keynes to emphasise 'animal spirits, a spontaneous urge to action rather than inaction' (see Keynes, *Collected Writings* [1936] 1972, vol. VII: 161).

Animal spirits are neither subjective expectations nor the source of them. They are the springs of action in a world where reason must default for lack of data (Koppl 1991). It is the default of reason that makes long-term expectations necessarily 'subjective' for Keynes in the extreme sense of disconnection from underlying scarcities. In Keynes's scheme of thought, the actions to which animal spirits impel us cannot be grounded in a rational calculation of future consequences. The extreme unknowability of the future ensures as much. The expectations behind such actions are psychological beliefs and more or less independent of market data. Subjective expectations are determined by an autonomous process of mass psychology. They are therefore fundamentally exogenous to the market process.

The exogeneity of subjective expectations in Keynes contrasts with the criterion stated above, namely, that a Lachmannian theory of expectations must represent expectations as endogenous to the market process. Lachmann was right to see Keynes as a pioneer in the theory of subjective expectations. But Keynes's pioneering work is not one on which we might build a theory of expectations that meets the challenge Lachmann put to the science of economics.

Alfred Schutz and the Lachmann problem

Schutz on anonymity

The works of F. A. Hayek and Alfred Schutz give us a way to solve the Lachmann problem. The work of Schutz teaches us that radical subjectivism can sometimes make use of a less psychologically detailed picture of action than Lachmann seems to have thought possible. The work of F. A. Hayek may be used to infer something about when it is appropriate to use those less detailed pictures. Putting together the insights of these two great subjectivists allows us to construct a theory of expectations that builds from the subjectivism of active minds to a picture of orderly and endogenously determined economic expectations.

A subjectivism of active minds must start with a picture of thought. Schutz gives us such a picture. The key notion in Schutz's phenomenological description of thought and action is 'typification'. A typification is just a stereotype.[2] All thinking, Schutz taught, is stereotypical. When we form an idea, we form a typification. Typifications of people are 'personal types'; typifications of actions are 'course-of-action types'. The structure of our thoughts, then, is a structure of typifications. Some of these typifications are filled with many particulars; others are quite empty. My typification of, say, my old pocket knife is quite particularistic. I know the heft of it and where the blade is nicked. By contrast, my typification of, say, a postal worker is rather empty. In ways I don't quite understand, the faceless postal worker sorts and delivers. The personal types containing more particulars have a low degree of 'anonymity'. At the other end are the personal types with a high degree of 'anonymity'.

What has been said about types of higher and lower anonymity is still true if the typifications are those of social science. The scientist's ideal types are of higher or lower anonymity according to the problem he studies. Whether we are speaking of everyday thought and action or of our scientific understanding of that thought and action, our thoughts spin a web of stereotypes, some of which are very spare or *thin* descriptions of their objects, others of which are very detailed or *thick* descriptions.

The stereotypes I must rely on when I think about social life are gotten by taking 'a cross-section of our experience of another person and, so to speak, "freezing it into slide"' (Schutz 1932: 187). Thus, the personal types of my mental picture of the world know no freedom. They cannot act out of character. The real people corresponding to them may, of course, act out of character, but not my typifications of them. The personal types of scientists and social participants are equally unfree.

Max Weber's method of ideal types 'consists', for Schutz, 'in replacing the human beings which the social scientist observes as actors on the social stage by puppets created by himself' (Schutz 1967, vol. II: 17). The puppet is a personal ideal type. Each puppet's 'destiny is regulated and determined beforehand by his creator, the social scientist, and with such a perfect pre-established harmony as Leibniz imagined the world created by God' (ibid.: 83).

Schutz showed that the propositions we make about highly anonymous (ideal) types are more reliable guides to our expectations than those we make about (ideal) types of low anonymity. Schutz's concept of anonymity helps us to understand how social order is achieved in spite of the subjectivism of expectations. We can co-operate with anonymous others precisely because of their anonymity. The types of high anonymity are thin descriptions of rather robot-like beings. We know that each real postal worker is unique. But we rely on a stereotyped picture of him that quite effaces his personality. To the extent that I can rely on such anonymous types, I can ignore the idiosyncrasies of my fellow social actors.

I can predict the actions of the typical postal worker with confidence. My usual carrier is a named individual. I cannot guess what he does off the job, nor how often he calls in sick or shows up late. This named individual is more or less a cipher to me. But I can be reasonably sure that he or someone like him will show up mid-morning to drop letters in my box.

Social co-operation with strangers is possible because we may rely on highly anonymous personal types in formulating our picture of the world and our expectations of the future. When our expectations may reasonably rely on personal types of high anonymity only, we have reason for confidence in those expectations. When, instead, we must formulate expectations on the basis of personal types of relatively low anonymity, we have reason to doubt the reliability of our expectations.

Here is a case where 'Austrian' economists may make use of a Keynesian concept. In his *Treatise on Probability*, Keynes distinguished between the 'probability' of proposition and its 'weight'. The weight of a probability judgement measures how confident we may be in it. I'm quite sure that the chance of a seven at craps is one in six. I may judge the chance of civil unrest to be one in six, but I cannot have confidence in that judgement. 'The weight, to speak metaphorically, measures the *sum* of the favorable and unfavorable evidence, the probability measures the *difference*' (Keynes, *Collected Writings* [1921] 1972, vol. VIII: 77). This notion of weight resurfaces in Chapter 12 of the *General Theory* (*Collected Writings* [1936] 1972, vol. VII: 148; see also Runde 1990.) Frank Knight may have been getting at more or less the same point when he distinguished the 'favorableness' of an opinion from 'the amount of confidence in that opinion' (Knight [1921] 1971: 227).

We may apply Keynes's notion of weight to restate Schutz's point about anonymous types. Expectations relying only on personal types of high anonymity may have high weight. Those relying in part on personal types of low anonymity should generally have low weight.

Economic actors can better predict the actions of anonymous than non-anonymous personal types. Something similar may be said of economic theorists. Social scientists may be able to predict confidently the results of processes whose descriptions are given using only personal ideal types of high anonymity. But when the description of a social process requires the use of some personal type(s) of low anonymity, the predictions of social science are more or less unreliable. This point is illustrated by three propositions discussed by Fritz Machlup (1978) in a paper intended to convey some of Schutz's ideas to an audience of economists (see also the discussion in Langlois 1986 and Langlois and Koppl 1991).

> Statement (1): 'If, because of an abundant crop, the output of wheat is much increased, the price of wheat will fall.'
> Statement (2): 'If, because of increased wage-rates and decreased interest rates, capital becomes relatively cheaper than labor, new labor-saving devices will be invented.'
> Statement (3): 'If, because of heavy withdrawals of foreign deposits, the banks are in danger of insolvency, the Central Bank Authorities will extend the necessary credit.'
>
> (Machlup 1978: 64)

The first statement is more reliable than the second and the second is more reliable than the third. Why? As we go down from the first statement, we reach ideal types of lower anonymity. Machlup explained that:

> the causal relations such as stated in (2) and (3) are derived from types of human conduct of a lesser generality or anonymity. To make a statement about the actions of bank authorities (such as (3)) calls for reasoning in a stratum of behavior conceptions of much less anonymous types of actors. We have to know or imagine the acting persons much more intimately.
>
> (Machlup 1978: 68)

That greater intimacy implies a greater chance that the actor will surprise us by acting out of character. (Later I will discuss the role of the 'system constraint' in determining when to use anonymous types.) We cannot be sure the central bank authorities will extend credit. It is a good guess they will; but they may surprise us with an act of monetary restraint. We can be much more confident in the coming reduction of wheat prices. We can rely on an anonymous typification of the wheat farmer. We need non-anonymous typifications of the central bank's high officials.

The Lachmann problem again

I identified the Lachmann problem as the need to have a theory of expectations that builds on the idea that each person's actions are animated by the spontaneous activity of a free human mind. Lachmann's recognition of this problem led him to his 'subjectivism of expectations' according to which expectations must be seen as *neither* data *nor* variables. They are 'interpretations', each one more or less unique to the interpreting individual. Lachmann calls for thick description.

The personal and interpretive quality of expectations spells trouble for any theory of expectations. We seem to require a detailed psychological portrait of each economic actor if we are to say anything at all about the market process. Moreover, each actor seems to require the same sort of psychological detail in his mental portrait of each of his fellow actors.

Schutz's discussion of anonymity shows that we do not always need to rely on a psychologically rich picture of economic actors. Both economic actors and economic analysts may sometimes forgo thick description in favour of thin description. When the observer or his subject requires reference to non-anonymous types, we may not be able to say much about expectations. In that case the results of the market process will be hard to predict.

In other words, the 'Lachmann problem' is more acute in some contexts, less acute in others. When it is most acute, the market process will be hard to fathom and economic theory of limited predictive value. When the Lachmann problem is least acute, the market process will be more transparent and economic theory will have greater predictive value.

F. A. Hayek and the Lachmann problem

I have argued that sometimes thin description is good enough. The trick is to know when. On this point, to my knowledge, Schutz is silent. Lachmann did emphasise institutions, calling them 'nodal points' to guide the individual. I think he was right about that, but the notion of nodal points is not a very detailed analysis. I think it is fair to say that 'radical subjectivism' has so far failed to tell us much about when economic actors might get along with anonymous types.

Perhaps we should not be surprised if radical subjectivism has not told us when thin description is enough. A radically subjectivist account would have to run in terms of the thoughts of economic actors. What we want to know is when those thoughts employ non-anonymous types. But a radically subjectivist account would be obliged to begin with the thoughts of the agent. It is hard to see how a pure subjectivist could get beyond the circular claim that agents use thin description when they use thin description. What we seem to require is a set of 'objective' conditions under which the 'subjective' thoughts of agents may be represented as employing only anonymous types.[3] Similarly, we need a set of objective conditions under which our own thinking as scientific observers may employ only anonymous types.

Consider again Machlup's three statements. Statement (1) asserted that if, 'because of an abundant crop, the output of wheat is much increased, the price of wheat will fall'. What is it that lets our reasoning be guided by anonymous types in this case? Why is a thin description enough? As Langlois and I have argued, it is the 'system constraint' (Langlois and Koppl 1991: 92). Imagine we have one or a few idiosyncratic wheat farmers or wheat traders. They may act foolishly or arbitrarily. But these few oddballs cannot reverse the tide of events. And if they try, they risk losses and banishment from the market. The large numbers of competitors involved and the discipline of profit and loss ensure that we may safely ignore any idiosyncracies of behaviour in the wheat market. Thin descriptions will do for economic observers.

Now consider the positions of participants in the wheat market. If they are operating under a tight system constraint, their actions will be driven into approximate conformity with the underlying situational logic. Those whose actions stray too far from this logic will suffer losses which, if uncorrected, will drive them from the market. A tight system constraint produces a relatively high correspondence between action and circumstance. Under such conditions, we may represent the thoughts of agents as expressing the same correspondence; agents act as if they had prescient expectations. The condition that lets us represent agents in this as-if way is the tight system constraint. But this is also the condition that lets observers rely exclusively on anonymous types. When the system constraint is tight, economic actors forgo thick description in favour of thin description.

Butos and I have developed some of these points in a paper drawing on Hayek's theories of mind and of social evolution (Butos and Koppl 1993). We argue that the market's evolutionary selection mechanism sometimes keeps anticipations in line, but sometimes does not. We identify two conditions that promote prescient expectations. The first is that the rules of the game of market competition are stable. The second is that competition is atomistic.

The rules of the game are stable when changes in them are small and infrequent. The rules that count here are both formal and informal. Indeed, the only formal rules that count are those that are enforced at least some of the time. Human habits are constantly changing piecemeal. Thus, perfect stability is impossible. But we can often say that the rules of the game are more stable in this market, less stable in that one.

Competition is atomistic when it is rivalrous. When each supplier considers his own actions to have an insignificant impact on the overall market, when there is little 'rival consciousness' (Machlup 1952), then competition is 'atomistic' in the relevant sense.

Under these conditions of stability and atomism, Butos and I have argued, evolutionary selection mechanisms of the sort Hayek analysed will produce relatively prescient economic expectations and relatively high levels of economic efficiency. Stable evolutionary environments produce prescient expectations in the social world, goodness of fit in the biological world.

The evolutionary and Hayekian considerations of the present section may not seem to fit well with the phenomenological and Schutzian considerations of the previous section. Butos and I adopted the Hayekian view of expectations as (mostly) dispositions to act. The Schutzian framework takes expectations to be psychological states. It is not immediately obvious that these are consistent perspectives. Some definitions may help to clarify the issues.

Let the term 'dispositional expectations' refer to the Hayekian view and the term 'psychological expectations' refer to the phenomenological or hermeneutical view of expectations. Psychological expectations refer to people's thoughts. Dispositional expectations refer to people's actions.

The 'expectations' of economic theory are often dispositional expectations. We say that creditors 'expect' zero inflation if they do not insist on an inflation premium. This 'expectation' may be nothing more than the conformity to old habits and ways of doing business. Conceivably, some creditors might even have a psychological expectation of inflation. If they don't understand the effect of inflation on purchasing power, they won't ask for an inflation premium. The case imagined is not purely hypothetical. Recently, an important Italian labour leader expressed concern over the government's low inflation target. Such low inflation, he claimed, would reduce the purchasing power of workers' wages.

Methodological subjectivists insist that one must be able to give a reasonable account of the psychological expectations animating the actions of economic actors. This is a kind of test. If your model requires that we imagine agents acting on unreasonable psychological expectations, the model is unreasonable. If the psychological expectations at work are reasonable, the model passes the test.

Dispositional and psychological expectations are distinct objects. On narrow logical grounds, any combination of them is possible. But it seems reasonable to suppose the two typically fit together. A theory of dispositional expectations without a correlated theory of psychological expectations is tenuous. We may wonder if any plausible psychological expectations could correlate with the posited dispositions. Rational expectations, for example, are an assumption about dispositional expectations. Traders act as if they had, on average, the true model in mind. The assumption is reasonable under some circumstances. But rational expectations are not reasonable assumptions when the implied psychological expectations entail, say, superhuman powers of calculation.

A theory of psychological expectations without a correlated theory of dispositional expectations is also dubious, and for a parallel reason. Without the latter we cannot be sure the posited psychological expectations would really come to prevail. Expectations are, as Lachmann insisted, endogenous to the market process. If we do not correlate our understanding of psychological expectations with a story of the emergence of dispositional expectations, we have to doubt that the imagined psychological expectations would really survive the test of market competition.

An example may clarify some of these issues. Consider the operation of a modern asset market. Traders must anticipate future values at least passably well if they are not to be forced out of the game by losses. Profits will encourage those with unusually good foresight to keep at it. An evolutionary selection mechanism works to keep anticipation more or less in line with underlying values as revealed by future returns. If the market filter of profits and loss works well, prices will reflect fundamental values. If the filter works badly, prices may wander freely from fundamental values. Whether the filter works well or not is an empirical question.

Efficient market theories predict that market prices will reflect all available information. An important implication of such theories (together with a few subsidiary assumptions) is that the past changes in an asset's return give no evidence about future changes. In consequence the expected value of an asset's return in any period is simply its return in the previous period. This property of the return series defines a 'martingale'. (A random walk is a special case of a martingale in which the higher moments are not expected to change over time. See LeRoy 1989 for a review of basic issues.)

The statistical evidence for the efficiency of asset markets is strong enough to have persuaded many serious and competent judges. Others doubt. There are many apparent counterexamples. Evidence reviewed below suggests that observable market conditions help determine how efficient asset markets are. The degree of efficiency may be an endogenous variable.

According to the 'Big Players theory', the order-giving properties of the filter of profit and loss are corrupted when 'Big Players' derange markets (Koppl and Yeager 1996; Butos and Koppl 1993). Yeager and I define a Big Player as 'anyone who habitually exercises discretionary power to influence the market while himself remaining wholly or largely immune from the discipline of profit and loss' (Koppl and Yeager 1996: 368). An interventionist finance minister is our paradigm of a Big Player. But a Big Player may be any actor who combines three things, namely, the power to influence markets, a degree of immunity from competition and use of discretion in the exercise of his power. We produce qualitative and statistical evidence that Big Players induce herding in asset markets and thus reduce market efficiency.

The point of the Big Players theory can be put in Schutzian terms. It is a matter of psychological expectations. Big Players divert each trader's attention from underlying conditions of supply and demand towards the personality of the Big Player. It is hard to know what a Big Player will do. Traders must base their expectations on a picture of the market in which a highly non-anonymous personal type is prominent. But this picture is always more or less dubious. Traders come to place a lower weight on their own expectations and more weight in the opinions of other traders. The importance of this non-anonymous type and the ignorance and uncertainty traders feel regarding the Big Player encourage them to follow the trend. Big Players encourage herding in asset markets.

The point may also be put in Hayekian evolutionary terms. It is a matter of dispositional expectations. The presence of Big Players destabilises the evolutionary environment. The disposition to follow trends is less likely to bring losses; the disposition to respond to fundamentals is more likely to produce losses. Big Players make luck count for more, skill count for less. Traders who survive market competition under Big Players will have a higher average propensity to herd. Big Players encourage herding in asset markets.

In the Big Players theory psychological and dispositional expectations fit together. This complementarity is a strength of the theory. Keynes's treatment of long-run expectations runs mostly in terms of psychological expectations. It is not clear, in his analysis, what institutional properties of asset markets encourage the perversities he identifies and what properties discourage them. (Keynes refers only to liquidity.) Rational expectations models refer, presumably, to dispositional expectations. They seem to imply that psychological expectations are perfectly plastic, taking on whatever form is needed to generate the predicted behaviour. As Thomas Sargent has noted, this may imply that economic agents know with certainty the very structural parameters of the economy that econometricians can only estimate with uncertainty (Sargent 1993: 21). The examples of Keynes and rational expectations help to show that we should prefer economic arguments that combine and correlate plausible treatments of both psychological and dispositional expectations.

Distinguishing dispositional and psychological expectations helps us to see how we might fit Schutz and Hayek into a consistent theory of expectations. The Big Players theory suggests the utility of doing so. The proposed integration seems to yield testable hypotheses. It may be true, then, that integrating Schutz and Hayek will help to solve the Lachmann problem.

Conclusion

The Lachmann problem was stated at least as early as 1943. For the most part it has remained unsolved. Some progress has been made by Lachmann and others through the recognition of the co-ordinative function of institutions, 'nodal points' of co-ordination as Lachmann called them. But much remains to be done. I conjecture that this intractability has been due in part to a tendency by researchers following Lachmann to look for either Keynesian or Misesian solutions. If instead we try to place considerations of anonymity raised by Schutz in a Hayekian context of social evolution, we may make more progress.

Acknowledgements

I thank William Butos for useful comments. Any deficiencies of the text are my fault.

Notes

1 For an interesting discussion of 'vision' and analysis in economics see Boettke 1992.
2 Today the term *ideal* type is commonly used only for the typification of science, especially social science. In his *Phenomenology of the Social World* (1932) Schutz used the term 'ideal type' to refer to both the typifications of common sense and those of science.
3 I have been ignoring the difference between the thoughts of agents and our representations of those thoughts. This difference can matter. As far as I can tell, however, it doesn't matter for the points being made in this paper.

References

Boettke, P. J. (1992) 'Analysis and vision in economic discourse', *Journal of the History of Economic Thought*, 14 (1): 84–95.

Butos, W. N. (1997) 'Toward an Austrian theory of expectations', *Advances in Austrian Economics*, 4: 75–94.

Butos, W. N. and Koppl, R. G. (1993) 'Hayekian expectations: theory and empirical applications', *Constitutional Political Economy*, 4 (3): 303–29.

—— (1997) 'The varieties of subjectivism: Keynes and Hayek on expectations', *History of Political Economy*, 29 (2): 327–59.

Keynes, J. M. ([1921] 1972) *Collected Writings of John Maynard Keynes*, vol. VIII, *A Treatise on Probability*, London: Macmillan.

—— ([1936] 1972) *Collected Writings of John Maynard Keynes*, vol. VII, *The General Theory of Money, Employment, and Interest*, London: Macmillan.

Knight, F. H. ([1921] 1971) *Risk, Uncertainty and Profit*, Chicago: The University of Chicago Press.

Koppl, R. G. (1991) 'Animal spirits', *Journal of Economic Perspectives*, 5 (3): 203–10.

—— (1997) 'Mises and Schutz on ideal types', *Cultural Dynamics*, 9 (1): 63–76.

Koppl, R. and Yeager, L. (1996) 'Big players and herding in asset markets: a case of the Russian ruble', *Explorations in Economic History*, 33: 367–83.

Lachmann, L. ([1943] 1977) 'The role of expectations in economics as a social science', in Lachmann, L., *Capital, Expectations, and the Market Process*, ed. by Grinder, W. E., Kansas City, Missouri: Sheed Andrews and McMeel, pp. 65–80.

—— ([1969] 1977) 'Methodological individualism and the market economy', in Lachmann, L., *Capital, Expectations, and the Market Process* ed. by Grinder, W. E., Kansas City, Missouri: Sheed Andrews and McMeel, pp. 149–65.

—— (1976) 'From Mises to Shackle: an essay on Austrian economics and the Kaleidic Society', *Journal of Economic Literature*, 14 (1): 54–62.

Lakatos, I. (1976) *Proofs and Refutations: The Logic of Mathematical Discovery*, Cambridge: Cambridge University Press.

Langlois, R. N. (ed.) (1986) 'Rationality, institutions, and explanation', in *Economics as a Process: Essays in the New Institutional Economics*, New York: Cambridge University Press.

Langlois, R. N. and Koppl, R. G. (1991) 'Fritz Machlup and marginalism: a reevaluation', *Methodus*, 3 (2): 86–102.

LeRoy, S. R. (1989) 'Efficient capital markets and martingales', *Journal of Economic Literature*, 27 (4): 1583–621.

Machlup, F. (1952) *The Economics of Sellers' Competition: Model Analysis of Sellers' Conduct*, Baltimore: The Johns Hopkins Press.

—— (1978) *Methodology of Economics and Other Social Sciences*, New York, San Francisco and London: Academic Press.

Mises, L. von ([1933a] 1981) 'Conception and understanding', in *Epistemological Problems of Economics*, New York and London: New York University Press.

—— ([1933b] 1981) 'The science of human action', in *Epistemological Problems of Economics*, New York and London: New York University Press.

—— (1943) ' "Elastic expectations" and the Austrian theory of the trade cycle', *Economica*, N.S. 10 (39): 251–2.

—— ([1957] 1985) *Theory and History: An Interpretation of Social and Economic Evolution*, Auburn University, Alabama and Washington, DC: The Ludwig von Mises Institute.

—— (1963) *Human Action*, New Haven: Yale University Press.

Runde, J. (1990) 'Keynesian uncertainty and the weight of arguments', *Economics and Philosophy*, 6 (2): 275–92.

Sargent, T. (1993) *Bounded Rationality in Macroeconomics*, Oxford: Clarendon Press.

Schumpeter, J. A. (1939) *Business Cycles*, 2 vols, New York: McGraw-Hill.

Schutz, A. ([1932] 1967) *The Phenomenology of the Social World*, Evanston, Illinois: Northwestern University Press.

—— (1967) *The Collected Papers*, vol. II, The Hague: Martin Nijhoff.

Vaughn, K. (1994) *Austrian Economics in America: The Migration of a Tradition*, New York: Cambridge University Press.

5

SUBJECTIVISM AND IDEAL TYPES

Lachmann and the methodological legacy of Max Weber

Lásló Csontos

Introduction

The following essay is based on the conviction that a better under-standing of Ludwig Lachmann's and Max Weber's methodological views is vital for a proper interpretation of the methodological groundwork of the social sciences. Two key elements in Max Weber's much debated and multifarious methodological legacy are the subjectivism of the method of understanding and the notion of ideal types. In what follows, I want to contrast and compare what I believe to be Weber's authentic methodological position on these issues with Lachmann's ideas about the subjectivism of the social sciences and his critique of Weber's concept of ideal types.

Subjectivism

Lachmann considered himself an advocate of subjectivism in the central area of economic theory. 'Subjectivism' and 'subjectivist methodology' are phrases with many meanings, however. They are not very helpful when it comes to identifying and describing a particular methodological tradition. There is a thick conceptual underbrush surrounding the very idea of subjectivism in the philos-ophy of science that should be removed before we embark upon clarifying Lachmann's methodological position. As a result, instead of maintaining that his methodological attitude exemplifies this or that, or some 'true' version of subjectivism, I'd rather create a clean terminological slate, and argue that Lachmann's views can be best described as belonging to the general category of *methodological solipsism*.

I consider methodological solipsism as a variety of methodological individualism.[1] The programme of methodological solipsism seems to be especially relevant to a thorough understanding of the methodological underpinnings of economic theory.

Methodological solipsism, just like methodological individualism, is founded on a distinct and definite view of the nature of social reality. Methodological solipsism's ontological doctrine, as a more or less coherent picture of the world, can be reconstructed on the basis of scattered remarks in the works of Hayek, Mises, Lachmann and others.

The world, more precisely the world of human action is, according to these authors, unimaginably complex, involved and multifaceted (see Hayek 1952a; Mises 1940). Its elements are constantly changing (Lachmann 1976) and its phenomena are infinitely diverse (Hayek 1952b, 1964). These complex phenomena and states of affairs are produced by the interplay of an endless number of individual circumstances and qualitatively different causal sequences; and they are always given to us as a tangled web of countless individual causes and effects (Mises 1940: 45). Everything hangs together with everything else in the world of human action, but social reality lacks any kind of objective structure. It doesn't comprise regulatory principles that would bring order into the chaos of individual phenomena. I want to emphasise, however, that, according to the authors whose views we are discussing here, the world of natural sciences, as opposed to social reality or the realm of human action, is homogeneous, ordered and governed by causal uniformities (Hayek 1964: 25; Mises 1940: 63).

In Lachmann's words:

> From a methodological point of view we may regard the economic thought of the last hundred years as marked by a long drawn-out struggle between two contending forces, *subjectivity* and *formalism*. While the formalists present models characterized by constant relationships between formal entities (even though these are in general supposed to reflect measurable magnitudes), subjectivists see social phenomena as the outcome of human action guided by plans (even though these often fail) and prompted by mental acts. While subjectivist models also of course depict

relationships between formal entities these need not, and in a world of changing knowledge cannot, remain constant.

(Lachmann 1986: 22–3)

Or, as Lachmann (1986: 48), quoting Shackle (1972: 76) approvingly notes, 'ours is "a *kaleidic* society, interspersing its moments or intervals of order, assurance and beauty with sudden disintegration and a cascade into a new pattern"'.

Finally, Lachmann (1986: 30) fully shares Shackle's view that 'economics, concerned with thoughts and only secondarily with things, the objects of those thoughts, must be as protean as thought itself. To adopt a rigid frame and appeal exclusively to it is bound to be fatal.' The fact that

in the real world knowledge requisite to action as a rule involves A's knowledge of B's knowledge of C's knowledge compounds the difficulty for the economist as observer no less than for the agents having to face it in reality.

(Shackle 1972: 246)

It was not Hayek, Mises, Shackle or Lachmann, however, who first thought out, formulated and brought to their logical conclusions the basic tenets of methodological solipsism, including the ontological beliefs discussed above. Although the most elemental components of this methodological position can be traced back to Carl Menger, its consequences as to the methodology of the social sciences, most notably economic theory, were first noted and systematically explored by a now practically unknown, but at the turn of the century very highly regarded, German economist and philosopher of science, Friedrich von Gottl-Ottlilienfeld.

I want to present a small collection of some of the metaphors that express very clearly Gottl's overall *Weltgefühl* and, at the same time, reveal the roots of the methodological position under discussion.[2] Gottl compares and contrasts repeatedly 'the greenness of life' with grey theories; talks about 'the green reality of thinking'; 'the entangled web of experience', 'current of events', 'events whirling around us'. He claims that 'the occurrence of an act is a variation on the endless melody of life' and he discusses 'the surge of the colorful world', 'the endless sea of action', 'the warm life', 'the endless stream of the world of human action', and finally 'the confusing totality of connections'. There is no need to comment extensively on the ontological imagery of Gottl. Clearly, if the world of human action can adequately be described only in terms of these and similar metaphors, then social reality is unpredictable and irrational, and as such not fully accessible to discursive reasoning and can at most be only partially understood by the human mind.

If this is what social reality looks like, that is, enigmatic, incomprehensible, although everything hangs together with everything else, then how do methodological solipsists describe social relations and how do they explain the emergence of society? In their view, society is made up of independent and isolated individuals (Hayek 1952b: 50–1) who not only lack a common social knowledge or common experiences but who are made even more isolated by their existing knowledge because the latter is scattered, imperfect, specific knowledge based on familiarity with particular circumstances (Hayek 1952b: 29–30).[3] Isolated individuals organise into societies as a result of utilitarian considerations, although the emergence of organised societies can be an unintended by-product of their actions. According to the proponents of methodological solipsism, the exchange relationship is the social relation *par excellence*, and the cement that holds society together is a general normative consensus (Mises 1940: 125, 128, 167, 180–1).

The main epistemological difficulty of this methodological programme lies in the assumption, however, that the 'dispersion and imperfection of all knowledge is one of the basic facts from which the social sciences have to start' (Hayek 1964: 30). If this is the case, and if individuals – as implied by the ontological position described above – are bound together only by social relations modelled after the exchange relationship, then how do they understand – or, as social scientists, what kind of epistemological guarantees do we have that we will be able to understand – the meaning and sense of the words, gestures and actions of other human beings?

On the basis of the premises sketched above, adherents of methodological solipsism seem to suggest there is only one possible answer to this question. We have to make the further assumption that there exists a mental structure common to all men, that is, the structure of thinking is the same for every human being, or, in other words, the structure of human thinking is constant (Hayek 1964: 23–4, 33–4; 1952b: 77–8, 102; Mises 1933: 126). To put it more simply: we can understand human action only by accepting the heuristic and scientifically unverifiable principle according to which the uniformity of human nature guarantees that the acting individual has the same *kind* of mental outfit, intentions and objectives as we do. (The phrase 'a mental structure common to all people' refers in this context to this alleged fact, and not, as it usually does, to the universal validity of the laws of logic.) Accordingly, to recognise something as a mind means to recognise it as something analogous to our own mind (Hayek 1964: 76–7; 1967: 15, 18, 60). As a result, we understand human action by imputing to the agent intentions and objectives similar to ours. We are epistemologically entitled to this analogical inference for two reasons. First, because of the postulated similarity of mental structures, and second, because we are acting human beings as well, that is, we have a first-hand knowledge of what it means to act in a certain way. In Gottl's openly irrationalistic language: the a priori and holistically given personal experience of acting makes it possible that we directly understand human action on the analogy of our own past and present actions (Gottl 1925: 154, 161–2, 169, 244–5).

These two assumptions, i.e., the ontological supposition of an inconceivably complex, ever-changing world of human action and the epistemological postulate of the direct intelligibility of human action by virtue of a legitimate analogical inference, are meant to bolster another fundamental tenet of methodological solipsism. Representatives of methodological solipsism advocate rather extreme forms of methodological dualism (see Wright 1971).

Methodological dualists tend to hold the following views: (i) The subject matter of the social sciences is fundamentally different from that of the natural sciences. It is human action in the first case° and brute facts and lifeless uniformities in the second. (ii) The methodological autonomy of social sciences is grounded in social scientists' unique and immediate access to the subject matter of their disciplines.[4] (iii) Consequently, social scientists are able to use epistemic techniques, methods of analysis and explanatory arguments unavailable and superior to those used by natural scientists. According to Gottl (1925: 203), an early and radical methodological dualist, the scientific outlook is delirious with causality and drunken with laws.

The heavy emphasis on methodological dualism seems even more paradoxical considering the fact that the origins of the ontological world view of methodological solipsism can in all probability be traced back to the late nineteenth century 'scientific' positivism of Mach and Avenarius. While Gottl's views, as Max Weber had already pointed out (Weber 1975: 211–12), could directly be linked to this source, Hayek, Mises and Lachmann were indirectly influenced by this sort of positivism through their Austrian connections. Let me illustrate this by presenting some striking similarities.

In the view of Avenarius (1891: 6–7), the 'naturalistic conception of the world' is made up of two components. One of them is a general experience, the other is a hypothesis. The experience in question 'encompasses me and my environment, together with its constituent parts (including my fellow human beings), plus certain relationships'. The hypothesis under discussion 'lies in the interpretation I give to the motions of fellow human beings (including the linguistic instruments and the noises and sounds used and made by them) – in the interpretation that is, according to which these motions are *assertions* (*Aussagen*) that refer to sounds, noises or tastes or wills or feelings, etc. again, just like my words and deeds do.' Somewhat later Avenarius has this to say about the hypothesis under discussion:

> To say that other people are human beings just like me and I am a human being just like they is nothing but to assume that motions (and sounds) made by humans have not only mechanistic meanings. This form of the hypothesis could be called the *cardinal empiriocriticist assumption of basic human equality*.
>
> (Avenarius 1891: 9)

The objective structure of the world and reality, according to Mach, falls apart into unanalysable elements – sensations – and there are no permanent, constant or autonomous entities over and above the amorphous and chaotic mass of these sensations (Mach 1905: 435–6; 1915: *passim*). Moreover, in Mach's view, observing 'other people's behavior . . . makes me assume . . . that my recollections, desires etc. exist *for them* only as a result of a compelling inference by analogy just as their recollections, desires, etc. do *for me*' (Mach 1905: 6).

Notice, however, that although the hypothesis underlying and vindicating this inference by analogy is intimately related to the world view of methodological solipsism, it is not an ontological but an epistemological assumption, and as such belongs to the general category of *epistemological isolationism*. I want to emphasise again though that its compelling force (and the compelling force of the inference by analogy) derives from the world view under discussion.

To fix ideas, let me review the epistemological stance of methodological solipsism. Suppose that on the basis of previous experience we know what *acting* means, that is, we know that human action always involves beliefs, desires, objectives and intentions. Suppose also that these beliefs, desires, objectives and intentions are not only the subjective data of actors but are also inaccessible to outside observers because outside observers can hardly do more than to establish the fact of an action. If we make the further assumption that the thought processes of the actors are just like ours, then we are allowed to attribute beliefs, desires, objectives and intentions to them on the analogy of our own mental states, making their actions thus directly and empathically understandable to us.

How do we learn about our own mental states and thus how do we get to know the mental states of other people? According to one of the fundamental epistemological postulates of methodological solipsism, we can learn about our own mental states only by way of introspection (Hayek 1964: 44–5, 50, 75–6; Mises 1933: 41, 122). Introspection is a kind of inner perception, independent of any bodily organ of sense, through which we can acquire (so the theory goes) a singularly reliable form of self-knowledge. This introspectively gained self-knowledge, as a result of the basic similarity of the human mind and the commonalities of our mental structures, gives us direct access to those thoughts, concepts and objectives with the help of which we can understand individual and collective attitudes and actions observable in the world around us. In the view of the advocates of methodological solipsism, this introspective knowledge is not only the methodological starting point for the social sciences, but in its subjective nature lies the ultimate explanation for the systematic subjectivism of these sciences (Hayek 1952a: 192–3; 1964: 50). This unique method of acquiring knowledge and information stretches the methodological rift between the social and the natural sciences even further. While the natural sciences approach their subject matter mechanistically and externally (Mises 1940: 27; Gottl 1925: 255), social scientists possess a kind of a priori and internal knowledge of their field of study, superior to the shallow knowledge of simple causal connections (Mises 1933: 122).

The principle of epistemological isolationism has some very unpleasant substantive and methodological consequences, however. To avoid them, methodological solipsists tend to qualify their position by saying, as Hayek (1952b: 89–90) does, for example, that the assumption of the basic similarity of human consciousness is true only under certain circumstances and that the likelihood of understanding the actions of other human beings diminishes as we move away from our habitual and familiar social environment. Moreover, methodological solipsists are forced to admit that from their epistemological point of view 'crazy' or mentally ill people cannot be considered part of humanity (Hayek 1964: 79; Gottl 1925: 161), because it is doubtful that their mental structures are sufficiently similar to that of social scientists to provide for a direct and empathic understanding of their actions.

Notice, however, that one of the unwelcome consequences of this methodological principle would be to ban cultural and economic anthropology from the family of social sciences. It seems, for one thing, very unlikely that researchers of tribal–religious rites or of economic transactions in tribal societies, for instance, could rely on the kind of introspective knowledge that guides them more or less successfully through the mores of their own societies and cultures. Bringing the principle of epistemological isolationism to its logical conclusion implies a denial of the adage, first formulated and vaguely explained by Simmel and later fully vindicated by Max Weber (1978: 5): 'one need not have been Caesar in order to understand Caesar.'

The third tenet of methodological solipsism is concerned with the logical–methodological status of models and theories in the social sciences. Adherents of the methodological programme under discussion tend to believe that the information provided by intro-spection and the knowledge based thereupon are true simply by virtue of our privileged access to this kind of knowledge and this kind of information. In Mises' view, the theoretical statements of the social sciences are apodictically certain and a priori, that is, independently of any subsequent factual evidence, true (Mises 1933: 12, 26–7; 1940: 18, 21; see also Hayek 1952b: 51–3).

Moreover, the social sciences do not strive for causal explanations; their cognitive goal is to understand human behaviour through introspection, and to classify and order introspectively understood forms of behaviour (Hayek 1952b: 91–2). Theories in the social sciences are not sets of laws, that is, hypotheses with explanatory power and informative content to be bolstered by empirical evidence, but are, like logic and mathematics, collections of tautologies furnished by the above mentioned process of introspection. In other words, theories of complex phenomena are not nomological (Hayek 1967: 41); they cannot be used to establish causal connections. Thus economics, which, according to Mises (1933: 12, 27–9), is only a part of praxeology, i.e., the general theory of human action, is not an empirical but an a priori science, the theorems of which are timeless and unchanging, and cannot be verified or falsified on the basis of empirical data or evidence. A given theory remains true as long as mental errors or fallacious inferences don't blemish it and as long as it is free of internal contradictions. Marginal utility theory or general equilibrium theory both belong to the realm of the 'pure logic of choice', i.e., both of them are tautological constructs used to classify action types created or generated by introspection and the researchers' theoretical imagination.

Methodological solipsism imputes eternal validity to the theoretical statements of the social sciences just because they were formulated on the basis of data to which we allegedly have privileged access, thus repudiating the trivial insight according to which the truth and reliability of our knowledge is guaranteed by its testability and not by the royal or less royal method that helped us acquire it. Notice, however, that the same argument is also being used to neutralise the theoretical social sciences against the impact of any eventual corrective measure grounded in empirical evidence.

Let me recapitulate the reasoning that makes methodological solipsists question the empirical nature of social sciences and reject the idea of factual verification or falsification. The argument illustrates the interconnections between the basic postulates of methodological solipsism. In Hayek's view (1964: 42, 65; 1967: 21), for instance, the social sciences can aim not at the 'detailed explanations' supplied by the natural sciences, but at 'explanations of principle' only; that is, at most they can, with the help of simplified models, provide an intuitive understanding of general principles. The truth value of an explanation of principle cannot be decided on the basis of some kind of a mechanical test.

The social sciences have to be content with explanations of principle because their subject matter is strikingly complex and the number of constraints and specific conditions to be taken into account when trying to construct a genuine explanation is so large that not even computers, not to mention the human mind, are able to master them. Because the social sciences cannot devise simplified experimental conditions, it is the same complexity that prevents them from checking the validity of their explanations by subjecting them to the critique of facts and of reality.

It is noteworthy that Menger, although from a somewhat different methodological perspective, had already made a similar argument. In his view:

> the main objective of the method to be called *exact* in the future is . . . to establish strict laws of phenomena; . . . laws which not only appear to be uniform to us but their uniformity is guaranteed by the cognitive routes leading to them.
>
> (Menger 1883: 38)

Accordingly, 'to check the *exact theory* of the national economy on the basis of the totality of empirical reality is a methodological absurdity.' Or:

> trying to corroborate the pure theory of the national economy by matching it to the full reality of experience would be similar to the procedure followed by a mathematician who would want to correct the theorems of geometry by measuring objects of the real world.
>
> (ibid.: 64)

For Menger, the 'full empirical reality of phenomena' is just another name for the complexity and totality of the real world, that is, for the impenetrable mass of concrete events and sensations surrounding us in the world of human actions. Of course, this full empirical reality cannot be used to verify or refute the laws of economic theory, and thus our methods of discovering them, combined with the laws of logic, should vouch for their validity. This is, according to Menger, only a temporary solution, however. Although these laws are basically instruments of causal explanation for him, they are also founded in one particular segment of empirical reality, namely the economic aspect of the heterogeneous empirical phenomena. Hence the empirical validity of economic laws can only be decided if we have at our disposal the comprehensive and 'exact' theory that is able to embrace all important aspects, that. is, the full reality, of these phenomena. This digression was necessary to point out the similarities, implied by the common world view, between the position of Menger and that of methodological solipsism.

Finally, I want to say a few words about the alleged apodictic certainty or a priori validity of the introspectively obtained theoretical statements of the sciences of human action. Max Weber had already answered some of these questions when he made a distinction between the clarity and certainty of interpretation and understanding on the one hand, and the validity of adequate causal explanations on the other. According to Weber, it is easy for us to comprehend clearly and with great inner certainty the meaning of forms of behaviour and types of action that we are either able to perform or that can be made empathically accessible to us through sympathetic participation. The same is true of the rational understanding of mathematically or logically related propositions, the meaning of which can be grasped immediately and unambiguously.

Although 'every interpretation', says Weber, 'attempts to attain clarity and certainty', it does not really matter 'how clear an interpretation as such appears to be from the point of view of meaning, it cannot on this account claim to be the causally valid interpretation. On this level it must remain only a peculiarly plausible hypothesis' (Weber 1978: 5) – a hypothesis, we may add, the truth value or validity of which can be decided only by comparing it with the facts of experience. Although the behaviour of Caesar or a mentally ill person may not be immediately accessible to our empathic understanding, we may still be able to come up with a rational interpretation or causal explanation of their behaviour with the help of our nomological knowledge and the behavioural uniformities of psychopathology.

The nomological knowledge Weber talks about is nothing but a loose collection of intersubjectively valid rules of experience, assigning particular means to particular ends in a given society. Acquisition and consistent application of this nomological knowledge in a causal explanation or rational interpretation is the precondition for the 'understanding' of a tribal or religious rite or of an economic transaction that happens to take place in a social or economic setting different from ours. Possessing this kind of nomological knowledge and not the special status of information obtained through introspection enables the social scientist to cope in his own society, and to understand the behaviour and actions of his fellow human beings. It is simply not true that 'a mind has a twofold "privileged access" to its own doings, which makes its self knowledge superior in quality, as well as prior in genesis, to its grasp of other things' (Ryle 1966: 154).

The last assumption would imply the absurdity that society consists of windowless monads who obtain information about their own minds and souls by a continuous process of non-sensuous inner perception, and who would have to peek into the other monads through the missing window to get a direct knowledge of their minds and souls. In reality, however,

> the problem is . . . simply the methodological question of how we establish, and how we apply, certain sorts of law-like propositions about the overt and the silent behaviour of persons. I come to appreciate the skill and tactics of a chess-player by watching him and others playing chess, and I learn that a certain pupil of mine is lazy, ambitious and witty by following his work, noticing his excuses, listening

to his conversation and comparing his performances with those of others. Nor does it make any important difference if I happen myself to be that pupil. I can indeed listen to more of his conversations, as I am the addressee of his unspoken soliloquies; I notice more of his excuses, as I am never absent, when they are made. On the other hand, my comparison of his performances with those of others is more difficult, since the examiner is himself taking the examination, which makes neutrality hard to preserve and precludes the demeanour of the candidate, when under interrogation, from being in good view.

(Ryle 1966: 169)

By getting rid of the myth of the epistemological inevitability of analogical inference in the social sciences, rejecting the fantasy of the absolute certainty of introspective knowledge, and realising that causal explanations do not necessarily tarnish the vibrant and irrational reality of human action, we can get a more adequate picture of the methodological discrepancies between the social and natural sciences. The alleged extreme methodological dualism of the social and natural sciences turns out to be a misconception of their true relationship, since in fact neither the natural sciences are able to offer detailed explanations as Hayek seems to assume, nor are the explanations of principle in the social sciences 'something of an art' (Hayek 1967: 18). The logical structure of explanations claiming empirical validity shows far-reaching similarities in both groups of sciences.

If we reject the tenets of methodological solipsism, we can also dismiss the case against attempts at constructing theories with explanatory power and informative content in the social sciences in general, and in economics in particular. Similarly, the arguments put forward against methodological solipsism raise serious doubts about the legitimacy of stripping much of modern economic theory of any connection to reality, of shielding it from the control of empirical tests and of interpreting it as a pure logic of choice, serving solely heuristic and classificatory purposes. To avoid a possible misunderstanding, let me emphasise that I do not want to banish the logic of choice from economic theory. What I have been trying to argue against in this chapter is simply the fallacious characterisation of the methodological foundations of the social sciences offered by eminent researchers who, unfortunately enough, happen to be advocates of the tenets of methodological solipsism.

Ideal types

This section offers an analysis of the logic of intentional explanations by way of a partial rational reconstruction of Max Weber's
views on the methodological foundations of economic theory. My
aims are, first, to demonstrate that Lachmann, in at least one important respect, misconstrued Weber's methodological legacy; and
second, to shed new methodological light on the notion of ideal
types. The discussion will largely be based on Weber's writings in
the philosophy of science, including a neglected early article that
was first published in 1908 in the *Archiv für Sozialwissenschaft und
Sozialpolitik*.

Whereas the natural sciences, behaviouristically conceived
psychology included, deal with brute facts, the subject matter of the
social sciences proper, argues Weber, is human action. Human
action, however, whether individual or collective, cannot be taken as
a *factum brutum*, because it is not something given to us *ex ante*. That
is, it is not something given before or without analysis. On the
contrary, human action is something that must be interpreted or
properly understood before we go about explaining it. Lachmann is
seemingly in complete agreement with Weber. 'Phenomena of
human action', he maintains:

> unlike phenomena of nature, are manifestations of the
> human mind. Action has a meaning to the agent. We are
> unable to understand phenomena of human action other-
> wise than as outward manifestations of human plans which
> must exist before action is taken and which subsequently
> guide all action. To understand phenomena of action we
> therefore have to elucidate those acts of the minds of agents
> which shape and steer their plans which in turn guide their
> overt action. In other words, our task as social scientists is
> primarily an interpretative one: we have to elucidate the
> meaning observable human acts have to their respective
> agents.
>
> (Lachmann 1986: 49)

The upshot of this argument is that the 'facts' of the social sciences
are 'artifacts', in the sense that in the process of a pre-explanatory
interpretation we make them. In other words, when we set out to
explain human action, first we have to construct the raw material
for our explanations.

Economists, argues Weber, take it for granted that people, in general, act purposefully or intentionally.[5] This, Weber might have said, is a theoretically more fruitful hypothesis than (aping the natural sciences) to conceive of human actors as puppets on the strings of obscure psychological stimuli or of mysterious social forces.[6]

Second, economists not only assume that people in general are capable of intentional action, but they add to this the further assumption that people – at least in economic matters or, more generally, in matters relating to their own interests – do act calculatively, that is, in this sense rationally. In Weber's words:

> Marginal utility theory, in order to attain specific objects of knowledge, treats human action as if it ran its course from beginning to end under the control of *commercial calculation* – a calculation set up on the basis of *all* conditions that need to be considered. It treats individual 'needs' and the goods available (or to be produced or to be exchanged) for their satisfaction as mathematically calculable 'sums' and 'amounts' in a continuous process of bookkeeping. It treats man as an agent who constantly carries on 'economic enterprise', and it treats his life as the object of his 'enterprise' controlled according to calculation. The outlook involved in commercial bookkeeping is, if anything, the starting point of the constructions of marginal utility theory.
>
> (Weber 1908: 32)

If individual people, in the light of everyday experience, really do act intentionally and calculatively, then in the great majority of economically relevant cases, we can regard their actions as means to achieve a desired end.[7] This is equivalent to saying that we can frequently explain individual actions and collective outcomes by referring to the particular ends people are seeking to achieve. We can call explanations couched in terms of means and goals *intentional explanations* of individual actions and *teleological–functional explanations* of collective outcomes.

In a similar vein, Lachmann suggests, 'actors, individuals as well as groups, pursue many purposes simultaneously and have to establish an order of priority among them. Moreover, the manifold constraints imposed upon the pursuit of our ends by the scarcity of means as well as by the ubiquitous presence of obstacles, actual or potential (negative means), compels all of us to bring all our means and ends within the framework of a comprehensive computation before we set out on our course of action' (Lachmann 1971: 34).

The social sciences, according to Lachmann, should follow what he calls the *praxeological* method. In a brief outline of the scope and nature of this method, Lachmann presents the following characterisation:

> Human action is not determinate, but neither is it arbitrary. It is bounded, firstly, by the scarcity of means at the disposal of actors. This circumstance imposes a constraint on the freedom of action. It is bounded, secondly, by the circumstance that, while men are free to choose ends to pursue, once they have made their choice they must adhere to it if consistent action with a chance of success is to be possible at all. In other words, human action is free within an area bounded by constraints. Obstacles of various kinds further limit the area of freedom.
>
> (Lachmann 1971: 37)

The praxeological method has to take these circumstances into account. Causal explanation in the field of action cannot hope to attain determinateness, but this does not mean that we must give up all hope of explanation. What we may hope to accomplish here is to be able to show to what ends, means and obstacles human action is oriented. *Orientation* thus emerges as a concept as fundamental to praxeological study as determinateness is to natural science (ibid.: 37).

Let me try to elucidate the logical structure of the above arguments and the logic of teleological explanations of individual human action with the help of a simple example.[8] Suppose we observed the conduct of a certain individual, B, and we found, after intentionalistically interpreting her action, that she did x, where x denotes a particular action type or action. In other words, we suppose that we have succeeded in giving an empirically sound answer to a 'What did B do?' type of question, and the answer, astonishingly enough, turned out to be: 'B did x.'

Now suppose that, as good and curious scholars, we do not stop here, but go a step further, and decide to find out: 'Why did B do x?' How can we answer, or, for that matter, how do economists answer these kinds of 'Why?' questions? Of course, by constructing ideal types of human action and putting forward empirical generalisations, Weber replied. Lachmann, however, finds this answer unsatisfactory. He not only repudiates the use of empirical generalisations in the social sciences as tenuous at best and irrelevant at worst,[9] but also rejects the very notion of ideal types. His argument is worth quoting in full:

> there is one (to us overwhelming) reason why we are unable to accept the ideal type as our fundamental concept. The reason lies in the simple fact that Weber's ideal type lacks any specific reference to human action and seems to be as readily applicable to the animal kingdom or the plant world as to the human sphere. It seems better to start our journey on more promising ground and adopt as our fundamental concept a notion germane to human action, a notion, that is, in which the meaning of action is preconceived even before the very moment at which the course of action begins to unfold.
>
> (Lachman 1971: 29)

Lachmann then proceeds to make a case for substituting his notion of a 'plan' for that of the ideal type. Weber, argues Lachmann:

> points out that causal explanation is just as necessary in culture as in nature. But in the former case 'its specific significance rests only in that we are able, and want, not merely to state but to *understand* human action'. The possibility of such understanding is warranted by the purposive character of human action. But 'purpose', he says, 'is for us an imagined end which becomes the cause of an action; we take account of it in the same way as we have to take account of any other cause which does, or may, contribute to a significant effect.
>
> (Lachmann 1971: 32–4)

Then Lachmann adds:

> It is readily seen (with the benefit of hindsight) that this conception of the nature of causal explanation of human action in terms of purpose would have provided a firmer and more convenient starting point for the methodology of the social sciences than the controversial notion of the Ideal Type. It is also easy to see how it is naturally linked to our concept of Plan. In fact, 'plan' is but a generalization of purpose.
>
> (ibid.: 32–4)

But what exactly do the terms 'ideal type' and 'plan' mean in this context?[10] My purpose in proposing a rational reconstruction of these notions is again twofold. First, I want to substantiate my earlier claim that Lachmann misunderstood, and consequently misconstrued, Weber's methodological legacy at least in one important respect. Second, I want to show that the concepts of plan and ideal types can be fruitfully united under the methodological umbrella of the idea of intentional explanation.

Let us return to the 'Why did B do x?' question. Suppose we know from the outset that B wanted and managed to achieve y, where y stands for some desired end. For simplicity's sake, let's make the further assumption that the only means to be taken into account, if a means is to be taken into account at all, or the only means B had considered if she had considered any means at all, was nothing else but the action x. Could we then put forward the following argument?

1   B wanted to achieve y.
2   The only means to achieve y was action x. Therefore,
3   B did x.

Clearly, we cannot always explain B's action this way. First, B may not have known that x was a means to achieve y, in which case she did x perhaps for some other reason, and obtained y only as a fluke. Second, B may have acted on a wrong reason, that is, she may have believed, mistakenly, that x was the only means to achieve y, whereas in fact x was not an effective means to this end at all.

We can take care of these possibilities, Weber came to argue later, in either of the following two ways. The first option is to show, by factoring in the agent's epistemic situation,[11] that B, given her beliefs about the relevant means–ends relationships, acted in a subjectively rational way. The second route is to examine what B should or could have done, had she acted in accordance with the objective logic of the situation, that is in an objectively rational fashion.[12] It is easy to see that construction of what Weber calls subjectively rational ideal types, *pace* Lachmann, produces straightforward intentional or teleological explanations of individual action. Objectively rational ideal types, however, as explanatory frameworks have only, as Weber points out, instrumental and heuristic value.[13]

Thus the logical structure of a subjectively rational ideal type is the same as that of an intentional explanation. In the simplest possible case the explanatory argument runs as follows:

1   B wanted to achieve y.
2   B thought (believed) that she could achieve y best by doing x.
    Therefore
3   B did x.

When we construe empirically adequate ideal types of this kind, then, according to Weber, we arrive at a motivational, as distinct from actual, understanding of human action. 'Actual' understanding is equivalent to selecting the 'right', i.e., the empirically adequate, intentionalistic description.[14] Motivational understanding, argues Weber, rests on our nomological knowledge. To have the required type and amount of nomological knowledge at our disposal is the same as to know – either by acquaintance or by description – the rules of experience that in the eyes of people living in a particular society or culture assign given means to given ends.

In the case of objectively rational ideal types the reasoning is hypothetical, and, in the instrumental or technical sense of the word, normative. Taking as our paradigm the simplest possible situation again, we have the following constrained maximisation type argument.

1   Let us assume B wanted to achieve y.
2   In the light of the available evidence, and under the existing constraints, B could have achieved y only if she had done x. Therefore
3   B should have done x.

It requires only a modicum of methodological imagination to recognise in the foregoing primitive models the germ or analytical core of marginal utility or, for that matter, modern microeconomic theory. In fact, argued Weber, economic analysis is founded not on some allegedly fundamental psychological laws, but on the use of the categories 'ends' and 'means', that is, on the use of more or less sophisticated 'praxeological' ideal types (Weber 1908: 3).

Conclusion

Economic analysis, for both Weber and Lachmann, is possible only because we are capable of *understanding* individual human conduct. By imputing intentions (or, in Lachmann's terminology, plans) to persons, we interpret individual behaviour as deliberate, subsume it under some specific 'action type' (utility maximisation, cost minimisation, etc.), and clear the ground for an *intentional explanation* of a particular instance of the action type in question. This is the rational core, if there is one, of the more radical subjectivist claims of methodological solipsism.

Intentional explanations of individual actions in economic theory, Lachmann's misguided criticism notwithstanding, are based on ideal types. Ideal types, in turn, are theoretical constructs, the *logical* structure of which is just about the same in both the natural and the social sciences. Moreover, the use of properly constructed ideal types is methodologically fundamental, because these constructs fulfil indispensable classificatory, heuristic, and explanatory functions (Weber 1978: 21). The constrained maximisation models of standard economic theory, for instance, help us pigeonhole economic behaviour into the categories of expected utility maximisation, profit maximisation, price discrimination, etc. Furthermore, if we want to explain a particular instance of any of these categories (the actions taken by the managers of a specific firm, for example), and it turns out that these actions deviate from the course of action 'prescribed' or predicted by our pet model, we are still going to have to use our ideal type as a benchmark, because without having that heuristic device at our disposal we will not be able to arrive at meaningful hypotheses about the possible causes of this clash between theory and reality.

Notes

1 For a good overview of different forms of methodological individualism see Bhargava (1992). The term 'methodological solipsism' itself was first used in a somewhat different sense from the one intended here (Carnap 1928).

2 We should heed Schumpeter's advice with regard to Gottl's work: 'I fear that the only way of appreciating Professor F. von Gottl-Ottlilienfeld, who held a conspicuous place and found many adherents . . . is to read him' (Schumpeter 1954: 854). For a sympathetic and tolerant, but in the end devastating, criticism of Gottl's views on the epistemology of the social sciences, see Weber's essay on 'Knies and the problem of irrationality' (Weber 1975). In Weber's view, Gottl:

> scrupulously eschews conventional, conceptually bound, and, from his point of view, 'denatured' language. Instead, he attempts to reproduce the contents of immediate 'experience' in some sort of ideogram. Admittedly, many of Gottl's views, including the principal theses of his work, are controversial. Nor has he succeeded in establishing genuine

conclusions. Nevertheless, this idiosyncratic work must be recognised for what it is: a subtle and intellectually stimulating illumination of the problem.

(Weber 1975: 212)

3 Although the logic of this reasoning is very similar to Hayek's epistemic argument against central planning and socialism, the methodological status of the two arguments is very different.

4 According to Lachmann:

Natural phenomena exist in time and space only, and observability is the only criterion of their existence. The fact, on the other hand, that human action exists in the form of plans, i.e. mental design, permits us to study the relationships between human action and the plans which guide it. The method of interpretation in the social sciences ultimately rests on the possibility of, and the need for, such comparative study. In this sense, then, we may say that we are able to give an 'intelligible account' of human action by revealing the plans which guide it, a task beyond the grasp of the natural sciences. The mere fact that this possibility exists is the foundation of the method of interpretation and thus offers a vindication of the plea for the methodological autonomy of the social sciences.

(Lachmann 1971: 30)

5 Cf. Weber:

In the economic theory of marginal utility and in every 'subjective' value theory . . . there is, to begin with, *not* an external 'stimulus' but a 'need'. This is of course the reverse of the situation we have in the case of the fundamental law of psychophysics. Accordingly, if we wish to express ourselves in 'psychological' terms, we deal with a complex of 'sensations', 'feeling-states', states of 'tension', 'discomfort', 'expectation', and the like, which may at any time be of most intricate character. And these, moreover, combine with 'memory images', 'purposes', and perhaps conflicting 'motives' of the most various kinds. Also, while the fundamental law of psychophysics instructs us about how an *external* stimulus evokes psychic conditions, . . . economics, rather, is concerned with the fact that in virtue of such 'psychic' conditions a specifically oriented *external* behaviour (action) is evoked.

(Weber 1908: 27–8)

6 According to Weber:

It is not only that, at least by and large, the most general hypotheses and assumptions of the 'natural sciences' (in the usual sense of this term) are the most irrelevant ones for our discipline. But further, and above all, precisely as regards the point which is decisive for the peculiar quality of the questions proper to our discipline: *In economic theory ('value theory') we stand entirely on our own feet.*

(Weber 1908: 31)

7 'Marginal utility theory and, more broadly, any subjective theory of value are not psychologically, but – if a methodological term is desired – "pragmatically" founded, that is, on the use of the categories *"ends"* and *"means"* ' (Weber 1908: 33).

8 On what follows see also Langlois and Csontos (1993).

9 According to Lachmann:

Some readers may feel that in doubting whether there is much scope in economics for empirical generalisations of a comprehensive character, applying equally to future and past, we have gone too far. They may remind us that in the Austrian tradition all economic action is embedded in a network of means and ends. . . . Mises even attributed *a priori* character to the network of means and ends, and Hayek in 1937 spoke of this part of economics as the 'pure logic of choice'. It is indeed evident that all human activity is purposeful. Why should such a body of thought have to be regarded as incapable of providing a solid basis for empirical generalisations of the kind mentioned?

The answer has to be that our network of means and ends, precisely by virtue of the logical necessity inherent in it, is impotent to engender empirical generalisations. Its truth is purely abstract and formal truth. The means and ends it connects are abstract entities. In the real world the concrete means used and ends sought are ever changing as knowledge changes and what seemed worthwhile yesterday no longer seems so today. We appeal in vain to the logic of means and ends to provide us with support for empirical generalisations of the kind mentioned.

(Lachmann 1971: 31)

10 According to Weber:

Now the tenets which constitute specifically economic *theory* do *not* represent, . . . 'the whole' of our science. These tenets afford but a single means (often, to be sure, an underestimated means) for the analysis of the causal connections of empirical reality. As soon as we take hold of this reality itself, in its culturally significant components, and seek to explain it causally, economic history is immediately revealed as a sum of 'ideal-typical' concepts. This means that its theorems represent a series of *conceptually* constructed events, which, in 'ideal purity', are seldom, or even not at all, to be found in the historical reality of any particular time.

(Weber 1908: 33–4)

On the structure and functions of ideal types, see further Weber (1978: 6, 9, 20; 1949: 50–113).

11 Lachmann is plainly wrong when he asserts that hypotheses or empirical generalisations cannot be tested in the social sciences because it is impossible to specify knowledge. Cf. the following characteristic stricture:

> The scientist who proposes an experiment to test his hypothesis must pay close attention to specifying the conditions in which the experiment is to take place. But in the case of human action, even were we to grant the existence of 'universal laws', it is impossible to specify such an initial situation for the simple reason that it is impossible to specify knowledge. Evidently the knowledge of the actor is an important element of his action. Were we to test hypotheses concerning action, the canon of scientific method would require us to describe in detail all the knowledge possessed by the actors – an evident impossibility. We see thus that while 'description of the initial situation' is a fairly innocuous requirement in nature, where all we have to do is enumerate objects in time and space, for human action this requirement cannot be met because we should have to include something unspecifiable – knowledge! A human situation without specific knowledge makes no sense. It follows that the 'scientific method' of the natural sciences will be of little use to the student of action because he is unable to use the testing procedure this method prescribes.
>
> (Lachmann 1971: 35–6)

12 Weber (1913) distinguishes between subjectively rational and objectively rational ideal types (the latter he calls *Richtigkeits-Typen*) in 'Über einige Kategorien der verstehenden Soziologie'; this essay represents his first attempt at a positive and systematic exposition of his methodological views.

13 According to Weber:

> [T]hese theorems – since in fact their elements are derived from experience and intensified to the point of pure rationality only in a process of thought – are useful both as heuristic instrumentalities of analysis and as constructive means for the representation of the empirical manifold.
>
> (Weber 1908: 34)

14 On the distinction between actual and motivational understanding see Weber (1978: 8–13). 'Actual' understanding (*aktuelles Verstehen*) is rendered in the English translation, somewhat misleadingly, as 'direct observational' understanding.

References

Avenarius, R. (1891) *Der menschliche Weltbegriff*, Leipzig: O. R. Reisland.

Bhargava, R. (1992) *Individualism in Social Science*, New York: Oxford University Press.

Carnap, R. (1928) *Der logische Aufbau der Welt*, Berlin-Schlachtensee: Weltkreis-Verlag.

Gottl-Ottlilienfeld, F. von (1925) *Wirtschaft als Leben*, Jena: Fischer Verlag.

Hayek, F. A. von (1952a) *The Sensory Order*, Chicago: University of Chicago Press.

—— (1952b) *Individualismus und wirtschaftliche Ordnung*, Erlenbach-Zürich: E. Rentsch Verlag.

—— (1964) *The Counter-Revolution of Science*, Glencoe, Ill: The Free Press of Glencoe.

—— (1967) *Studies in Philosophy, Politics, and Economics*, Chicago: University of Chicago Press.

Lachmann, L. M. (1971) *The Legacy of Max Weber*, Berkeley: Glendessary Press.

—— (1976) 'From Mises to Shackle', *Journal of Economic Literature*, 14: 55–6.

—— (1986) *The Market as an Economic Process*, Oxford: Blackwell.

Langlois, R. N. and Csontos, L. (1993) 'Optimization, rule following, and the methodology of situational analysis', in B. Gustaffson, C. Knudsen, and U. Müki (eds) *Rationality, Institutions, and Economic Methodology*, London: Routledge.

Mach, E. (1905) *Erkenntnis und Irrtum*, Leipzig: J. A. Barth.

—— (1915) *Die Analyse der Empfindungen* (6, vermehrte Auflage), Jena: Fischer Verlag.

Menger, C. (1883) *Untersuchungen Ober die Methode der Sozialwissenschaften*, Leipzig: Duncker and Humblot.

Mises, L. von (1933) *Grundgrobleme der Nationalökonomie*, Jena: Fischer Verlag.

—— (1940) *Nationalökonomie*, Genf: Ed. Union.

Ryle, G. (1966) *The Concept of Mind*, London: Hutchinson.

Schumpeter, J. A. (1954) *History of Economic Analysis*, New York: Oxford University Press.

Shackle, G. L. S. (1972) *Epistemics and Economics*, Cambridge: Cambridge University Press.

Weber, M. (1908) 'Die Grenznutzenlehre und das "psychophysische Grundgesetz"', transl. as 'Marginal utility and "the fundamental laws of psychophysics"', *The Social Science Quarterly* (1975), 56: 21–36.

—— (1913) 'Über einige Kategorien der verstehenden Soziologie', in *Gesammelte Autsätze zur Wissenschaftslehre*, 4th edn, Tübingen: J. C. B. Mohr [1973].

—— (1949) '"Objectivity" in social science and social policy', in *The Methodology of the Social Sciences*, Glencoe, Ill: The Free Press of Glencoe.

—— (1975) *Roscher and Knies: The Logical Problems of Historical Economics*, New York and London: The Free Press.

—— (1978) *Economy and Society*, Berkeley: University of California Press.

Wright, G. H. von (1971) *Explanation and Understanding*, Ithaca, NY: Cornell University Press.

6

ENDOGENOUS CHANGE, OPEN SYSTEMS AND PROVISIONAL EQUILIBRIUM

Maurizio Caserta

Although he dismissed it as an essentially inadequate construct for a proper understanding of the market process, equilibrium was a recurrent theme in the work of Ludwig Lachmann. He rejected the idea of equilibrium as an attainable position of rest in which individual plans become mutually compatible; he also rejected the idea of equilibrium as a position towards which the economy tends but may never actually reach. The only notion of equilibrium that Lachmann thought should be retained was the notion of individual equilibrium.[1] This is the axiom of the purposeful individual.

For Lachmann, the market process was to be viewed as a sequence of actions and interactions. It would be understood by means of a voluntaristic theory of action where the freedom of individuals' will would represent a fundamental assumption.[2] The inclusion of this chapter in a memorial volume for Ludwig Lachmann is justified by this emphasis on action, which it shares with all Austrian thinking. Such an emphasis enlarges the scope of economic analysis: in mainstream economic analysis only reactions, that is, responses to known stimuli, are permitted; equilibrium is precisely a state of affairs where no further reaction is justified. When action is contemplated, equilibrium can be either dismissed altogether, or reconceived as identifying a less definitive state of affairs. The latter route is followed here.

Introduction

Among the different notions of equilibrium in economic theory, one contends that equilibrium is a state of affairs that can be disrupted only by an exogenous change. This fundamentally implies that all foreseeable changes have been discounted and that what is there to be learned has been learned. This notion of equilibrium, therefore, is inconsistent with the emergence of novelty. Continuity cannot be preserved if novelty emerges; such an occurrence will necessarily break continuity. As far as economic theory goes, such novelties remain inexplicable.

In Chick and Caserta (1994) a different notion of equilibrium is put forward, in which it is argued that equilibrium and the possibility of novelty are not necessarily incompatible. Equilibrium can be dissolved from within as well as from without. Continuity can be preserved without having to portray equilibrium as encompassing all possible developments. All this becomes sustainable if equilibrium is not seen as the outcome of a fully specified model, where all contingencies have been taken into account and where choice is predetermined.

A partially specified model implies that not all aspects of relevant behaviour have been spelled out nor that all the relevant actors have been included in the picture. This partial specification, however, does not render the model necessarily wrong. This would be the case if those aspects of behaviour or those actors were fully operative in that particular situation. Let us take, for instance, the neoclassical model of economic growth. There entrepreneurial propensities are altogether neglected. One can deem entrepreneurial propensities relevant or not relevant. If the latter is the case, it would be right to ignore them in the model; if the former is the case, the neoclassical model of economic growth would be incorrectly specified. There is a third option, however: entrepreneurial propensities may be considered relevant, but in a state of quiescence in that particular situation. What this means is that they are suspended but not suppressed. Since suspension presupposes resumption, the state of rest that is represented in the model may be dissolved from within rather than from without.

It must be noticed that the difference between a partially and a fully specified model is not the same as that between a short-term and a long-term model. The difference between a short-term and a long-term model turns on the number of variables that are kept constant, this number decreasing as we move from a short-term to a long-term model. The difference between a partially and a fully specified model is one between a model whose functions, through ignorance of the agent or the analyst, cannot all be precisely specified, and a model where nothing impedes such specifications.[3] Thus a short-term model can be fully specified if what is treated as given is not liable to generate at some point in time an unpredictable dynamics, either because fixity of that variable is a realistic assumption or because the analyst is not prepared to take into account the possibility of change. That assumption, therefore, is not concealing the inability of the theorist to properly specify that function.

If this argument is accepted, equilibrium will cease to convey necessarily the idea of finality, that is, the idea of a state of affairs that can be changed only by external occurrences. More generally, it might become associated with endogenous as well as with exogenous change. The notion of provisional equilibrium, introduced in Chick and Caserta (1994) mentioned above, was designed precisely to represent a state of rest that has within itself the seeds of its own destruction. Thus, equilibrium becomes consistent with innovation, learning and evolution.

The purpose of this chapter is to pursue further the notion of provisional equilibrium. In particular, what kind of theoretical purpose is served by this notion will be discussed. Then attention will be devoted to the idea that equilibrium is consistent with learning. To do so, Hahn's notion of equilibrium is taken as the starting point.[4] Finally, an example, taken from the theory of economic growth, of what implications the notion of provisional equilibrium could have for actual theorising will be suggested. It will be argued that the need to ensure continuity to the economic discourse can be served by an approach to growth based on a multiplicity of growth regimes, each of which is associated with a different set of exogenous and endogenous variables. Such an approach can cope with novelty in a non-traditional way: instead of having shifts in the parameters of the functions (which obviously can still take place), it handles novelty by means of shifts from one regime to another. This implies that there is a higher level in the analysis, a general framework, which is what is required for the notion of provisional equilibrium to make any sense.

The nature of change

Any account of change in theorising is bound to be unsatisfactory. If change is viewed as the emergence of novelty, one can only trace its consequences. If, on the other hand, one wants to explain change, it must be deprived of its novelty. The treatment of change in economic theory reflects this inadequacy, for change is portrayed either as entirely exogenous, or as entirely generated within the model. When it is entirely exogenous, no explanation can be given within the realm of economic theory; when it is entirely generated within the model, it becomes indistinguishable from an equilibrium relation, as all changes have been pre-reconciled. One cannot fail to see that a pre-reconciled change is not a kind of change that displays any novelty. Novelty and explanation appear therefore as mutually exclusive categories.

This difficulty in the treatment of change might be thought to be easily overcome by taking one of the following routes. When change is portrayed as entirely exogenous, one could have recourse to a different field of study other than economics and supply an explanation in terms of the factors relevant to that field. But this would just shift the problem onto a different area, as change will then be portrayed as entirely explicable within that model. Novelty would be preserved only as far as economic theory goes.

In the case of model-generated change, there is no novelty to speak of. All change is governed by pre-determined relations. In fact, some degree of novelty could be introduced by assuming uncertainty. However, as long as uncertainty is associated with probabilistic knowledge, instead of having deterministic pre-reconciliation, we would have pre-reconciliation of the probabilistic type. Novelty would here appear under the guise of chance, and thus hardly be explicable. Consider, for example, the growth of the capital stock. In a model of growth the change in the capital stock is generated within the model. The model outcome ensures that all changes are reconciled. Growth of the capital stock could be assumed to depend on the growth of demand. When this is the case, the model outcome ensures that capacity and demand grow at the same rate. With uncertainty, the growth of the capital stock will depend on the expected growth of demand. A growing capital stock will thus be consistent with a growing demand only on average. Deviations from this average will just be chance deviations.

It appears impossible therefore, as one tries slowly to move away from one treatment of change in order to include some aspects of the other, to remain halfway and have novelty and explanation at the same time. As one tries to make novelty less novel and introduce some explanation, novelty is totally lost. Similarly, as one tries to reduce the degree of pre-reconciliation by introducing random events, explanation is totally lost. All this goes to show that the question of change should be approached in a different way.

The following suggestion of Loasby's might be a useful starting point:

> The distinction between incremental and discontinuous change is an imposed distinction. All change involves at least one discontinuity; no change obliterates the past. The invention of such categories as revolutionary and normal science, or the hard core and protective belt of a research programme, like the familiar distinction between short- and long-run effects (. . .) is part of the process through which we try to make sense of the world by imposing manageable categories upon it. If driven hard, all such distinctions break down.
>
> (Loasby 1991: 19)

Instead of portraying change as an unexpected event, thus stressing discontinuity, or as a fully known development, implying strict continuity, it might be possible to think of change as an underlying process whose developments are, as yet, unknown. Such a process may not impinge on the established relations that are being studied, but may produce some consequences at a later date. Here novelty is preserved, but a line of development is identified. When this is acknowledged in the establishment of a set of equilibrium relations, equilibrium by its very nature becomes provisional.

This argument could appear to be very easily countered by the remark that there is always something going on in the world that is beyond our understanding. There is always something left out of the picture that is difficult to fit into it. When it becomes possible to fit the new piece in, the picture will be enlarged. Thus, despite the perception that there is more to the world than we can make out, we should say no more than what our coherent model allows us to say. In fact, this counter-argument can be questioned. Just as the analyst perceives that there is more to the world than he or she can make out, so there is no reason to rule out that the actors of the theoretical model entertain the very same perception. It will be argued below that it is through this line of reasoning that Loasby's remarks can be supported and a different treatment of change suggested.

Hahn's notion of equilibrium

Hahn's notion of equilibrium is well known: 'an economy is in equilibrium when it generates messages which do not cause agents to change the theories which they hold or the policies which they pursue' (Hahn 1984: 59). According to Hahn, an agent's theory is the result of the processing of the messages from the economy and nature received by the agent up to the date t. An agent's policy is a mapping from messages to acts. It is in the nature of the equilibrium position that the agents are not learning in equilibrium, which means that the agents' theory is independent of the date t. It is also in the nature of the equilibrium position that policies are not changing, which requires that agents are not learning and that their objectives are not changing.[5]

As long as agents are learning, the economy is not in equilibrium. The economy is generating messages that do not cause agents to maintain their theories.[6] Hahn contents himself with the hypothesis that theories are abandoned when they are 'sufficiently and systematically falsified'. Any such message from the economy will prompt a reconsideration of the theories entertained that far and a change in regime. How the new theory and hence the new equilibrium are reached is not known. However, if a 'higher-level' theory of the learning process were available, such a change in regime would not cause any discontinuity, as it would represent an equilibrium behaviour of the economy being studied. If such a theory were available, analysts and agents alike would know how to discard a theory and put another one in its place.[7]

Strictly speaking the process whereby theories are rejected and replaced does not imply, on the part of agents, any learning in Hahn's sense. Therefore, equilibrium and learning carry on being two incompatible ideas. The argument put forward here is that equilibrium and learning can indeed coexist. What this argument is built on is the equal treatment of economic agents and economic analysts.[8] Let us see what is a typical attitude of economic analysts. Responding to an objection on the axiomatic method Hahn says:

> Axioms, like special hypotheses, are there to specialise. It is not that they are divorced from experience or observation but rather that they mark the stage beyond which one does not seek to explain. The axiom that firms maximise some function of profits is stated as such

because the theorist is not proposing to answer the question why firms should do so.

(Hahn 1984: 6)

Once this axiom is accepted, agents and theorists can develop a theory of the determination of the rate of profit. It is true that the assumption of profit maximisation may conflict with a different objective on the part of firms. Such an objective, however, is not contemplated: one has to start somewhere. Hahn continues: 'My own position is that economists are at their most useful when they give an account of the alternative scenarios which the present state of our knowledge allows' (ibid.: 8) This implies that economists do their job properly only when they set very clearly the limits of their analyses. Even when they perceive that something interesting could be said of what lies beyond those limits, they should confine themselves only to what can be said with sufficient clarity. However, future developments of the subject are not ruled out. On the contrary, they are sought and encouraged. In fact, the need for clarity is emphasised precisely in view of the future development: 'It is one of the great virtues of the way good economic theorizing proceeds that it allows us to pinpoint difficulties precisely and to be precise about the difficulties' (Hahn 1984: 50–1).

It is fair to say, therefore, that good economic theorists always perceive the limits of the present state of their knowledge. Such a perception, however, is not preventing them from constructing sound logical arguments. They perceive the complexity of the world, but nevertheless try to make some sense of it. Thus, they hold to a theory, but never rule out that a new development might put into question the current state of their knowledge. In fact, they might be even directly involved in pursuing such developments, which means that they might be learning.

Thus learning is compatible with adherence to a theory. In fact, adherence to a good theory will facilitate the evolution of knowledge, as it will mark clearly the boundaries of current knowledge. This means that adherence to a theory is always done with reservations. Theorists know that their theory may be supplanted by a new one but they do not know which theory will supplant the old one. Now, if we want to treat economic analysts and economic agents equally, we must assume that agents, too, can adhere to a theory and carry on learning at the same time.

The important implication of this equal treatment is that learning and equilibrium are no longer incompatible ideas. Agents can entertain theories and follow policies such that equilibrium results. But there is no reason why they should not do it with reservations, which means that a process of learning may be taking place. Hahn's claim that: 'it will be a condition of the agent being in equilibrium that he is not learning' is therefore put into question by this argument. Agents may fail to have a fully comprehensive theory of the world, but may content themselves with a less comprehensive one that leaves out a subset of the messages from the economy and nature.[9] The benefit from this partitioning is that a coherent set of propositions can be put together and a policy can be defined. But just like economists, agents will select a line of research and pursue it until some new theory is ready to be used. The new theory may be more comprehensive than the previous one or consist of an altogether different set of propositions.

It is the perception of complexity, on the part of economic analysts and economic agents alike, that this argument is based on. Any theory entertained by both groups is entertained with reservations. Such reservations, however, do not prevent them from using that theory. This is especially true for economic agents who need theories to act. What these reservations imply is that a tendency is continuously at work to try new lines of research whose possible developments and final outcome are as yet unknown.

We have reached a point when Loasby's remarks can be reconsidered to see whether they can be substantiated by the arguments put forward so far. As quoted above, Loasby questions the adequacy of the distinction between discontinuous and incremental change, arguing that it is an imposed distinction. The question we have to ask, then, is whether this distinction breaks down when learning is shown to be compatible with equilibrium, which is precisely the conclusion reached above. The answer is that it does break down. When learning is compatible with equilibrium in the way that was described earlier, change is no longer discontinuous or incremental or, alternatively, is both discontinuous and incremental. This is the case because the change that results from the process of learning has an element of discontinuity and an element of continuity. The element of discontinuity originates from the fact that the unknown outcome of the process of learning might disrupt the established equilibrium relations. The element of continuity comes from the simple fact that a process of learning is assumed, with the result that a line of development is identified.[10] This is just another way of saying that novelty and explanation are both preserved. For this kind of change the most appropriate definition seems to be that of endogenous change. The final implication of this line of reasoning is that the notion of provisional equilibrium is strengthened. When equilibrium is correctly associated with a process of learning, equilibrium by its very nature becomes provisional.

One may wonder at this point whether there is any difference between provisional equilibrium and Hahn's equilibrium. Both equilibria are disrupted by a change in the theory entertained and in both cases no disequilibrium dynamics are spelled out. There is a fundamental difference, however. Hahn's equilibrium presupposes that agents form theories that, however simple, are comprehensive, that is, theories which result from the processing of all messages received from the economy and nature. Provisional equilibrium, on the other hand, does not rule out that a subset of messages, although perceived, are not processed or are just partially processed. This means that a subset of messages is provisionally, as it were, put on one side, while a theory is formed on the basis of another subset of messages and acted upon. However, the processing of the other subset does not necessarily stop, so that a new theory may result at some point in time. The new theory may or may not be compatible with the set of propositions the old theory consists of; as a result it may or it may not include the material covered by the old theory.

It should become clear then that while Hahn's equilibrium can be disrupted when the theory is sufficiently and systematically falsified, this is not a necessary requirement for provisional equilibrium to be disrupted. Provisional equilibrium can be disrupted because the theory that results from the ongoing process of learning is not compatible with the old one, regardless of whether the old theory is falsified or not. Therefore, the notions of equilibrium and disequilibrium do not coincide in the two different stories. While Hahn's equilibrium is not compatible with learning, provisional equilibrium is; while Hahn's disequilibrium originates from systematic falsification of theories, disruption of provisional equilibrium does not have to originate from that.

The important implication of this difference is that whereas disruption of Hahn's equilibrium represents a discontinuity in the process of learning that does not proceed smoothly, disruption of provisional equilibrium does not alter the fundamental unity of the process of learning. It is this fundamental unity that lies at the heart of provisional equilibrium and serves as its main distinguishing point. But when it comes to economic analysis, is there any possibility of discriminating between the two notions? In other words, is it possible to tell a model of provisional equilibrium apart from a model of static or final equilibrium? Can the notion of provisional equilibrium make any difference for actual theorising? A tentative answer to this question will be given below.

Models of provisional equilibrium

When the theorist comes to construct a model of provisional equilibrium, the difference between endogenous change in the sense of this chapter and endogenous change of the pre-reconciled type becomes more striking. Unlike the change of the pre-reconciled type, endogenous change does not imply any actual change: no change is generated by a *model* of provisional equilibrium. In this respect a model of provisional equilibrium is more similar to a model of static equilibrium, where change can only be imposed from outside the model. What is different in a model of provisional equilibrium is the interpretation of equilibrium; equilibrium is no longer thought to be a state of affairs which can be disrupted only by exogenous occurrences. Thus the concept of provisional equilibrium is compatible with the proposition that change will occur, while the concept of static or final equilibrium is not.

However, different interpretations are relevant in so far as they carry implications for actual theorising. Just a different interpretation of the positions of provisional and final equilibrium would not by itself take us very far. It is argued here that one can go further than that. Since provisional equilibrium is based on a non-fully comprehensive theory, that is a theory with a clearly limited scope, it becomes possible to associate different non-fully comprehensive theories with different models. This possibility is not without consequences.

Despite the fact that each model will carry on looking indistinguishable from a static model, the simple fact that a number of alternative models is *simultaneously* considered carries important implications. It shows that there is a higher level of analysis where the individual models and their relations can be understood as parts of a single conceptual framework. The different models, however, will not be related to each other in the same way as short-term models are related to long-term models: there will be no hierarchy among them. Shifting from one model to another will not be due to the relaxation of some previously fixed variable. It is not simply a matter of making endogenous what was previously exogenous. That would certainly not disturb the above-mentioned novelty-*versus*-explanation dichotomy. Similarly this dichotomy would not be disturbed by models that differ because they are based on different fully comprehensive theories: shifting from one model to another would be the result of a structural break. On the contrary, the collection of models based on different non-fully comprehensive theories *will* disturb the novelty-*versus*-explanation dichotomy. Shifting from one model to another will not be the result of a structural break, but the result of the evolution of one regime into another within the same ongoing process of learning. What would be preserved in this case is the unity of the process of learning: the various models would appear as different closures of the same general system. Provisional equilibrium, therefore, turns out to be a quite appropriate notion of equilibrium to associate with this kind of approach.

It is not neglected here that the approach sketched above is just a tentative answer to the question of the relevance of the notion of provisional equilibrium. There is at least one other route that would be interesting to take. It concerns the possibility of modelling a process of learning that is neither deterministic, which would kill novelty, nor evolving through exogenous changes, which would kill explanation. This line is not pursued here.

The reason why emphasis is placed on an approach based on a multiplicity of models lies in the fact that there is already an example in the literature, in particular, in the theory of economic growth. By playing with endogenous and exogenous variables a number of growth regimes is established. Each of these regimes is here reinterpreted as being associated with a non-fully comprehensive theory. The whole approach is thus reinterpreted as an application of the notion of provisional equilibrium. It is to the discussion of this approach that the rest of this chapter is devoted.

An open-system approach

An analytical approach that admits of a multiplicity of solutions was the subject matter of an article Sen published in 1963. This article has become the source of inspiration for a number of growth theorists. What Sen argues in this article, which focuses on distributional problems rather than on growth, is that it is not possible to satisfy simultaneously an investment function independent from saving, full employment of capital and labour, and the marginal productivity theory of distribution.

Sen uses the following equations:

$$X = X(L^*, X^*) \qquad [1]$$
$$w = \partial X / \partial L \qquad [2]$$
$$X = \pi + wL^* \qquad [3]$$
$$I = s_p \pi + s_w wL^* \qquad [4]$$
$$I = I^* \qquad [5]$$

Equation [1] is a production function where X is the flow of the only good produced; L^* the amount of labour available in the economy and X^* the stock of capital in existence; the output and the capital comprise the same good. Equation [2] says that the wage rate must be equal to the marginal product of labour. Equation [3] requires profits and wages to exhaust the product. Equation [4] requires investment to be equal to saving. In this equation s_p and s_w are the marginal propensities to save out of profits and wages, respectively. Finally, Equation [5] represents the independent investment function. There are five equations, but only four unknowns: X, w, π, I. The problem, then, is a problem of overdeterminacy: one equation should be dropped or a further unknown introduced. Therefore, something must be given up. It could be, in turn, the independent investment function, marginalist distribution, full employment, etc.

The approach adopted by Sen in the treatment of distributional problems has been revived in the treatment of growth. Works by Marglin (1984a, b), Dutt (1987, 1990) and Taylor (1991) have followed Sen's procedure by starting from a general framework and presenting different growth regimes as different ways of closing the same general framework. Such a procedure amounts to deciding on which variables are going to be exogenous and which ones are going to be endogenous in each particular case. Thus, by playing with exogenous and endogenous variables, various combinations are obtained. It is argued here that this procedure proves appropriate for generating a set of models, each of which is associated with a non-fully comprehensive theory. In any case such a combination must be compatible with the purpose of producing a determinate system, that is, a system that yields an equilibrium solution.

In presenting the analytical foundations of the approach, Dutt's formulation will be followed.[11] However, while in Dutt's work the emphasis is on closures, that is, on what is assumed to be exogenous, here the emphasis is on what is given up, that is, on the variables made endogenous for the sake of having a determinate system. The purpose of this shift of emphasis is to highlight which set of messages is provisionally left out and not processed to form a theory. Here an exogenous variable is a variable that underlies a particular policy, and hence a particular theory, while an endogenous variable is a variable that can assume whatever value, as there is no policy and no theory for it.

Dutt assumes a closed capitalist economy that produces one good using two factors only: homogeneous labour and capital. Technology is given and exhibits fixed coefficients and constant returns to scale. Moreover, capital is eternal and all firms are identical. No government or money is included in the model. The basic structure of the system is made up of two equations, a production equation and a price equation. Production is either consumed or invested. So we have:

$$X = CL + gK$$

where X is total output, C consumption per worker, L employment, g the rate of growth of capital and K productive capacity. Since constant returns to scale have been assumed, unit coefficients can be used instead. Thus we get:

$$1 = Ca_0 + ga_1$$

where a_0 is the labour coefficient and a_1 the capital coefficient, obtained by dividing L and K by X. K/X, however, is made up of two different components, a technical coefficient and a given degree of capacity utilisation. This becomes clear when we divide both K and X by full capacity output X_f:

$$(K/X_f)/(X/X_f)$$

where the numerator represents the capital coefficient proper, and the denominator the degree of capacity utilisation. Only if current output equals full capacity output, i.e. when $X = X_f$, will the capital–output ratio be equal to the capital coefficient. It follows that in the general case the capital–output ratio will be different from the capital coefficient a_1. Thus the production equation is best kept in this general form:

$$1 = Ca_0 + g(K/X).$$

Price per unit of production goes to wages or profits. We have therefore the following price equation:

$$P = Wa_0 + rP \ (K/X)$$

where P, W and r have the usual meaning: the price, the money wage and the rate of profit, respectively. Assuming $P = 1$ we get:

$$1 = Wa_0 + r \ (K/X)$$

with W now representing the real wage rate. The reason for using (K/X) instead of the capital coefficient a_1 is the same as before.

The equations presented above can be said to constitute the common analytical core of any model of growth. They imply no more than the following propositions: for any given degree of capacity utilisation (a) production can be either consumed or invested; (b) what is not paid as wages is paid as profits. This means, for example, that only if we know the degree of capacity utilisation, the consumption rate and the real wage rate can we determine the accumulation rate and the profit rate. In other words, we have five unknowns, but only two equations to play with. So three additional explanations, in the form of independent relations, have to be supplied. Provided no further unknown is introduced, the system will yield a determinate solution. At the same time no more than three independent relations can be added to the model, otherwise the model will become overdetermined. A particular model of growth, therefore, will be distinguished by what set of independent relations is added to that common analytical core, in particular, by what is going to be exogenous and what is going to be endogenous. This choice is not obviously unconstrained: if, for example, independent relations are introduced to determine the degree of capacity utilisation, the accumulation rate and the profit rate, the consumption rate and the real wage rate must be determined endogenously. In other words, if all actors in the economy had theories on all the relevant variables, no consistency of plans or policies could be possible. This implies that any particular choice can be characterised by what one is prepared to sacrifice in order to avoid overdeterminacy.

What follows will be devoted to a brief illustration of four possible alternative choices. In each case emphasis will be placed on the relations that could not be added because otherwise the system would become overdetermined. Such relations are associated with the set of messages from the economy and nature, which are provisionally not included in the currently entertained theory.

It must be noticed that any regime that is associated with a non-fully comprehensive theory cannot be said to be in final equilibrium. The whole approach, based as it is on a multiplicity of regimes, provides a solution to the problem posed by the provisional nature of the equilibrium position: a different regime will replace the old one when the set of messages previously neglected are processed to form a theory. Thus, the overall picture which one gets from the adoption of this approach is that of a succession of growth regimes brought about by the creation of new knowledge and the undertaking of new policies.

Four regimes of growth

Let us consider one possible selection of independent relations to be added to the common analytical core. The market-clearing hypothesis, typical of neoclassical thinking, defines one. This implies adding to the price and production equations two independent relations requiring full employment of labour and equilibrium in the goods market. So we can write:

$$g = n$$
$$K/X = a_1$$

where n is the rate of growth of the labour force. The two equations imply, respectively, that accumulation is going on at a rate equal to the rate of growth of the labour force and the capacity is being used at its normal level. Finally we need a relation linking distribution to growth. This is provided in the form of a saving function. A classical saving function is assumed, implying that workers save nothing and capitalists save a constant fraction of their income. The fifth relation we need is therefore the following:

$$g = sr$$

where s is the capitalists' propensity to save. We are now endowed with five independent relations that determine five unknowns: the degree of capacity utilisation, the accumulation rate, the profit rate, the consumption rate and the real wage rate. It is clear that the introduction of an independent investment function, allowing for entrepreneurial investment propensities, would overdetermine the system. This case can be assumed to be characterised, therefore, by the absence of an independent investment function. There is no room in this world for independent investment decisions.

In this model of a growing economy the agents who are usually supposed to make investment decisions are passively accepting the equilibrium rate of accumulation. Various reasons explain their behaviour. Here emphasis is placed on the possibility that investors have not yet formed a theory of the growth of the economy, with the result that they do not act on that. No theory implies no policy. The fact that the rate of accumulation is determined as the rate that clears the labour market shows that no theory is currently entertained by entrepreneurs on the variables relevant to their potential investment decisions, like, for example, the rate of profit. Otherwise investment decisions would be changed according to some established behavioural function. Precisely because of the absence of any such behavioural function, equilibrium cannot but be provisional.

If accumulation is supposed to be governed by decisions of firms, the equation linking the rate of accumulation with the rate of growth of the labour force can be replaced by an equation linking accumulation with something more congenial to firms, such as the expected rate of profit on invested capital. This replacement is the distinguishing characteristic of another regime of growth, which has a clear Keynesian flavour. The set of independent relations to be added to the common analytical core to obtain this case is the following:

$$g_s = sr$$
$$K/X = a_1$$
$$g_i = g(r)$$

where g_s and g_i represent desired saving and desired investment per unit of capital. Again we have a set of independent relations that determine the usual set of five unknowns. Clearly, the addition of a further relation requiring accumulation to be carried out at the natural rate would overdetermine the system. Thus, this particular regime of growth implies in the general case $g \neq n$. It also implies that distribution can no longer be explained as the result of the market-clearing hypothesis. The rate of growth of employment and income distribution are turned into residual variables. Individual behaviour in the field of employment and income distribution is not modelled then: the supply of labour is presented as perfectly elastic, the real wage rate is just a consequence of entrepreneurs' investment decisions.

What is left out in this regime, then, is the behaviour of individuals as labour suppliers. Such individuals are not supposed to react to the endogenous rate of growth of employment or to the endogenous wage rate. No policy and hence no theory exist on this account. A learning process can be assumed to be in place, however, to form such a theory. Only when the theory becomes available can a policy be developed. Again, this kind of equilibrium is necessarily provisional in nature.

When, unlike the previous case, distribution is not allowed to be residually determined, but is supposed to play a crucial role in the system, a different regime of growth is established. We then have a situation where the state of class conflict, reflected in a particular income distribution, acts as a binding constraint on the capability of the system to grow over time. To see why this is the case suppose that the equation:

$$W = W^0$$

where W^0 represents the exogenously given real wage rate, is added to the previous system. Since we already have five independent relations that determine five unknowns, this additional relation would clearly overdetermine the system. As a consequence, one independent relation has to be given up to make room for the relation reflecting the state of class conflict over the distribution of income. If the sacrificed relation is the investment function, we would get what in the literature is known as the neo-Marxian case.

Unlike the previous case, here distribution determines accumulation. Thus, accumulation is no longer determined by the desire of firms to grow, but serves the interests of the class conflict. Again, as in the full-employment neoclassical case, animal spirits have been suppressed; entrepreneurial investment propensities have not been modelled. No policies are pursued, no theories are checked in the light of the messages received from the economy and nature.

In the cases considered so far the degree of capacity utilisation has not figured among the variables that are determined residually. The assumption $K/X = a_1$ has always ensured that the degree of capacity utilisation remains fixed at its normal level. A theory of the degree of capacity utilisation is somehow included in the model. When that assumption is relaxed, a new regime of growth can be obtained where the degree of capacity utilisation turns into a variable to be determined endogenously. If this assumption is replaced by another one fixing income distribution, we have a model that

Dutt has named after Kalecki and Steindl. The following equations define the model:

$$1 = a_0 C + g(K/X)$$
$$1 = Wa_0 + r(K/X)$$
$$g = sr$$
$$1 = Wa_0 (1+z)$$
$$g = g (r, X/K).$$

Given the mark-up rate z, the propensity to save s, the labour coefficient a_0 and the parameters of the investment function (which is here kept implicit), the model will determine C, W, g, r and X/K. The forces affecting income distribution will here manifest themselves through the determination of the mark-up rate z. This implies that the rate of profit r can change without this placing any constraint on such forces. This can be realised by means of a variable degree of capacity utilisation whose variations will produce the saving per unit of capital required to sustain desired accumulation. As a further consequence of the variability of capacity utilisation, desired accumulation g will now depend on the degree of capacity utilisation as well as on the rate of profit.

There is no theory of the degree of capacity utilisation in this model. It will be fixed at the level required to make saving per unit of capital equal to investment per unit of capital. It is, therefore, a residual variable. No theory implies no policies. The messages from the economy showing a degree of capacity utilisation different from any pre-determined one will not cause any revision or confirmation of theories. No theory of the degree of capacity utilisation is being checked against reality. However, such a theory may be in the process of being formed. When this process is completed it may bring about a change in regime. Again, equilibrium is provisional.

The concept of provisional equilibrium, therefore, has an implication for actual theorising. By playing with exogenous and endogenous variables, different combinations are obtained, where the exogenous variables are the variables for which a theory exists, and the endogenous those for which a theory is not yet formed. It is this extraordinary flexibility that renders this approach particularly suitable for treating change as neither deterministic nor inexplicable. The succession of regimes that results from the adoption of this approach can adequately reflect the formation of new theories and the undertaking of new policies. What this approach cannot do is explain how new theories are formed and old theories are discarded. It only shows that learning and equilibrium are not necessarily incompatible.

Conclusion

The fundamental proposition of this chapter is that learning and equilibrium are not incompatible ideas. This is argued starting from Hahn's notion of equilibrium where, however, equilibrium and learning are said to be incompatible. The argument rests on the equal treatment of economic analysts and economic agents. Just as economic analysts cannot afford a fully comprehensive theory of the economy, but need to set clear limits to what they can say in an orderly way, so economic agents form theories which cover only a subset of the messages received from the economy and nature. No one could deny, however, that while theories are propounded and applied by economic analysts, a process of learning is taking place aimed at generating new and better theories. Similarly, no one could deny that economic agents, while using the available theories for action, continually process information that has not yet found its way into a theory. The question posed in this chapter is whether this recognition bears any relevance to the notion of equilibrium. The answer is that it does, and that the notion of provisional equilibrium is thus substantiated.

Another question concerns the relevance of the notion of provisional equilibrium to the method of analysis. The answer again is in the positive. It has been argued that a method of analysis based on a multiplicity of models or regimes proves adequate for the purpose of fitting the creation of new theories into an analytical framework. It must also be noticed that such an approach is compatible with the axiom of the purposeful individual typical of Lachmann's thinking.

Acknowledgements

I wish to thank Gary Mongiovi and Roger Koppl for helpful comments and suggestions. However, the responsibility for the views expressed in this chapter lies entirely with the author.

Notes

1 See, for example, Lachmann 1976.
2 See Lachmann 1990: 137.

3 The difficulty in specifying a particular function should immediately place it outside the interest of economic theory. If some function cannot be properly specified, how would one go about it or why should one introduce it in the analysis at all? The sensible thing to do in such a case is to put it off until somebody comes up with an acceptable specification. However, when the function in question is for instance the production of new knowledge, there is no acceptable specification to speak of as it is logically impossible to predict the content of new knowledge. The question in this case is whether the production of new knowledge is to be left out of economic discourse. The answer given in this chapter is that it is not.

4 See Hahn 1973.

5 See Hahn 1984: 56.

6 According to Hahn, agents are learning if, for example, having observed rain at time $t + 1$ the probability they attach to rain at time $t + 2$ is different from the probability they attached to that event at time t conditional on rain at time $t + 1$.

7 Loasby makes an interesting comment on this:

> Such meta-theories and meta-policies cannot be precisely specified, because it is logically impossible for the content of new knowledge to be predicted in advance or, what comes to the same thing, to be specified as the output, determinate or probabilistic, of a well-defined process. This may be why, in 1973, Hahn placed the generation or revision of theories and policies beyond the scope of economic analysis. He now (1991) believes that we cannot deal adequately with some important problems without extending that scope, and recognizes that such extensions imply substantial revisions of the theories and policies which economists use.
>
> (Loasby 1991: 48)

8 Loasby starts his book with this comment:

> I would like to direct readers' attention to a basic similarity between the problems faced by economists and by the economic agents whom they attempt to study. Both sets of people are trying to make sense of the world in which they find themselves, and to behave intelligently in it. . . . So the behaviour of economists may help us to understand the behaviour of economic agents, and vice versa.
>
> (Loasby 1991: 2)

9 As an example of bounded rationality Hahn mentions the possibility that agents peer only a short distance into the future, or that a whole class of messages is ignored despite their relevance. However he does not pursue this point any further (see Hahn 1984: 56).

10 This assumption can be viewed as an aspect of the axiom of the purposeful individual typical of Austrian thinking.

11 Dutt (1990) represents the most comprehensive treatment of this approach.

References

Chick, V. and Caserta, M. (1994) 'Provisional equilibrium and macroeconomic theory', discussion paper, University College, London.

Dolan, E. G. (ed.) (1976) *The Foundations of Modern Austrian Economics*, Kansas City: Sheed and Ward.

Dutt, A. K. (1987) 'Alternative closures again: a comment on "Growth, Distribution and Inflation"', *Cambridge Journal of Economics*, 11 (1): 75–82.

—— (1990) *Growth, Distribution and Uneven Development*, Cambridge: Cambridge University Press.

Hahn, F. H. (1973) 'On the notion of equilibrium in economics', in Hahn (1984).

—— (1984) *Equilibrium and Macroeconomics*, Oxford: Basil Blackwell.

Lachmann, L. M. (1976) 'On the central concept of Austrian economics: market process', in E. G. Dolan (ed.) *The Foundations of Modern Austrian Economics*, Kansas City: Sheed and Ward.

—— (1990) 'Austrian economics: a hermeneutic approach', in D. Lavoie (ed.) *Economics and Hermeneutics*, London: Routledge.

Lavoie, D. (ed.) (1990) *Economics and Hermeneutics*, London: Routledge.

Loasby, B. J. (1991) *Equilibrium and Evolution*, Manchester: Manchester University Press.

Marglin, S. A. (1984a) 'Growth, distribution and inflation: a centennial synthesis', *Cambridge Journal of Economics*, 8 (2): 115–44.

—— (1984b) *Growth, Distribution and Prices*, Cambridge, MA: Harvard University Press.

Sen, A. K. (1963) 'Neoclassical and neo-Keynesian theories of distribution', *Economic Record*, 39: 53–64.

Taylor, L. (1991) *Income Distribution, Inflation, and Growth*, Cambridge, MA: MIT Press.

7

RADICAL SUBJECTIVISM AND AUSTRIAN ECONOMICS

Carlo Zappia

Introduction

In her vivid description of the conference held at South Royalton in 1974 to revitalise the Austrian tradition in the US, Karen Vaughn considers Ludwig Lachmann as 'the odd man out' at the conference, mainly because he was the 'only speaker who seemed to see much theoretical work still to be done in defining and developing an Austrian economics'. It is by following the way in which Lachmann influenced the subsequent evolution of Austrian thinking that Vaughn mainly reconstructs the Austrian paradigm in her recent book on *Austrian Economics in America: The Migration of a Tradition* (1994).[1]

Vaughn proposes an exhaustive reconstruction of the traditional Austrian school of thought – ranging through Menger, Mises, Hayek and their followers – which mainly stresses those aspects of the Austrian approach that have remained outside neoclassical developments. Vaughn's view is that it is the rediscovery of those aspects of Austrian thinking eschewed by the mainstream that has brought about the emergence of an American tradition of Austrian economics. Vaughn's explicit purpose is thus to highlight those 'American Austrians',[2] who have successfully managed to draw on that tradition of thought.

Vaughn's book is an important attempt to answer the question: What is Austrian economics? Needless to say, this is the kind of question one must address in trying to assess any paradigmatic alternative to the dominant corpus of the discipline. It is also the kind of question that often generates only negative heuristics (i.e. a set of methodological options that does not necessarily entail a clear positive analytic content).

The answer provided by Vaughn in her attempt to give analytic content to her definition of the Austrian paradigm is that if Austrian economics is to be something different from mainstream economics – a fact that is seen as essential for the survival of a separate tradition of economic thinking – then it must be founded on a continuous effort to develop a radically subjectivist approach. Vaughn contends that many fundamental concepts of Austrian economics such as the market process and spontaneous order can be consistently opposed to neoclassical equilibrium constructs only if they are based on an approach to individual choice which stresses not only the subjectivity of agents' preferences and decisions, but also the subjectivity of knowledge and expectations. Lachmann's legacy is thus central to the whole of Vaughn's analysis, because of the way in which Lachmann forced the Austrians to deal with subjectivism. In fact, the overall purpose of the book is to define a more comprehensive concept of 'order', which can take into account both Lachmann's viewpoint and the traditional Austrian reference to co-ordinated patterns of behaviour.

In what follows I intend to argue that while one may agree with Vaughn's emphasis on the necessity of further developing the subjectivism proper to the Austrian tradition, it might be argued that the way in which this methodological option is implemented is unconvincing, at least with respect to one central issue. I will maintain that with respect to the analysis of economic institutions – which Vaughn considers essential for the notion of order she suggests – some distinguished Austrian arguments are not only critical of the mainstream, but also inconclusive. This is mainly because these arguments are derived from an analysis of economic institutions, which is limited to the usual comparison between decentralised and centralised economies and devoid of appropriate reference to a number of interesting developments – generated within the mainstream, even if critical of the standard account of it – which try to deepen the understanding of the organisation of exchanges in decentralised economies. To be specific, I will argue that the Austrian attitude towards the mainstream sometimes shows little knowledge of the relevance of certain recent developments for a number of distinctive Austrian themes. In order to provide the background for my argument, I will give a preliminary account of the relationship between the Austrian approach and the mainstream, with specific regard to the question of how to deal with decisions under uncertainty. It is from this preliminary question that my argument will start.

Rational ignorance

It is usual to find reconstructions of the Austrian tradition which emphasise a Kirznerian and a Lachmannian vein (for example, see O'Driscoll and Rizzo 1985). But the way in which Vaughn presents the former as a 'supplement to neoclassical economics' and the latter as the only possible way to a meaningful 'alternative conception of order' is uncommonly persuasive. The most prominent example can be found in the consideration of the analytical tools needed to deal effectively with uncertainty and the passage of time.

Vaughn argues that Kirzner has been successful in providing an analysis of the process through which competitive markets may reach equilibrium. His notion of the alert entrepreneur is a definite step forward in the appreciation of the role of those economic agents who 'notice opportunities that others miss and act upon that knowledge to bring markets closer to equilibrium' (165). But when real time and genuine uncertainty are taken into account there is no longer any reason to argue that each entrepreneur is 'correct' in his or her action, and thus no reason for expecting their joint actions to be equilibrating, as Kirzner assumes. This is why any attempt to formalise entrepreneurial behaviour as a problem of constrained maximisation under uncertainty is bound to be unproductive. Genuine uncertainty must imply that the entrepreneur cannot anticipate all possible future consequences of his action. Therefore equilibrium cannot be considered an *ex ante* reference point for analysis.

Lachmann's contribution, on the other hand, takes stock of the traditional Austrian emphasis on heterogeneous and incomplete knowledge and comes to the conclusion that only those descriptions of economic activities that consider endogenous and unpredictable change are apt to understand agents' behaviour. The market process driven by individuals whose acting is 'undetermined creative choice' (152) is necessarily an open-ended process. Not just the possibility of anticipating it *ex ante*, but the very notion of equilibrium is called into question.

The main point of disagreement between the two alternative views of Kirzner and Lachmann not only originated in a different attitude towards the modelling of individual behaviour, but also in the explanation of what the achievable aggregate outcomes are.

They both recognise that the question is not so much that of incorrectly perceived opportunities by individual agents – which is usually dealt with in neoclassical economics – as that of unperceived opportunities. Still, Kirzner admits that equilibrating actions can be consistently defined, thus sticking implicitly to a (perhaps generalised) constrained optimisation approach in the Robbinsian tradition. As Vaughn contends, 'he has improved upon a model of market behaviour that still fails to capture the central problem of human action' (150). In fact, 'he rejects the notion that entrepreneurs create anything *ex nihilo*, instead arguing that by discovering opportunities already "there" to be discovered, they are introducing genuine novelty into the system' (148). Thus it would seem that, from Vaughn's viewpoint, 'genuine novelty' and unperceived opportunities are distinct.

In contrast, Lachmann thinks that, if equilibrium is no longer a useful tool, then the notion of equilibrating action is unintelligible. Therefore he argues for an entirely different approach. Following Shackle, Lachmann maintains that it is the undetermined nature of the future that explains why the consequences of creative choice are unpredictable. 'Genuine novelty' rests in the fact that 'no two minds are alike' (153), so that neither individual choices nor their outcome can be fully predicted. As a consequence, economic theory must draw on the notion of a plan 'to make the world intelligible in terms of human action'. But the passage of time accounts for the fact that 'revision of plans is the norm rather than the exception' (154), thus rendering co-ordination almost unachievable as a state of the economy. Lachmann's suggested solution, Vaughn contends, is then to be sought in the study of those institutions that can favour order even in the face of unco-ordinated patterns of behaviour. But, as regards the possibility of having a formal theory of economic decisions, we are only left with a series of negative statements. In Vaughn's words 'Lachmann, in an attempt to take radical subjectivism and real time seriously in his interpretation of economic action, tries to devise an alternative to equilibrium theorising but fails to produce the kind of overall theoretical structure that would seriously challenge the neoclassical hegemony' (161). In particular, one might add, Lachmann does not provide any description of the characteristics of the domain encompassing not only unperceived but also inconceivable opportunities.

The fact that the modelling of individual behaviour is crucial to the whole of Vaughn's reassessment of the Austrian tradition is demonstrated in her attempt to summarise what aspects can be considered as 'hard core' Austrian. She points to a widely agreed opinion on the assumption of perfect knowledge used in neoclassical economics as heading the list of commonly shared beliefs among Austrian scholars:

> Austrians agree with neoclassical economics that human beings attempt to act rationally to achieve their purposes. However, because human action always takes place in time and always under conditions of partial ignorance about the present and total ignorance about the future, a theory of market processes can be neither static in nature nor based on the assumption of perfect knowledge. *Nor is rational ignorance a promising assumption for Austrians who deny that all the relevant future states of the world are listable by the choosing agent.*
>
> (163, my italics)

Given that perfect knowledge is obviously not a common assumption in most modern economic theory, the real meaning of rational ignorance deserves closer investigation. Austrian economics, Vaughn stresses, 'cannot usefully be considered merely a variation on the economics of rationality and constrained maximisation' (162). This statement accounts for her position, which is critical of Kirzner's ideas and supportive of Lachmann's. But the main question that the analysis of the two different positions leaves open is the following: what does rational ignorance really mean?

If one looks at the theory of decision adopted by mainstream economic theory for the last forty years, things appear to be plain. The theory of economic decisions has been based – starting from Savage's definition of states of nature – on Bayesian decision theory, which requires that the possible events must be 'listable' and that their (subjective) probabilities of realisation add up to unity. Indeed, the basic assumption of decision theory under uncertainty is that economic agents know with certainty the domain of their uncertainty. This is of course not a theoretically appealing assumption if one is interested, as the Austrians are, in 'themes such as the importance of dynamic growth and development, the generation and function of knowledge in economic action, the uncertainties associated with processes in time and the pivotal importance of diversity and heterogeneity in economic life' (162).

But one should notice that in recent years some perceptive mainstream theorists have shown that they share with the Austrians the same discomfort. The difficulties in representing formally how the knowledge of individual agents changes – which is the upshot of Lachmann's insistence on the subjective nature of knowledge – has troubled many neoclassical economists. More and more of them have increasingly acknowledged these difficulties. This is apparent in the evolution of the notion of equilibrium towards a more dynamic conception, as in the works of Hahn (1973) and Fisher (1983).[3]

What is more important with respect to the Austrian themes is that there is now an increasing number of attempts to deal explicitly with the question from a choice theoretic perspective (among others, see Kreps 1992 and Hahn 1995a). Let us take as an example Kreps's analysis of unforeseen contingencies. In an effort to give choice theoretic foundations to Williamson's contention that many of the forms of contractual arrangements one can observe in markets and organisations are to be attributed to the need to adapt to contingencies which cannot be anticipated at the date of the signature of the contract, Kreps provides a model of choice in which the individual agent is aware, at the outset, that unforeseen contingencies may arise. In other words, the individual agent might not have been able to imagine at an earlier date an event which he now has to face up to. The analytical trick is to leave room for a state of nature which can be called 'none of the other states', whose content is not conceivable *ex ante*. In this way one can imagine different degrees of flexibility preserved by agents for future decisions about possibly new events (Kreps 1992: 259–61).[4] One can also refer to the related, and probably more powerful, notion of unawareness presented in Modica and Rustichini (1994), where the discussion involves unforeseeable contingencies. In other words, the individual agent might have been unable not only to think of the event but even to understand it before its realisation. It is also worth stressing that this kind of approach hints at a departure from traditional choice theory, which is not in principle limited to exogenous uncertainty as indicated by Hahn's conjecture (1995a) about the possibility of introducing endogenous uncertainty into equilibrium theory via the notion of unawareness. I believe that the notion of unawareness can account for certain aspects of Vaughn's idea of 'genuine novelty'.

The aspects of decision theory just mentioned do not represent an isolated contention by certain leading authors. The astonishing increase in studies concerned with informational asymmetries, incomplete contracts, non-additive probability theory and so on do not simply entail a major extension of formal exercises in constrained maximisation. They indicate the attitude of modern economic theory towards the question of rational ignorance. The traditional formulation of the problem of decision under uncertainty is still dominant, above all because of the central role assigned to utility-maximising individuals; but an increasing number of papers are devoted to alternative ways of formalising uncertainty. The literature on incomplete contracts is a notable example. The argument for signing an incomplete contract conceives fully rational agents who decide not to spend time in describing states that in principle can be described (for instance, because they are not easily observed from outside by a judge, as suggested in Hart and Holmstrom 1987). In this instance agents may form beliefs that can be represented as probabilities over the set of unexplored states.

It might be argued that there are different, and much more convincing, reasons for justifying an analysis of ignorance, as argued in the Austrian tradition. But it is difficult to understand why one should not take stock of the effort of 'erroneously' justified analyses. If the main analytical point is the one that concerns the possibility of listing the future events, it is counterproductive to deny that there are many studies seriously confronting it.

One possible objection to my point might be that it is difficult to say which contributions can be labelled as part of the mainstream and which not. Of course, Williamson is not a typical neoclassical representative. But his contribution draws on opportunistic behaviour at least as much as other neoclassical work. If the crucial point is whether or not we are dealing with utility maximisers, all the studies I have mentioned can be considered mainstream. It might also be argued that these studies do not constitute a coherent entity. For instance, Kreps's formalisation holds only if the 'sure-thing principle' is assumed, while studies in non-additive probability theory are based precisely on its denial, which emerges from the Ellsberg paradox (for example, see Machina 1987 and Camerer and Weber 1992). But that does not change the substance of the argument: the question of how to formalise decision making under uncertainty is central in much of modern economic theory, and the suggested solutions cannot be simply considered variations in constrained optimisation.[5]

To sum up on this question of rational ignorance: my point is that the comparison between neoclassical theory and alternative paradigms, such as the Austrian, should take into account the multiple aspects of neoclassical theory. It is unhelpful to compare the Austrian insights on knowledge and time with a mere travesty of neoclassical theory. Even if one points at the efforts of general equilibrium theorists, it can be shown that they are now involved in accounting for endogenous uncertainty and information asymmetries. The standard framework is one of missing markets and impossibility of complete insurance against future events. Indeterminacy of equilibria, that is multiplicity, is regarded as the norm; Pareto-constrained efficiency of equilibria is not guaranteed (Hahn 1995b).

We have seen that while she considers Kirzner's analysis too closely linked to the mainstream, Vaughn finds it difficult to clarify the Lachmannian alternative. Of course, Lachmann's attitude towards what other Austrian scholars have characterised as 'theoretical nihilism' leaves economic theory without a clear path to follow, at least as regards the study of individual behaviour. As we shall see in a moment, Vaughn's viewpoint is that the solution to this problem can be found in an elaboration of the notion of order which takes the role of institutions into due account.

But the attitude that denies the possibility of any solution at the individual level is unconvincing. Moreover, it is fruitless in the comparison between Austrian insights and the mainstream, because it makes it difficult to understand whether the mainstream has actually understood the Austrian message. To take an example, in the Austrian literature the influences of Hayek's work on the economics of information are often noted, as Vaughn points out (165). But the unanimous conclusion by the Austrians is that Hayek's profound insights have been misunderstood and not properly dealt with. It is worth noting that non-Austrian theorists show an opposite attitude on this historiographic matter. Hahn (1990) has recently contended that a typical Hayekian theme such as that prices may reflect the different expectations of agents and thus reveal information has been carried well beyond Hayek's vague remarks, and 'fully absorbed' in neoclassical economics, only by virtue of the literature on revelation of information prompted by Radner (1979) and Grossman (1989). Milgrom and Roberts (1992: Chapter 4) consider Hayek's notion of personal knowledge central but insufficient on its own for the comparative analysis of organisations and the market. Similar viewpoints can be found in Arrow (1994), with respect to the notion of personal knowledge as compared to that of technological knowledge, and in Bowles and Gintis (1993) and Stiglitz (1994), with respect to those functions performed by the market that are not simply allocative. I have argued elsewhere that an attitude different from Vaughn's with respect to the relationships between Hayek's insights and modern attempts to deal with asymmetries of information may be more fruitful (Zappia 1997). I shall now turn to this issue.

Economic order and economic institutions

The most important of Vaughn's recurrent themes is the necessity for current Austrian economics to consistently develop an analysis of economic institutions in the direction indicated by Menger and Hayek. Her book is written under the firm, and clearly argued, belief that the unorthodox component of Menger as a founder of the neoclassical paradigm – his theory of economic institutions – is the cornerstone of the Austrian approach. Thus, although equilibrium is the dominant organising principle in most economic theory, the Austrians, especially since Hayek's reconsideration of Menger's theory of the origin of economic institutions, have turned their attention to the more general notion of social order. The ultimate goal of this shift of focus is not, as the evolution of Hayek's thought might suggest, the search for a qualitative notion of equilibrium to counterbalance the quantitative notion of the mainstream. (This has been argued even recently in Donzelli 1993 and Moss 1994.) In fact, Vaughn maintains, it is in the way order is conceived, as 'a system of rules established to enable individuals to achieve their own objectives' (123), that the impact of Hayek's work (especially *Law, Legislation and Liberty*) can best be appreciated. A corollary of this view of order is that the objectives of individuals and the specific action they set in motion:

> depend upon their [the individual's] perception of opportu-
> nities, . . . but the process for taking these actions depends
> upon the legal and informal rules structure in which they
> operate, a rules structure that includes rules of business
> trading as well as of cultural norms and legal prescriptions.
> (124–5)

Vaughn's view is that Hayek's insistence on the heterogeneous and dispersed nature of market knowledge not only implies a vision of the market order as a discovery procedure, 'a means of inducing individuals to learn more about the opportunities available to them and to create new products and new methods of production'. It also allows an 'evolutionary theory of social institutions wherein those that survived only did so because they better helped individuals within a society to achieve their goals.... It is indisputable', Vaughn concludes, 'that [Hayek's] theory of social evolution helped to point Austrian economists toward the study of economic institutions and evolutionary orders in a systematic way' (126–7). The Austrian alternative to conventional equilibrium theorising is thus to be found in the development of an evolutionary theory of institutions.

The implicit assumption in Vaughn's reading of Hayek and the subsequent evolution of the Austrian paradigm is that a specific analysis of individual behaviour no longer matters once the methodological implications of Hayek's work are correctly drawn. The Hayekian notion of spontaneous order is not to be interpreted simply as a fundamental shift in thinking about the meaning of the type of co-ordination that is conceptualised by general equilibrium (as in Moss 1994). Neither can it be interpreted as a qualitative equilibrium construct within which formal economic theory can help in clarifying the phases of plan co-ordination. On the contrary, it is a definite step towards an understanding of economics largely as 'a study of economic institutions within a nonequilibrium context' (127). This is why Kirzner's approach to individual behaviour is regarded merely as a variation in constrained optimisation. As for Lachmann, his inability to give analytic content to his insights on the inherently continuous revision of individuals' plans is deemed unimportant in comparison to the alternatives to conventional equilibrium theorising suggested in his work. One might even argue that Vaughn's assessment of Lachmann's role in the development of Austrian thought points to the 'beneficial' influences of Lachmann's belief that no formal theory of individual decision making can be arrived at.

Vaughn's proposal, then, is to follow the implications of her reading of Hayek's abandonment of general equilibrium analysis, that is to investigate a different notion of order. But the notion of spontaneous order in itself cannot accomplish this task. For Vaughn's contention about the impossibility of giving formal support to the analysis of individual behaviour when new knowledge is prompted by the passage of time implies that the market tendency towards a spontaneous order is not guaranteed. Here Lachmann makes his contribution; he improves on Hayek's idea of spontaneous order by pointing out 'that markets are subject to both disequilibrating and equilibrating tendencies' and that pure economic theory cannot help in showing 'which kind of tendencies dominate the system' (160). Lachmann's most fruitful suggestion is thus to abandon the search for alternative equilibrium constructs, and to pursue the analysis of those institutional settings that favour the market's order. But Lachmann's drawback is that he failed to provide a 'clearly articulated theory of institutions' (157). As a consequence, in order to move forward in the development of an Austrian alternative to the mainstream, it is necessary to address the question of how institutions can evolve, persist and justify the desirability – if not the efficiency – of the market order.[6]

The upshot of Vaughn's assessment of the Austrian paradigm is clearly summarised in the following:

> Economics is a social science that by definition is concerned with understanding order in human society. As human beings we recognise many recurrent patterns of behaviour that result in orderly social processes – customs, manners, laws, institutions and relationships. In addition, often what seems disorderly and chaotic at first glance, upon further investigation, can be shown to reflect some deeper unsuspected principles of order, usually some purposeful response to perceived constraints. . . . The question is, how do we explain this social order that goes beyond our immediate perceptions while remaining true to our recognition that humans act not only to make themselves better off, but they do so in a world of limited resources, incomplete knowledge and radical uncertainty?
>
> (164)

In their continuous search for an alternative theoretical structure that would provide a better explanation of economic order than neoclassical economics, the Austrians have provided a number of interesting equilibrium constructs, including Mises's notion of an evenly rotating economy, Hayek's notion of plan co-ordination and O'Driscoll and Rizzo's notion of pattern co-ordination. These three notions are all carefully examined by Vaughn, but the one she seems most supportive of is O'Driscoll's and Rizzo's. Their approach is an attempt to develop a definition of co-ordination that is intended to describe an economic system in which new endogenous knowledge is fostered by the actions of individual agents and thus to accommodate endogenous and unpredictable change.

But even though pattern co-ordination has its attraction for

Vaughn, the major component of a satisfying notion of order is still missing. Economic institutions can be considered as 'points of orientation' for individual agents and thus favour pattern co-ordination – that is co-ordination among the typical, recurrent features of individual actions – even if specific aspects of individual actions 'fail to mesh', as O'Driscoll and Rizzo contend. On the other hand, even those specific aspects of human action that do turn out to be unco-ordinated are relevant for the endogenous change of prevailing institutions. What the Austrian tradition has hinted at, but not dealt with as much as it should, is the fact that 'errors that consti-tute part of the market process should be construed as both integral and beneficial'. Therefore, the proper approach to learning is 'how can mistakes and error be channelled into productive knowledge' (173). At this point, Vaughn abruptly concludes that a cogent explanation of the market process as a process of trial and error thus requires an evolutionary theory of institutions, where experimenta-tion and learning, which lead to 'new modes of human interaction', can explain 'the origin, persistence or failure of human institutions, those regular observable patterns of action that lend stability and predictability to human life' (175).

So Vaughn seems to be supporting a definitive withdrawal from the traditional ways of economic theorising, by arguing in favour of a shift of focus from spontaneous to social order, and for almost the same reasons that prompted Hayek's withdrawal from equilibrium towards spontaneous order. But Vaughn's discussion of those insti-tutions that 'permit the use of new knowledge in human action' (174) is not very satisfying. She only refers to the tradition of those economists, notably Nelson and Winter, who have attempted to adapt evolutionary reasoning to economic processes, and to the similarities between certain features of evolutionary theory and the Austrian viewpoint, as represented by Witt (1992) and Horwitz (1992). She also concedes, 'there is much work to be done' (175). Indeed, the need for the Austrian research programme to abandon the equilibrium metaphor and to elaborate an evolutionary notion of social order is supported only by a few suggestions for future research. This inevitably leaves the reader feeling discontented, for Vaughn does not even discuss the difficulties of reconciling method-ological individualism with group selection processes on which the evolutionary approach hinges. Moreover, it seems to imply that the analytic content of the Austrian paradigm is yet to be developed.

The future relevance of Austrian economics might probably depend on the viability of Vaughn's suggestions, although current

Austrian researchers are still divided on the research strategies to be followed in order to avoid the sidelining of Austrian economics (for example see Rizzo's (1992) and White's (1992) sharply differentiated positions). Although it is not an aim of my chapter to make conjectures about the future Austrian impact on economic research, let me conclude by making some remarks on a different implication of Vaughn's proposal.

One issue Vaughn leaves undiscussed is why the analysis of economic institutions cannot be based on the study of individual behaviour, as is traditional in the Austrian approach. She argues that:

> people carry out their projects and plans within a variety of social institutions, all of which have both tacit and explicit rules of behaviour. . . . Indeed, an agreement between two people to engage in a recurrent pattern of behaviour *vis à vis* each other is also a form of 'institution' or typical behaviour.
>
> (171)

But here Vaughn neglects to refer to the fact that a leading interpretation of the recent developments in the economics of information is that if opportunistic behaviour is properly taken into account, then the typical contract between two asymmetrically informed agents can be interpreted as the outcome of tacit rules of behaviour (for a summary, see Bowles and Gintis 1993). A more thorough inspection of the market as an institution reveals that many aspects of economic activity such as repeated interaction for exchange purposes do not necessarily involve the emergence of organisations, but can be explained instead as the emergence of conventional behaviour among distinct market participants, and that this can be interpreted as 'a form of "institution" '. This view is consistent with the Austrian view of the market as represented by Hayek. Hayek's conception of the superiority of the market over alternative organisational settings is not exclusively linked to the impersonal working of the price system and its efficiency in diffusing existing knowledge and creating the incentives for discovering new knowledge. It also emphasises the role of those forces of competition, such as imitative behaviour, rules and traditions, which were excluded by the Walrasian interpretation of competition. The view that the exchange of information that is dispersed throughout the system is achieved through a process that is more complex than the Walrasian process of impersonal allocation through prices is not only compatible with Austrian thought, but has also been strongly supported by Hayek (1948 and 1968). I have argued elsewhere (Zappia 1997) that a superficial denial of the relevance of many recent microeconomic developments to understanding the market as an institution is inconsistent with Hayek's insights into the matter.[7]

Here a paradox seems to emerge: following Vaughn's reconstruction of Austrian thought, it might be argued (as in Bowles and Gintis 1993) that new developments of what Vaughn considers neoclassical theory have done more than the Austrians for providing an individualistically based explanation of those elements – such as habits and customary business procedures – which characterise economic institutions. But this is of course untrue, as Vaughn herself stresses in her reassessment of Hayek's theory of knowledge and the related efforts by O'Driscoll and Rizzo to develop an economics of time and ignorance in which 'the existence of private and tacit knowledge implies that nonprice signals can contain important market information' (136).

A similar issue arises as regards the application of game theory to the explanation of spontaneous orders (see Sudgen 1989) and the evolution of institutions. The Austrian explanation of economic institutions is essentially a causal–genetic theory, taking Menger's theory of money as exemplar. This explanation describes the development of institutions as the outcome of a sequence of actions by individual agents, where the aggregate outcome of these actions is not necessarily the intended outcome. Indeed, what distinguishes Austrian theory from the 'pure' methodological individualism of neoclassical theory is that it necessarily involves the explanation of a composition principle. It might thus be argued that to represent the process of composing the effects of distinct individual plans by means of the theory of games is a valuable complement to the evolutionary theory of institutions (see Langlois 1992; Bianchi 1994). Furthermore, this approach attributes a primary role to the decisions of individuals, which is contrary to the interpretation suggested by Vaughn.

Concluding remarks

In this assessment of Karen Vaughn's *Austrian Economics in America*, I have stressed that her call for a definitive shift in Austrian thought away from the search for equilibrium constructs and towards the analysis of those institutions that favour ordered outcomes of the market process, is not justified by the inability of pure economic theory to deal with rational ignorance. In fact, most Austrians seem to use this argument to avoid discussing the inevitable withdrawal from methodological individualism, which is implicit in the endorsement of an evolutionary approach to economic theory.

My aim here has not been to argue that future developments in Austrian economics should not follow this line of research, but rather to point out that a withdrawal from equilibrium theorising – which seems contradictory both to traditional Austrian thought in general and to Hayek's theory in particular – cannot be based on an inaccurate representation of recent developments in orthodox microeconomics.

Furthermore, a critical, but positive, attitude towards the attempts to formalise rational ignorance might suggest that the Austrian tradition may actually influence future research rather than merely constitute an optional supplement to it. As I have argued, the kind of formal representation of decision making under uncertainty one finds in recent developments in microeconomic theory is not intended to describe agents 'striving to formulate the correct vision of the future as if the future were something already implicit in the data and one's only problem is to guess correctly what the future will be' (147). On the contrary, it recognises as a starting point for research the view that ignorance is an inherent feature of every decision regarding future events. In this, it resembles the Shackleian – and Lachmannian – assertion that the future is the unpredictable consequence of creative choices made by individual agents. And it seems to point towards a re-elaboration of the notion of equilibrium that is compatible at least with Hayek's, if not with the whole Austrian, tradition.

Acknowledgements

I wish to thank J. Birner, L. Moss and the editors for their comments on a previous draft of this paper.

Notes

1 Throughout this chapter, unless otherwise noted, the page numbers in parentheses refer to this book. The passage quoted in this paragraph is taken from p. 108.

2 The inverted commas are of course necessary because it is generally considered that one of the most influential 'American Austrian' scholars is Lachmann.

3 In their examination of the models provided by Hahn and Fisher, Currie and Steedman (1990: 215) find it 'striking that much recent work has more in common . . . with Lachmann's conception of market processes than it does with the Arrow–Debreu economy'. Their opinion is relevant with respect to my argument because their analysis of economists who have dealt with the behaviour of economies over time highlights the importance of Shackle's and Lachmann's contributions.

4 A previous attempt is Loomes and Sudgen 1986. It is worth noting, however, that the predictive power that is usually attributed to the Bayesian process of updating beliefs seems bound to be lost in Kreps's representation.

5 A recent interpretation of the approach of non-additive utility theory points to the fact that while Bayesian decision theory is unable to deal with the influence that choices can have on future states of nature, a main point in the agenda of the non-additive utility theory approach is to address the issue of the degree of irreversibility that characterises the consequences of sequential actions (Vercelli 1995).

6 Vaughn mentions, but does not discuss, Lachmann's explicit retreat (1986) from the institutional issue.

7 But see also the 'Austrian rationale' for the existence of organisations provided by Minkler 1993.

References

Arrow, K. J. (1994) 'Methodological individualism and social knowledge', *American Economic Review*, 84 (2): 1–11.

Bianchi, M. (1994) 'Hayek's spontaneous order: the "correct" versus the "corregible" society', in J. Birner and R. Van Zijp (eds) *Hayek, Co-ordination and Evolution*, London: Routledge.

Bowles, S. and Gintis, H. (1993) 'The revenge of Homo Economicus: contested exchange and the revival of political economy', *Journal of Economic Perspectives*, 7: 83–102.

Camerer, C. and Weber, M. (1992) 'Recent developments in modeling preferences: uncertainty and ambiguity', *Journal of Risk and Uncertainty*, 5: 325–70.

Currie, D. and Steedman, I. (1990) *Wrestling with Time*, Ann Arbor: Michigan University Press.

Donzelli, F. (1993) 'The influence of the socialist calculation debate on Hayek's view of general equilibrium theory', *Revue Européenne des Sciences Sociales*, 31: 47–83.

Fisher, F. M. (1983) *Disequilibrium Foundations of Equilibrium Economics*, Cambridge: Cambridge University Press.

Grossman, S. (1989) *The Informational Role of Prices*, Cambridge, MA: MIT Press.

Hahn, F. H. (1973 [1984]) 'On the notion of equilibrium in economics', in *Equilibrium and Macroeconomics*, Oxford: Basil Blackwell.

—— (1990) 'Expectations', in J. Hey and D. Winch (eds) *A Century of Economics*, Oxford: Basil Blackwell.

—— (1995a) 'On economies with Arrow Securities', mimeo. Paper presented at the ISER on 'Decisions under uncertainty', Siena.

—— (1995b) 'Uncertainty in general equilibrium', mimeo. Paper presented at Annual Meeting of the Società Italiana degli Economisti, Firenze.

Hart, O. and Holmstrom, B. (1987) 'The theory of contracts', in T. Bewley (ed.) *Advances in Economic Theory, Fifth World Congress*, Cambridge: Cambridge University Press.

Hayek, F. A. (1948) 'The meaning of competition', in *Individualism and Economic Order*, London: Routledge and Kegan Paul.

—— (1968 [1978]) 'Competition as a discovery procedure', in *New Studies in Philosophy, Politics, Economics and the History of Ideas*, Chicago: Chicago University Press.

Horwitz, S. (1992) *Monetary Evolution, Free Banking and Economic Order*, San Francisco: Westview Press.

Kreps, D. M. (1992) 'Static choice in the presence of unforeseen contingencies', in P. Dasgupta, D. Gale, O. Hart and E. Maskin (eds) *Economic Analysis of Markets and Games. Essays in Honor of Frank Hahn*, Cambridge, MA: MIT Press.

Lachmann, L. M. (1986) *The Market as an Economic Process*, Oxford: Basil Blackwell.

Langlois, R. N. (1992) 'Orders and organizations: toward an Austrian theory of social institutions', in B. Caldwell and S. Boehm (eds) *Austrian Economics: Tensions and New Directions*, Boston: Kluwer Academic Publishers.

Loomes, G. and Sudgen, R. (1986) 'Disappointment and dynamic consistency in choice under uncertainty', *Review of Economic Studies*, 53: 271–82.

Machina, M. J. (1987) 'Choice under uncertainty: problems solved and unsolved', *Journal of Economic Perspectives*, 1: 121–54.

Milgrom, P. and Roberts, J. (1992) *Economics, Organizations and Management*, Englewood Cliffs: Prentice Hall.

Minkler, A. P. (1993) 'Knowledge and internal organizations', *Journal of Economic Behavior and Organization*, 21: 17–30.

Modica, S. and Rustichini, A. (1994) 'Awareness and partitional information structures', *Theory and Decisions*, 37: 107–24.

Moss, L. S. (1994) 'Hayek and the several faces of socialism', in M. Colonna, H. Hagemann and O. Homouda (eds) *Capitalism, Socialism and Knowledge*, vol. II, Aldershot: Edward Elgar.

O'Driscoll, G. P. and Rizzo, M. J. (1985) *The Economics of Time and Ignorance*, Oxford: Basil Blackwell.

Radner, R. (1979) 'Rational expectations equilibrium, generic existence and the information revealed by prices', *Econometrica*, 47: 655–78.

Rizzo, M. (1992) 'Afterword: Austrian economics for the twenty-first century', in B. Caldwell and S. Boehm (eds) *Austrian Economics: Tensions and New Directions*, Boston: Kluwer Academic Publishers.

Stiglitz, J. E. (1994) *Whither Socialism?*, Cambridge, MA: MIT Press.

Sudgen, R. (1989) 'Spontaneous order', *Journal of Economic Perspectives*, 3 (4): 85–97.

Vaughn, K. (1994) *Austrian Economics in America*: *The Migration of a Tradition*, New York: Cambridge University Press.

Vercelli, A. (1995) 'From soft uncertainty to hard environmental uncertainty', *Economie Appliquée*, 48: 251–69.

White, L. H. (1992) 'Afterword: appraising Austrian economics: contentions and misdirections', in B. Caldwell and S. Boehm (eds) *Austrian Economics: Tensions and New Directions*, Boston: Kluwer Academic Publishers.

Witt, U. (1992) 'Evolutionary theory – the direction Austrian economics should take?' in B. Caldwell and S. Boehm (eds) *Austrian Economics: Tensions and New Developments*, Dodrecht: Kluwer Academics.

Zappia, C. (1997) 'Private information, contractual arrangements and Hayek's knowledge problem', in W. Keizer, B. Tieben and R. Van Zijp (eds) *Austrians in Debate*, London: Routledge.

8

HIERARCHICAL METAPHORS IN AUSTRIAN INSTITUTIONALISM

A friendly subjectivist caveat

Steven Horwitz

Thanks in large part to the later work of Hayek and the varied contributions of Ludwig Lachmann, the post-revival generation of Austrian economists is rediscovering the importance of a theory of economic and social institutions for a healthy understanding of economic and social order. One can legitimately say 'rediscovering' because an emphasis on institutions was at the heart of Carl Menger's work that founded a distinct Austrian approach.[1] While Hayek's work on the evolution of institutions (e.g., Hayek 1988) put the notion of spontaneous order back at the centre of Austrian economics, Lachmann's enduring contribution can be seen as reminding us of the equal importance of seeing institutions in terms of the *meaning* that they have for actors. Lachmann's work on institutions can thus be seen as an attempt to extend subjectivism beyond tastes, knowledge and expectations to our understanding of the very institutions that help to co-ordinate our diverse subjectivities.

What I hope to accomplish in this chapter is to search for any unacceptable lingering objectivism in the treatment of institutions by both Lachmann and other post-revival Austrians. My point is not merely to be deconstructive (although that is important), rather I want to give the discussion of institutions a nudge towards being more completely subjectivist, and thus more true to Lachmann's own conception of economic theory and social order.[2] More specifically, there is a sense in Austrian discussions of institutions that there is a certain 'hierarchy' of institutions, or that, in Lachmann's (1971: 81) words, there are 'internal' and 'external' institutions. My argument is that this way of talking about institutions can easily lead us to posit incorrectly an objective structure or ordering of institutions that exists separately from either the particular questions posed by theorists, or the subjective perspectives of actors in those institutions. The argument will be fleshed out by borrowing some concepts from the Austrian theory of capital to sketch a different conceptual framework for discussing institutions, and by an illustration from the history of banking.

Austrian institutionalism

The focus of my critical attention will be the work on economic and social institutions by both Lachmann (1971, 1986) and Richard Langlois (1986a, b, c, 1992). The reason for this narrow focus is that these two authors have developed the most 'Austrian' treatments of institutions.[3] It is also in their work that notions of 'externality/internality' and hierarchy come to the fore. It should be noted that none of my critical comments should be seen as directed towards the general idea of an Austrian institutionalism. To the contrary, the analysis of the origin, evolution, and function of institutions is one of the most powerful contributions Austrians can provide and the hope is that a more thorough subjectivism can improve work along these lines.[4]

Lachmann's theory of institutions is most clearly sketched out in his book *The Legacy of Max Weber* (1971). After focusing on the plan as his central conception of individual human action, Lachmann asks about 'the interrelationship between the actions of various actors' (1971: 49). When the success of each individual's plan depends on the success or failure of the plans of millions of others, how are we able to acquire information about those plans of others? In the face of this apparent ignorance of others' plans, how does social co-ordination ever come about? The answer, according to Lachmann (as taken from Weber) is through social institutions.

This question, in a variety of forms, is one that has been woven through Austrian economics for many years. From Menger's (1985 [1883]) original emphasis on undesigned institutions, to Hayek's (1937) definition of equilibrium in terms of plan co-ordination, to O'Driscoll and Rizzo's (1985: 86) discussion of 'pattern coordination', which 'involves the coordination of plans but not of actual activities', Austrians have always asked a version of Lachmann's question.[5] The novelty of Lachmann's answer was that it reminded Austrians of their roots in the Germanic sociological tradition of Weber, Georg Simmel and Alfred Schutz.[6]

Central to that tradition, especially in its Weberian extensions, was the role of institutions as social co-ordination processes. In Lachmann's conception, institutions:

> enable each of us to rely on the actions of thousands of anonymous others about whose individual purposes and plans we can know nothing. They are nodal points of society, coordinating the actions of millions whom they relieve of the need to acquire and digest detailed knowledge about others and form detailed expectations about their future action.
>
> (Lachmann 1971: 50)

Lachmann ties the role of institutions into Austrian conceptions of divided and contextualised knowledge. In a generalised version of Hayek's (1945) pioneering work on how the price system enables us to have access to knowledge that would otherwise be incommunicable, Lachmann suggests that Weber's theory of institutions points us towards seeing all economic and social institutions as communication processes that make our diverse and often tacit knowledge socially usable.

This aspect of institutions figures prominently in Langlois's extensions of Lachmann's work. He describes institutions as 'interpersonal stores of coordinative knowledge; as such, they serve to restrict at once the dimensions of the agent's problem-situation and the extent of the cognitive demands placed on the agent' (Langlois 1986b: 237). In the context of game-theoretic applications, Langlois (1986c) discusses how institutions enable us to solve 'coordination' problems. By everyone agreeing (whether explicitly or tacitly) on a particular practice, we no longer have to out-guess or out-strategise other actors. The classic example of such a co-ordination problem is which side of the road to drive on. As long as all agree, the particular choice is irrelevant. Knowing which side others will drive on lowers 'the extent of cognitive demands' in specific situations. Important in Langlois's formulation is that by removing some elements of social interaction from conscious deliberation, institutions free us to focus on other situations that lack institutional solutions:

the existence at higher levels of institutions that stabilize the environment and reduce environmental entropy effectively frees behavioral entropy for use at lower levels. In a stable regime, the agent's reliability is high enough that he can add new actions to his repertoire ... at lower levels.

(Langlois 1986c: 186–7)

This idea parallels the oft-quoted dictum of Alfred Whitehead that 'Civilization advances by extending the number of important operations which we can perform without thinking about them' (as quoted in Hayek 1960: 22). In the light of an Austrian approach to institutions, we can interpret 'civilisation advances' as a proxy for 'as institutions evolve and mature'.[7] By serving as co-ordinative nodes, institutions reduce the knowledge needed to execute our plans, and enhance our ability to execute those plans successfully.

Given this description of what institutions do, Lachmann and others have pursued the question of how institutions come about. In short, institutions emerge as the unintended consequence of successful individual acts of rule-following behaviour. Individuals trying to improve themselves construct plans of action and attempt to carry them out. Individuals will continue to use modes of behaviour that are successful and will treat them as 'rules-of-thumb' as to how to act in certain circumstances. To the extent the ways of behaving exhibited in the successful plans can be observed by others, they will be imitated, increasing the number of actors behaving in particular ways. As this imitation process continues, and the number of users of particular rules-of-thumb increases, people learn to expect similar behaviour from others. A larger number of rule followers makes using the rule more attractive to potential newcomers as more users mean more opportunities to use the rule as a predictor of behaviour, enhancing the likelihood of co-ordinated outcomes.[8] When the behaviour in question is so widespread that we can call it 'generally accepted', the rule-of-thumb has become a social institution.

As Lachmann describes it:

Successful plans thus gradually crystallize into institutions. . . . Imitation of the successful is, here as elsewhere, the most important form by which the ways of the elite become the property of the masses. . . . Institutions are

the relics of the pioneering efforts of former generations
from which we are still drawing benefit.

(Lachmann 1971: 68)

Lachmann and others in the Austrian tradition point to Carl
Menger's (1892) theory of money as the exemplary story of institutional emergence and evolution.[9]

An Austrian conception of social order sees it as an interconnected set of institutions, most spontaneous, some designed and all
evolving and serving as communicative processes that enhance the
ability of individuals or collectivities (such as firms) to formulate
and execute their plans. The next, and perhaps more important,
question deals with the relationships among all of these institutions. In Lachmann's (1971: 69) words: 'how can we know that
these undesigned products of individual pursuit will all be compatible with one another?' Just how do the various institutional
arrangements of a modern society interact to form what might
legitimately be called an 'institutional order'?

Both Lachmann and Langlois offer us a way of conceptualising
this order that enables us to say something about the relationships
among institutions. For Lachmann, the crucial distinction is
between 'internal' and 'external' institutions:

> the undesigned institutions which evolve gradually as the
> unintended and unforseeable result of the pursuit of indi-
> vidual interests accumulate in the *interstices* of the legal
> order. The interstices have been planned, though the sedi-
> ments accumulating in them have not and could not have
> been. In a society of this type we might then distinguish
> between the *external* institutions which constitute, as it
> were, the outer framework of society, the legal order, and
> the *internal* institutions which gradually evolve as a result
> of market processes and other forms of spontaneous indi-
> vidual action.
>
> (Lachmann 1971: 81, emphasis in original)

Although Lachmann, on the following page, admits some short-
comings to this scheme, he also claims it is one in which a
'praxeological theory of institutions . . . most readily finds its place'
(ibid.: 81). As seen in the lengthy quote above, Lachmann's prime
example of an 'external' institution is the legal order in so far as
market institutions emerge and evolve by taking the law as a given

framework within which to develop. For example, given the framework provided by contract law, what sorts of practices will banks and their customers develop to engage in lending activities? The institution of a mortgage is internal to the external legal order of contract law.

Along the same lines, Langlois argues for a 'hierarchy' of institutions. For example: 'Highest-level institutions coordinate the highest level of plans. Institutions at lower levels coordinate lower-level or more concrete plans . . . lower-level institutions "grow" on the trellis of higher-level institutions' (Langlois 1986c: 185–6).

One can imagine all sorts of visual metaphors that capture the points both Lachmann and Langlois wish to make. One that seems in the spirit of both is to visualise institutions as concentric spheres, with the outermost spheres being the most 'external' or 'highest-level' institutions, which provide the framework within which the more inner spheres can arise. This image is compatible with all of the observations that Langlois (1992) makes concerning the relationship between internality and externality and Hayek's distinction between orders and organisations. My point is that such a visual metaphor seems to capture the essence of what both Lachmann and Langlois are articulating, even if it is not consistent with all of the details.

Before I proceed to argue why these hierarchical conceptions are problematic, let me recognise the important insight they contain. It is surely true that when we theorise or act, we treat many institutions as 'given' or at 'higher levels'. It is crucially important to realise that both describing and participating in the evolution of specific institutions always take place within a framework of institutional practices that are treated as stable. What Lachmann and Langlois are saying is largely correct. What I wish to object to is the implication, if not the explicit argument, that the hierarchy of institutions is something objective, even at a specific moment in time.

Subjectivism and the institutional order

One of the most important subjectivist insights of the past few years, particularly in its hermeneutical version, has been the emphasis on the actor's interpretive perspective in understanding both human action and economic theory. A thoroughgoing subjectivism sees 'the market' as the outward manifestation of the interpretive acts of the myriad actors who comprise it. What 'the market is saying' to individuals is not something objectively known by all, but can only be understood with, at the very least, some reference to the perspective of the individuals in question. Trying to define or explain market processes without taking into consideration the differing subjective perspectives of actors is highly problematic.

Starting where Lachmann surely would have, we note that Austrian economics began with Menger's subjective theory of value. In that theory, a good's value could not be defined by its objective characteristics, rather only by its role in the purposes and plans of individual actors. In contrast to the labour theory of value, which saw the value of outputs determined by the value of the labour inputs that comprised them, the subjective theory of value saw the value of inputs deriving from the value of consumer goods, which itself derived from the minds of choosing individuals. In the same way, I want to argue that which institutions are internal or external, or which ones are higher or lower, depends on either the question the theorist is asking or the plan an actor is considering. Just as a specific good has value only in the contexts of individual actors, so can institutions only be ordered hierarchically in the context of a specific theorist or actor.

Another way to see this is to analogise it to subjectivist epistemology for a moment. From the simple insight that all facts are theory-laden to more sophisticated work in the theory of knowledge, it is generally accepted that humans do not see the world unmediated. As Hayek's (1952) work on theoretical psychology argues, the mind is an ordering process. How we perceive the world today depends on the various abstractions that the mind has evolved in the past. Thus, any given sensory ordering depends to at least some degree on the particular history and experience of the perceiver. In language more congenial to interpretive philosophical approaches, we always understand 'from' somewhere. As noted earlier, this same idea appears in the work of Michael Polanyi (1958: 55ff.), who argued that our focal awareness (i.e. what we are focusing on now) depends upon a certain subsidiary awareness (i.e. the framework we take for granted when we focus). To some extent, these philosophical ideas cohere with the hierarchical conception of institutions in that they stress the givenness of some aspects of the world when we turn to examine others.

However, what the philosophical literature also emphasises is that what is given, or what is subsidiary, or which experiences have created certain neural linkages, *cannot be understood as objectively the same for everyone*. Each person's 'facts' are laden with different theories, for example. This is the fundamental challenge to the notion of a reality that is objectively knowable in its purest form.

The danger with the hierarchical conception of the institutional order (as in the sphere analogy from earlier) is that it implies that some institutions are objectively external to others. Notice, too, that the point is not that the 'position' of institutions might change over time. Most theorists of institutions agree that the hierarchy of institutions today may be different from the hierarchy tomorrow. That is clearly true. The point here is deeper; we cannot objectively define which institutions are where in the hierarchy even at a point in time. The 'hierarchical order' of institutions is contextual to the question or action under consideration.

It is also true that the different 'levels' of institutions can have feedback effects on one another. For example, changes in the structure of firms may call for a reinterpretation of aspects of property or contract law, or a new banking practice may lead to changes in the institutional arrangements of the money supply process. My point is not just to say that such feedback effects occur. Austrian institutionalists recognise this point. However, taking those feedback effects seriously should imply that as such effects occur, they force analysts and actors to reverse the hierarchical relationships among the institutions in question.

If one wants to understand the evolution of contract law since the mid-1700s, one will have to take certain institutions as 'external' to the law. Surely such an evolutionary explanation will show how actual commercial activities exposed 'gaps' in the law that were filled by judicial interpretation and application of the existing law to the new circumstances. When a legal historian performs this task, he can be seen as offering an explanation of the evolution of an institution within the framework provided by market institutions and the monetary order. Judicial decisions cause the law to evolve against a background of given market practices. In this story the 'fixed' institutions are those of the market, while the evolving practices are the legal rules. Of course if one wanted to explain why modern corporations have the structure they do, some portion of that story would illustrate how that structure emerged as a response to existing contract and property law. In such a case the legal order is external to the market process.

Moving away from theory to actual practice, the same point applies. The judge making case law is, in effect, treating his institution as internal to the market order, much as the owners deciding how to structure their firm have to treat it as internal to the legal order. Again, where particular institutions are in the hierarchical structure will vary depending on the perspective one is taking on the issue at hand.

To avoid any premature charges of nihilism, I am not arguing that we throw out all of the valuable insights provided by hierarchical metaphors. Instead I would suggest that we reconsider our metaphors to make them more consistent with a radically subjective understanding of both knowledge and the social order. After offering an alternative way of conceiving the institutional order, I will briefly discuss an application.

Parallels between Austrian theories of institutions and capital

An alternative way to conceptualise the institutional order might draw from Austrian analyses of another, equally complex, interconnected economic structure: capital.[10] In fact, Lachmann used the same phrase 'nodal points' to describe both institutions (see the quote above on p. 145) and capital goods: 'Capital goods are merely the *nodal points* of the flows of input . . . which they absorb, and of output . . . which they emanate' (Lachmann 1978: 58, emphasis in original). Austrian approaches to capital are the logical extension of subjectivist value theory. Once it is recognised that value is the product of consumer perceptions, then capital goods have to be understood in their roles as possible contributors to the production of valued goods. Since production does not occur automatically, but rather reflects the choices of producers/entrepreneurs, the way capital gets used will reflect the purposes and plans and expectations of its users. Whether a given good is capital depends on the role it plays in producers' attempts to anticipate the valuations of consumers. Production is inherently speculative as owners of capital 'bet' on it producing what consumers desire.

The implication of this theory of capital is that, as with value, the capital status of a good is not amenable to some objective definition. It is not the physical properties of a good that make it capital, rather it is the good's role in the plans of producers that give it the quality of being capital. The same slice of bread I use to make my ham sandwich at home would be considered capital if used for a restaurant sandwich and then sold to diners.[11] In a more complete discussion, stemming from Menger (1981 [1871]), we can recognise that capital goods can be 'ordered'. If consumer goods are 'first-order' goods, then the immediate inputs that comprise them are 'second-order' goods, and the inputs into those inputs are 'third-order' goods, etc. Such a schema gives the analyst a nice way to locate a specific good in the whole production process.

However, as with the hierarchical metaphors used in discussion of institutions, the danger here is in forgetting that the place of a specific good in this hierarchy is not objectively definable. For example, flour might be second-order for a bakery-made cake bought directly by consumers. On the other hand, the very same flour might be of a much higher order if it goes to a large commercial bakery that makes breads that are then sold to various food-supply wholesalers. Austrian capital theorists, especially Lachmann (1978), have long recognised the essential subjectivity of the concept of capital. In fact, one reading of the failure of Austrians to convince mainstream critics during the two debates of the 1930s (with Keynes and the market socialists), was that no one, including perhaps the Austrians, really understood the centrality of a subjectivist capital theory to understanding the market process. As we conceptualise the relationships among institutions, we should bear in mind the analogy from the capital 'structure'. Where a particular institution falls in the institutional order depends on the question we are asking.

Another set of concepts that can be taken from the Austrian theory of capital are 'complementarity' and 'specificity'. As Lachmann argues, capital is essentially heterogeneous implying that:

> each capital good can only be used for a limited number of purposes. We shall speak of the *multiple specificity* of capital goods. . . . For most purposes capital goods have to be used jointly. *Complementarity* is of the essence of capital use.
> (Lachmann 1978: 2–3, emphasis in original)

When producers formulate plans, they have to understand the range of possible uses for each capital good and how each good might fit with other goods needed to execute the plan at hand. In addition, as external circumstances (e.g., consumer demands) change, existing capital combinations may no longer be appropriate, and a reshuffling of capital must occur. How capital will be reshuffled depends greatly on how specific it is and how complementary it will be with other newly required capital goods. This constant arranging and rearranging of the capital structure is driven by the ever-changing demands of consumers.

Many of these same concepts could be applied to the institutional order. Certainly complementarity is a central concept in discussing institutions. How well institutions mesh together is crucial to their epistemological roles. One of Lachmann's (1971: 75ff.) four characteristics of institutional order is 'over-all complementarity'. He argues that clusters of related institutions might have high degrees of complementarity (e.g., all of those involving written or oral communication), but the relationships among clusters are not always so 'gapless'. For Lachmann, the 'gap' metaphor is a way of fleshing out how complementary a set of institutions is. He says of the legal system: 'It has no "gaps". A judge before whom a legal case is brought can never refuse to give a decision on the grounds that he knows of no legal norm to apply to it. He has to find one' (Lachmann 1971: 76–7).

Interestingly this same notion of 'gaps in the structure' appears in his discussion of capital and the way in which new investor-entrepreneurs see opportunities for profit: 'The shape in which new capital goods make their appearance is determined largely by the existing pattern, in the sense that "investment opportunities" really mean "holes in the pattern"' (Lachmann 1978: 10). In both cases, what is at issue is the *internal coherence* of each structure, rather than some externally observable objective pattern (ibid.: 57).

Rather than seeing institutions as in hierarchical relationships with each other, a more fruitful conceptual device might be an exploration of the ways in which they can work together and the limits to such complementarity. Concerns about institutional complementarity are inherently linked with real historical time and unexpected change. How social order can be preserved in the face of an unknowable but not unimaginable future may well rest on the ease with which different institutions can work together in various combinations to react to and anticipate (to the degree possible) future events.

The issue of specificity also comes into play with institutions. Rather than examining how a particular institution fits with others, the specificity of an institution might refer to its own adaptability in the face of social change. The flexibility of institutions may be crucial for providing social order. An example of this might be seen in the way in which many indigenous institutions in the Third World have changed and adapted to being further permeated by market forces.[12] Overly specific institutions may inhibit social order by being insufficiently flexible.

153

Linked with specificity is the fact that institutions display a high degree of path-dependency. Institutions always change and adapt from their earlier incarnations; they normally cannot be constructed whole cloth. Path-dependency also suggests that objectivist measures of optimality (such as Pareto criteria) are difficult to apply in an Austrian view of institutions. Institutions are never likely to be perfectly fitted for solving existing problems because they are the products of imperfect processes of historical evolution. Just as a relatively specific capital good refitted to perform a task different from its original one may not do so as well as a new machine, so are many institutions imperfect adaptations to existing social environments.[13]

Of course, completely non-specific institutions are likely to be problematic also, since they would have to be at a level of generality that would probably require other sorts of (complementary!) institutions in order to generate concrete co-ordinative results. An example here might be language. Language is extremely flexible (though perhaps not perfectly). However that very flexibility creates the problem of jargon or dialects that make linguistic co-ordination more difficult. Other social institutions might be necessary to enable language to adapt smoothly to outside change. An example of this might be the technospeak of the very computer-literate compared to the average person's understanding of such issues. The very flexibility of language can create communication barriers.

One problem all institutions face is being sufficiently flexible to adapt to the unexpected, yet sufficiently coherent to serve as nodal points for current attempts at co-ordination. With capital goods, complementarity and specificity are ways of conceiving these issues. As conditions change, producers have to work with capital goods of distinct specificity and reshuffle them into complementary combinations that will meet the new change. Transferring the same concepts to institutions might provide a useful way of conceiving the institutional order without positing some objectively given, hierarchical structure. Thinking of institutions as nodal points of co-ordination that are constantly in motion and shuffling and reshuffling their relationships with each other need not lead to theoretical chaos. The profundity and longevity of the Austrian theory of capital attests to how such a theory (even when insufficiently developed) can provide important insights and be radically subjectivist.

Banking and the law: an illustration

A quick overview of the relationship between the growth of financial intermediaries and the evolution of the relevant portions of the law can illustrate the complex and varied relationships among institutions and the difficulties of viewing them as hierarchical. The evolution of banking provides some excellent examples of complementarity and specificity and the flexibility/coherence balance.[14]

It is generally argued that what we now understand as financial intermediaries probably grew out of earlier institutions that were simply warehouses for storing precious metals. Traders who did not wish to undertake the risk of holding large stocks of gold could store them for safekeeping with goldsmiths or others who offered security for a fee. At first, transferring these gold 'balances' was cumbersome as the law often required the presence of both parties to the transfer and perhaps their legal representatives in order to execute the exchange of gold. At this point, the proto-banks were acting within the given legal order and using the accepted processes of transfer.

However, entrepreneurial gold storers realised that transfers could be made more easy by issuing receipts to gold in storage and allowing traders to simply exchange those receipts (via endorsement) rather than by actually meeting at the storage facility and signing the relevant paperwork. The issue facing this innovation was how the legal order would interpret those receipts and the use of signature endorsements to transfer them. This uncertainty reflects a missing complementarity between two institutions. In most cases, the law recognised the receipts as contractual obligations and endorsement as an acceptable transfer process.

This issue also illustrates a limit of hierarchical metaphors. To the extent that the popularity of this banking innovation put pressure on the legal system to decide on their status, it reflects the degree to which legal institutions were 'internal' to financial institutions and practices. However, once such a decision was made, banks could treat the legal status of such receipts as given and move to innovate further, thus treating the legal order as 'external'. The metaphor of complementarity seems much more appropriate here.

One of the next major steps in the evolution of banking was the move to fractional reserve banking. Once again, entrepreneurial warehousers realised they could profit by lending out deposited specie at interest to the extent that depositors had no direct use for it. The transferring of receipts had diminished the actual amount of metal that flowed in and out of the 'bank', facilitating the move to fractional reserves. Early bankers understood that the challenge was to maximise their interest returns while still maintaining sufficient reserves to meet the demands of depositors.[15] The question that needed to be answered was how the legal system would interpret deposit receipts in the absence of 100 per cent reserves.

Whereas deposit receipts under 100 per cent reserve banking are effectively bailments, not unlike the receipt one might have for furniture at a self-storage facility, fractional reserve bank notes cannot be seen this way. The exact legal standing of the contract between a depositor and a fractional reserve bank has been the subject of much discussion among Austrian monetary theorists.[16] Historically, however, the law has generally seen those contracts as *demand* deposits, in that the legal obligation of the bank is to redeem bank notes when customers demand it.[17] Under this inter- pretation, the bank is free to do what it pleases with the specie as long as it can deliver the required amount when demanded.[18] In this case again, the legal order had to respond to an innovation coming from the financial sector. As both note users and issuers generally began to find fractional reserve notes to be acceptable, judges worked within that set of practices in establishing the legal standing of the notes. Again, however, having established the acceptability of fractional reserve notes, banks now treated the law as external and were able to pursue other related innovations with the assumption that the legal order would treat such innovations the same way.

One example might be the decision to give borrowers bank notes (or deposit credits) rather than actual specie. Banking historians generally agree that banks first lent actual specie and somewhat later realised they could lend out notes rather than specie. With the uncertain legal standing of fractional notes, banks were likely to have been hesitant to use them for all customers at first. Once the law indicated it would accept such notes as redeemable on demand, then banks probably extended the practice to new borrowers rather than just to old depositors. The complementary interrelationships between banking and the law are clearly illustrated here.

One last banking innovation that reflects issues of complemen- tarity and specificity is the 'option clause'.[19] Scottish banks during their free banking period in the eighteenth century developed a way of dealing with the danger of massive withdrawals that could drain a fractional reserve bank by rewriting the contract contained in a bank note. Rather than being redeemable 'on demand', their notes were redeemable on demand or in six months at 5 per cent interest, at the bank's discretion. The notes gave the bank the option of suspending redemption for a limited period of time with compensation paid to the note holder.

This innovation can be viewed as an example of institutional flexibility in the face of uncertainty. Scottish banking practices were not so institutionally specific as to be unable to react to external change. At first, the Bank of Scotland simply unilaterally declared that note redemption would be suspended for some period and interest would be paid to note holders, without having specified this in writing on the note. This *ad hoc* policy was used on three occasions in the early 1700s (White 1984: 25–6). Eventually, such *ad hoc* manoeuvres faced legal challenges.

The period (1727–30) during which an actual option clause was added to Scottish notes was one of new entry and intense competition (Dowd 1991: 769). Faced with the uncertainty inherent in such a situation, the Bank of Scotland first used the *ad hoc* invocation of temporary suspension with interest to prevent itself from being drained of reserves by a new competitor, the Royal Bank of Scotland. In this case, however, a suit was brought charging the Bank of Scotland with violating the terms of its charter by not redeeming notes on demand. According to White (1984: 26): 'After much legal wrangling the note holder's right of "summary diligence" or immediate payment on Bank of Scotland notes . . . was upheld'. Shortly after this decision, the Bank of Scotland added an explicit option clause on the obverse of all of its notes indicating its right to suspend redemption and the corresponding payment of interest.

The problem facing both the banks and the law was how to be sufficiently flexible to deal with the challenges of innovation and uncertainty, while still maintaining a coherence and complementarity that could provide a stable institutional environment for market actors. The whole Scottish option clause episode can be seen as an attempt to fill in the 'gaps' in both the monetary and legal institutional orders.[20] Judges had to react to financial innovations, and banks had to wait to learn the official legal status of their innovations before extending or advancing on them. It would be difficult in this case to point to either the legal or monetary order as being internal or external or up or down in some hierarchy. Rather it seems more like a story of shuffling and reshuffling and searching for complementarity in the face of external change, much like the Austrian theory of capital.

This illustration indicates that the complexities of historical processes of institutional evolution cannot be fully captured by hierarchical conceptions of institutional order. A more subjectivist view of institutional order would seek out more circular or interactive relationships among institutions. The evolution of any specific institution will indeed proceed against the backdrop of other institutions, but may also *affect* the future evolution of those other institutions. Our approach to institutional evolution needs to be forward-looking as well, by understanding the unintended consequences that emanate from individual institutional change. The idea of 'co-evolution' and notions of complementarity and specificity should begin to play more prominent roles in Austrian conceptions of economic and social institutions.

Conclusion

One of the subtexts of this chapter has been the claim that it is not accidental that Ludwig Lachmann was a pioneer in both Austrian capital theory and the theory of institutions. Both theories and their subject matters share important characteristics. What they share most, though, is that they are both rooted in a subjectivist approach to social phenomena. That subjectivism is Lachmann's true legacy. However, consistently adhering to a subjectivist paradigm is a continual challenge. Debates over equilibrium theory among Austrians, and debates between Austrians and post-Keynesians concerning the theoretical and political implications of subjectivism demonstrate this challenge quite vividly. As subjectivists pursue a theory of institutions, we need to be careful not to accidentally drift from the friendly seas of subjectivism into the rapids of mechanistic, hierarchical or objectivistic conceptions of the institutional order. Extending Lachmann's legacy demands no less of us.

Notes

1 For a larger treatment of these issues in the post-revival generation of Austrians and their relationship to Menger's original work, see Vaughn (1994).
2 In that sense, my mission parallels that of Prychitko (1994) who argues that Lachmann's focus on 'the plan' is untrue to Lachmann's own professed hermeneutic orientation as it ignores or downplays the unintended consequences of the playing out of individual plans.
3 Of course there are numerous other treatments of institutions. A variety of perspectives can be found in Hodgson (1988); Mäki *et al.*

(eds) (1993); and Rutherford (1994), among others. Explorations of the relationship between Austrian economics and the Old Institutionalism (from each side) can be found in Boettke (1989) and Samuels (1989).

4 For my own partial attempts at such work, see Horwitz (1992a, 1993, 1994).

5 Philosophically this question is also at the bottom of modern phenomenology. As the Austrian philosopher Alfred Schutz put it: 'What makes my behavior social is the fact that its intentional object is the expected behavior of another person' (Schutz 1967: 149).

6 On Schutz and the Austrians, see Prendergast (1986). On Simmel and the Austrians, see Horwitz (1992b).

7 There is also a parallel here to Michael Polanyi's (1958) distinction between 'focal' and 'subsidiary' awareness. I shall return to this issue later.

8 This phenomenon is frequently referred to as a 'network effect', as in a telephone network. With any network or other communication process (like language), the more users there are, the more attractive is the process to potential participants. A phone network with only three users is not very attractive compared to one with millions.

9 Indeed, note my use of the phrase 'generally accepted', which is normally associated with the definition of money as a 'generally accepted medium of exchange'. One can extend that definition to other social institutions by changing the practice that is being generally accepted. For example, one might define law as a 'generally accepted set of rules for interpersonal interaction'. For more on the parallels between money and law, see Horwitz (1993).

10 Lachmann's capital theory is seeing a bit of a revival. See Horwitz (1994) and Lewin (1994 and 1997).

11 Of course one could argue that my bread is capital too, in that the sandwich is a 'capital' good that produces utility. Although that insight is in some sense true, it is also trivial. A better way of conceiving the issue is in terms of trade on a market. Capital goods have market prices, as do the items they produce. The ham sandwich I make and eat is, in Marxian terms, not a commodity; the restaurant sandwich is. The commodity status of the product confers capital status on the inputs. It is neither accidental, nor incorrect, that Marx started *Capital* with a discussion of the commodity.

12 See, for example, Chamlee (1993).

13 The analogies to evolutionary biology are obvious here. For more see Horwitz (1992a: Chapter 2) and Hodgson (1992). Darwin himself understood that existing biological species will not meet criteria of perfection: 'We cannot doubt that each structure is of use to each kind of squirrel in its own country . . . [b]ut it does not follow from this fact that the structure of each squirrel is the best that it is possible to conceive under all possible conditions' (Darwin 1859: 129).

14 This section draws on the work of Selgin and White (1987) and extensions of that work in Horwitz (1992a: Chapter 4).

15 The two criteria necessary for fractional reserve banking are that the medium of exchange is fungible and that withdrawal patterns are sufficiently random so that the law of large numbers can be said to hold. If

the law of large numbers holds, then the chance of any significant amount of withdrawals on any given day is small, enabling banks to hold fractional reserves.

16 See Rothbard 1983: Chapter 1.

17 One of the ironies of the 100 per cent reserve position is that its adherents correctly recognise the historicity of the particular goods that get used as media of exchange, but forget the importance of historical evolution when discussing the legal standing of fractional reserve notes. They wish to impose a legal/ethical theoretical position by *fiat*, despite the historical evolution of case law on that practice. To this extent, the more 'traditional' Austrian view on banking was very much non-institutional, and a more subjectivist and institutionalist view would stress the complementary evolution of financial institutions and legal practices.

18 One interesting issue here is whether the bank has a legal obligation to maintain the purchasing power of the specie while it is in its custody. Some Austrian defenders of 100 per cent reserve banking argue that fractional reserve banks by definition depreciate the value of specie, thus violating the bank note contract. The validity of this argument depends on one's definition of inflation/depreciation and the role of the demand for money, issues which are beyond the scope of this paper. See Horwitz (1988) for more.

19 A good overview and defence of this practice is in Dowd (1991).

20 Interestingly enough, option clauses were eventually outlawed in Scotland in 1765. Various players in the banking industry were willing to give up the right to the option clause in exchange for differing political favours. Provincial banks wanted full legal recognition and the chartered banks wanted to politically eliminate their competition. The provincial banks eventually won and the option clause and small denomination notes were the price. See the accounts in Dowd (1991) and White (1984).

References

Boettke, P. J. (1989) 'Evolution and economics: Austrians as institutionalists', *Research in the History of Economic Thought and Methodology* 6: 73–89.

Chamlee, E. (1993) 'Indigenous African institutions and economic development', *Cato Journal* 13: 1, Spring/Summer.

Darwin, C. (1859) *The Origin of Species*, New York: Modern Library edn.

Dowd, K. (1991) 'Option clauses and bank suspension', *Cato Journal* 10: 3, Winter.

Hayek, F. A. (1937) 'Economics and knowledge', in *Individualism and Economic Order*, Chicago: University of Chicago Press, 1948.

—— (1945) 'The use of knowledge in society', in *Individualism and Economic Order*, Chicago: University of Chicago Press, 1948.

—— (1952) *The Sensory Order*, Chicago: University of Chicago Press.

—— (1960) *The Constitution of Liberty*, Chicago: University of Chicago Press.

—— (1988) *The Fatal Conceit: The Errors of Socialism*, W. W. Bartley III (ed.), Chicago: University of Chicago Press.

Hodgson, G. M. (1988) *Economics and Institutions*, Philadelphia: University of Pennsylvania Press.

—— (1992) 'Institutional evolution and methodological individualism', in B. J. Caldwell and S. Boehm (eds) *Austrian Economics: Tensions and New Directions*, Boston: Kluwer Academic.

Horwitz, S. (1988) 'Misreading the "Myth": Rothbard on the theory and history of free banking', repr. in P. Boettke and D. Prychitko (eds) *The Market Process: Essays on Contemporary Austrian Economics*, Aldershot, UK: Edward Elgar, 1994.

—— (1992a) *Monetary Evolution, Free Banking, and Economic Order*, Boulder: Westview Press.

—— (1992b) 'Monetary exchange as an extra-linguistic social communication process', *Review of Social Economy* 50: 2, Summer.

—— (1993) 'Spontaneity and design in the evolution of institutions: the similarities of money and law', *Journal des Economistes et des Etudes Humaines* 4: 4, December.

—— (1994) 'Subjectivism, institutions, and capital: comment on Mongiovi and Lewin', *Advances in Austrian Economics*, vol. 1, Greenwich, CT: JAI Press.

Lachmann, L. M. (1971) *The Legacy of Max Weber*, Berkeley: The Glendessary Press.

—— (1978) *Capital and Its Structure*, 2nd edn, Kansas City: Sheed Andrews and McMeel.

—— (1986) *The Market as an Economic Process*, London: Basil Blackwell.

Langlois, R. (1986a) 'The New Institutional economics: an introductory essay', in R. Langlois (ed.) *Economics as a Process: Essays in the New Institutionalist Economics*, Cambridge: Cambridge University Press.

—— (1986b) 'Rationality, institutions, and explanation', in R. Langlois (ed.) *Economics as a Process: Essays in the New Institutionalist Economics*, Cambridge: Cambridge University Press.

—— (1986c) 'Coherence and flexibility: social institutions in a world of radical uncertainty', in I. M. Kirzner (ed.) *Subjectivism, Intelligibility, and Economic Understanding*, New York: New York University Press.

—— (1992) 'Orders and organizations: toward an Austrian theory of social institutions', in B. J. Caldwell and S. Boehm (eds) *Austrian Economics: Tensions and New Directions*, Boston: Kluwer Academic.

Lewin, P. (1994) 'Knowledge, expectations, and capital', *Advances in Austrian Economics*, vol. 1, Greenwich, CT: JAI Press.

—— (1997) 'Capital in disequilibrium: a reexamination of the capital theory of Ludwig M. Lachmann', *History of Political Economy*, 29: 3, Fall.

Mäki, U., Gustafsson, B. and Knudsen, C. (eds) (1993) *Rationality, Institutions and Economic Methodology*, London: Routledge.

Menger, C. (1892) 'On the origin of money', *Economic Journal* 2.

—— (1981 [1871]) *Principles of Economics*, New York: New York University Press.

—— (1985 [1883]) *Investigations into the Method of the Social Sciences with Special Reference to Economics*, New York: New York University Press.

O'Driscoll, G. P. and Rizzo, M. J. (1985) *The Economics of Time and Ignorance*, London: Basil Blackwell.

Polanyi, M. (1958) *Personal Knowledge: Towards a Post-Critical Philosophy*, Chicago: University of Chicago Press.

Prendergast, C. (1986) 'Alfred Schutz and the Austrian School of Economics', *American Journal of Sociology* 92: 1: 1–26, July.

Prychitko, D. L. (1994) 'Ludwig Lachmann and the interpretive turn in economics: a critical inquiry into the hermeneutics of the plan', *Advances in Austrian Economics*, vol. 1, Greenwich, CT: JAI Press.

Rothbard, M. N. (1983) *America's Great Depression*, 4th edn, New York: Richardson and Snyder.

Rutherford, M. (1994) *Institutions in Economics: The Old and the New Institutionalists*, Cambridge: Cambridge University Press.

Samuels, W. (1989) 'Austrian and institutional economics: some common elements', *Research in the History of Economic Thought and Methodology* 6: 53–71.

Schutz, A. (1967) *The Phenomenology of the Social World*, Evanston: Northwestern University Press.

Selgin, G. A. and White, L. H. (1987) 'The evolution of a free banking system', *Economic Inquiry* 25: July.

Vaughn, K. I. (1994) *Austrian Economics in America: The Migration of a Tradition*, Cambridge: Cambridge University Press.

White, L. H. (1984) *Free Banking in Britain*, Cambridge: Cambridge University Press.

9

LACHMANN'S POLICY ACTIVISM

An Austrian critique of Keynesian proclivities

Peter J. Boettke and Steven T. Sullivan

Introduction

W. H. Hutt, upon noticing that Ludwig Lachmann was to be one of the main lecturers at the first Austrian Economics Instructional Conference in South Royalton, VT in the summer of 1974, supposedly turned to a crowd of students and said, 'Why is Lachmann here? He is a Keynesian, not an Austrian.' Hutt, one of the foremost critics of Keynesian economics, was someone with authority to comment on this issue. Indeed, why was Lachmann there if he possessed Keynesian proclivities in public policy?[1] Roger Garrison, perhaps the leading contemporary authority on Austrian macroeconomics, often refers in lectures to Lachmann's approach to economics as 'Austro-Keynesianism'.[2] There can be no doubt that in the history of Austrian economics, Lachmann was the most charitable interpreter of Keynes within the Austrian tradition. Indeed, in a 1983 essay Lachmann sought to delineate the common ground that existed between Keynes and his followers and the Austrians.[3] Lachmann adhered so consistently to the 'principle of charitable interpretation' with respect to Keynes and many other of the Austrian School's rivals that it became known around the NYU colloquium as 'Lachmann's Law'.[4] Mises and Hayek certainly lacked both the patience and the intellectual sympathy required to deal with Keynes in the manner that Lachmann did. Those familiar with the history of Austrian economics will also note that when Lachmann's subjectivism is mentioned, Keynes and Shackle are never far behind.

There also can be no doubt that Lachmann played a significant role in the resurgence of Austrian economics in the late 1970s and 1980s. He was the catalyst for much of the internal development of Austrian economics among the resurgence generation, and his influence can be seen in the work of Gerald O'Driscoll and Mario Rizzo, *The Economics of Time and Ignorance* (1985), Karen Vaughn, *Austrian Economics in America* (1994) and Don Lavoie (ed.), *Economics and Hermeneutics* (1991) and *Expectations and the Meaning of Institutions* (1994). Lachmann's theoretical challenge to extend subjectivism from preferences to expectations has had a deep and lasting influence among his Austrian colleagues, including Israel Kirzner, who, despite his serious reservations about aspects of Lachmann's research project remained Lachmann's closest intellectual ally in the Austrian revival.

Most scholars of Lachmann's generation, as we know, had their faith in the operation of unhampered market economies shaken by the Great Depression of the 1930s. The Great Depression left an indelible mark on Lachmann as well. While working as F. A. Hayek's assistant, Lachmann wrote an M. Sc. thesis at the London School of Economics in 1935 entitled 'Capital structure and depression' – in which, despite his use of the Austrian theory of crises to explain the depression, he advocated a public works programme as a solution to the depression problem (Lachmann 1935, esp. Chapter IV). The instability of the stock market and of speculative investment were recurring themes throughout his long research career (see, e.g., Lachmann 1937, 1988). Lachmann was one of the most articulate spokesmen for the Austrian notion of a time structure of production, yet he was also a severe critic of any notion of a determinate equilibrium as the outcome of economic processes (including the unhampered market economy). These two positions are not unrelated, but it takes some teasing out of the issues to realise the implications for theory and application.

Can Lachmann be both radical subjectivist and policy activist? Could it be, as Garrison suggests, that Lachmann was both Austrian and Keynesian? And, if Lachmann's influence on the Austrian revival is as deep as it appears, then are contemporary Austrian economists Keynesians? Lachmann took subjectivism seriously – subjectivists, then, might best take Lachmann's subjectivism seriously. And so can we correctly infer from the activist positions of subjectivism's pre-eminent modern champion that the charge of 'nihilism' it so often faces is misplaced?[5] Lachmann presents us with quite a set of puzzles, and it seems only fitting that we should apply the principle of charitable interpretation to this subset of the writings of its main adherent in order to solve them.

In his 1956 book *Capital and Its Structure*, Lachmann provided his readers with a vision of the morphology of capital as an order in an exposition that was the clearest of its time. Drawing on a view of capital as physically and functionally heterogeneous combinations operated by planning acting human minds, Lachmann traced out his vision and catalogued its implications for the state of capital theory and macroeconomic policy. His interpretive and distinctly 'Austrian' system, thoroughly adhered to, would seemingly deny interventionist macroeconomic policies. Yet in the final analysis, Lachmann's vision of the economy as a system that does not necessarily possess a tendency towards equilibrium, and in particular, his view of the operation of the price system, led him to call for policy activism in times of general economic distress. This is something of a curiosity within the Austrian camp.

The purpose of this chapter is to trace out Lachmann's vision of capital as an order, stressing along the way those aspects of his vision (and the Austrian concept of spontaneous order) that most effectively deny interventionist macroeconomics in order to determine whether Lachmann ultimately leaves us with a set of policy prescriptions that (despite whatever theoretical validity they may be said to possess), could not rationally be carried out by anyone. We first present Lachmann's vision of capital as an order, and note those aspects that are most at odds with aggregate macroeconomics – the view constituting the problem environment of the interventionist policy maker. We then emphasise a second set of arguments extant in *Capital and Its Structure* (1956) (and elsewhere in Lachmann's writings) concerning the functioning of the price system, and in particular its role in any self-correcting tendency in the economy, in order to develop the setting for Lachmann's policy advocacy in times of massive plan discoordination. Finally, we survey the possibility of reconciliation and explore the following possibilities: That Lachmann: (1) contradicted himself in establishing the validity in principle of the policy positions he takes; (2) presented us with a fully coherent set of policy arguments; (3) established the validity in theory of the policy positions he takes but left no basis for their rational implementation.

Understanding the capital-using economy

The concepts Lachmann employed to understand the industrial structure of a contemporary economically developed society, namely functional heterogeneity, complementarity as joint use, multiple specificity, the individual's production plan and its physical mani- festation in the capital combination, are rooted in the Austrian tradition. At the core of Lachmann's system is the production plan – this is the means–ends framework of the individual in the capital- using economy. In other words, Lachmann's understanding of the 'macroeconomic' world was thoroughly choice-theoretic. The plan is a logical structure where objects and the causal relationships among objects are subjectively perceived; this focuses theoretical attention on how the planning individual organises the means of production at his disposal in order to generate output. The plan is shaped by the individual's subjective assessment of the economic environment, and its success or failure is judged by signals provided by the market process and filtered through that agent's perceptions. The individual's plan determines the relationship between already existing capital goods and prospective new capital goods – Lachmann viewed complementarity as joint use of items within the context of an existing plan, and substitution as a fundamental element of plan revision contingent on that plan's failure as perceived by its creator.

Capital heterogeneity in Lachmann's system, then, provides a different view of the investment relationship from that found in the aggregate macroeconomics or growth theory literature. The assumption of homogeneity, in light of the Lachmannian alterna- tive, can thus be seen to generate some analytical costs in terms of lost categories of capital relationships. It misleads the economist into presuming that new capital is a substitute for old capital, as Lachmann notes:

> As long as we cling to the view that all capital is homoge- neous, we shall only see, as Keynes did, the unfavourable effects of investment on the earning capacity and value of existing capital goods, since all the elements of a homoge- neous aggregate are necessarily perfect substitutes for each other. The new capital competes with the old and reduces the profitability of the latter. Once we allow for hetero- geneity we must also allow for complementarity between old and new capital. The effect of investment on the prof-

itability of old capital is now seen to depend on which of the various forms of old capital are complementary to, or substitutes for, the new capital.

(Lachmann 1956: 6)

The relationships between new and old capital are thus more complicated than a homogeneous aggregate conception would lead us to believe. The economics then becomes more complicated, and no small amount of damage is done to one of the central features of the Keynesian analysis of the macroeconomy:

> Looking at the matter in the way we have done also opens up a new vista on the problem of the 'incentive to invest'. New capital goods are being used in combination with existing ones. This form of complementarity means that the lower the price of existing capital goods the greater the profitability of the new goods. . .
>
> Keynes, to be sure, did not neglect the effect of prices of existing capital goods on new investment, but, treating in characteristic fashion all capital as homogeneous, only saw the possibility of substitution. So he held that prices of existing capital goods below reproduction cost would weaken the incentive to invest. But in reality capital is as a rule heterogeneous and complementary. Except in the case, which Keynes alone considered, where existing and new capital goods happen to be substitutes, low prices of the former will have a favourable effect on the incentive to invest. Neglect of the heterogeneity of capital thus vitiates the theory of investment.
>
> (Lachmann 1956: 49–50)

Such issues of standard economics, we shall argue below, while damaging to the particulars of the Keynesian analysis, are secondary in importance to the implications of the Lachmannian vision for the problem environment of the planner. To hint at arguments developed more fully below, one can imagine the increased degree of technical knowledge required to centrally plan investment in a capital-using economy if one recognises the heterogeneity of capital. Yet this daunting increase in the data requirements merely reflects the task of the investment planner in a world where knowing *that* is all the relevant knowing; the relevant knowing in Lachmann's framework is not merely a laundry list of engineering relationships but knowledge of *context* – knowing *how*.

Adding to this level of complexity, and generally raising the stakes of the intervention game, is another notion arising out of heterogeneity – that of *multiple specificity*. Capital goods are characterised by joint use, and are capable of many alternative combinations, but the scope for their alternative use is not unlimited. Some modes of joint use are not feasible – there only exist certain 'technically possible' modes of complementarity; furthermore, the schedule of 'economically significant' *and* technically possible combinations is not given at once to the entrepreneur. The entrepreneur must deploy resources (i.e. search) *and* be alert towards the discovery of such economical modes of complementarity, being careful all the while because specification mistakes are admitted into the theory. Without multiple specificity, there would be no need to ask why certain capital combinations are used and others are not – the problem facing the capital combination operator would be solved *ex hypothesi*.[6] Heterogeneity adds the possibility of *mis*-fits, or *mal*-investment, in the combinations of capital goods employed by agents. In a world of capital factor homogeneity, of course, each additional dK of capital is exactly like the last, except that its expected marginal value product is different. In Lachmann's world, an additional 'dK' *can* cause the capital combination to become incoherent and require costly revision of the plan. Furthermore, mistakes are durable – the failed combinations of the past may shape the current problem environment, therefore contributing a pronounced degree of path dependency.[7] Investment is an undertaking on a higher plane of uncertainty in Lachmann's view of the world. This further adds to the would-be planner's problems.

Heterogeneity and multiple specificity are not the end of Lachmann's vision, however, but rather the beginning. Investment planning is not the computationally simple affair that emerges from models that assume homogeneity of capital goods. The problem of the maintenance of capital, and the role of signals employed by actors within the economy in forming and revising capital-using plans, are minimised in alternative models.[8] The Austrian analytical contribution to capital theory represents, rather, a way of looking at capital that effectively denies the theoretical aggregation, which is often employed to motivate interventionist arguments. Why? Looking at the texts provides us with a revealing distinction. The difference between the outcome of plans as envisioned at the firm level and manifested at the level of the market is reflected in the concepts of 'plan complementarity' or 'designed complementarity', which refer to the relationship between elements in the firm's plan, versus 'structural complementarity' – which refers to the relationship of elements across firms and indeed across industries, *and therefore across planning consciousnesses*. 'Capital structure' is given to be the mode of complementarity expressed in the market as a whole, or 'a mode of the composition of the capital stock of society' (Lachmann 1986: 63ff). In *Capital and Its Structure*, Lachmann distinguishes between plan and structural complementarity along these lines: 'The first type of complementarity is brought about *directly* by entrepreneurial action. . . . Our second type of complementarity is, if at all, brought about *indirectly* by the market, viz. by the interplay of mostly inconsistent entrepreneurial plans' (Lachmann 1956: 54, italics in original). Again, in his last book *The Market as an Economic Process*, Lachmann draws the distinction:

> This second type of complementarity [here meaning structural complementarity] is not the direct result of planned action, but the indirect result of the interaction between the plans of different firms in the market. These latter plans need not have been consistent from the start, but were then made consistent by market forces.
>
> (Lachmann 1986: 63)

Structural complementarity is of the macro-level – on the order of the phenomena studied by policy makers; so is it valid to speak of policies on the macro-level, such as increasing the 'level of investment', without making reference to the coherence of individual plans? If we follow Lachmann's line of argument, we see clearly that structural complementarity is a surface relationship or by-product, merely a manifestation of the dovetailing (or failure to dovetail) of individual plans, which are the more fundamental units of analysis. The morphology of capital at the *structural* level is therefore an *order*, which is to say that it is the result 'of human action, but not of human design' – of individual and firm-level investment planning, but not of macroeconomic investment policy.

To recognise this argument in Lachmann's work is to drive the stake of subjectivism into the heart of aggregate capital theory, and thus into the heart of most arguments for macroeconomic interventionism as well. This is because standard investment theory fails to perceive the differences between conscious or intended *plan* complementarity at the firm level and manifested *structural* complementarity at the 'macro'economic level. Blind to the phenomenology of the capital structure, the decentralised choice-driven process of the *coming-to-be* of that capital structure, the macroeconomist speaks of the 'level of investment' without proper reference to the causal agents of the capital structure, namely planning individuals and firms. 'National' investment, good or bad, high or low, appropriate or misdirected, only makes sense if we can speak of a 'national' plan, a means–ends framework constructed by a directing and controlling mind. But such a plan is a fiction – at the level of structural complementarity, *there is no one directing or controlling mind.* Lachmann cites Hayek's *Pure Theory of Capital* in the development of this point:

> Of consistent capital change, on the other hand, we may speak where 'coincident expectations about the quantities and qualities of goods which will pass from one person's possession into another's will in effect co-ordinate all these different plans into one single plan, although this "plan" will not exist in any one mind. It can only be constructed.'
>
> (Lachmann 1956: 60)

Yet the macroeconomist engages in the familiar conceit of extending the individual's problem-solving acts of mind to the social level, with all the attendant hazards. In its restatement of the problem at the planner's level, it also departs from a fully subjectivist understanding of the problem world. Capital combinations are manifestations of logical structures composed of relationships among subjectively perceived objects, and the knowledge they embody is not fully available to anyone except their operators. The macroeconomist who employs an aggregate production technology with 'known' and stable characteristics of factor complementarity and substitutability presumes a level of knowledge that no one mind or group of minds can ever possess.[9] A Lachmannian capital theorist, then, might reasonably view macroeconomic investment policy as an undertaking with context-specific knowledge requirements that are simply impossible to satisfy. How, then, can Lachmann call for policy activism in times of widespread plan discoordination?

Lachmann on the price system and the trade cycle

Lachmann viewed the price system (including the interest rate) as a communications network through which individual operators of capital combinations could receive signals as to the opportunities *ex ante* and the performance *ex post* of their plans, and co-ordinate the time profiles of their productive activities:

> In a market economy . . . prices are not merely exchange ratios between commodities and services but links in a market-wide system of economic communications. Through price changes knowledge is transmitted from any corner of the market to the rest of the system. On each market buyers and sellers, by varying their bids and offers, signal to each other the need for action. Buyers learn about their opportunities growing or shrinking, sellers receive notice of the need for adjustment. In this way every economic change has market-wide repercussions. . . . We may thus conclude that via knowledge transmitted through the price system economic change tends, in general, to give rise to expectations consistent with itself.
>
> (Lachmann 1956: 62)

In Lachmann's work the above paragraph represents the zenith of market performance as a co-ordinator of plans. The institutional context of the real world, however, plays havoc with the idealised world of responsive, flexible prices. Rigid wages and administered prices degrade the signals in the system:

> But in reality the price system is not such an ideal system of economic communications as the picture just drawn might suggest. Our apparatus, we must remember, works by 'translating' demand and supply changes into price changes. Hence, whenever the translation does not take place, for instance, where prices are inflexible, our apparatus ceases to operate. Moreover, as we learnt before, transmission is often delayed and sometimes faulty. Where this is known to be the case the meaning of the messages received will lend itself to different, and perhaps contrasting, interpretations, both as to content and time of despatch. This all the more so where numerous, perhaps contradictory, messages follow each other within a short time over the same 'wire'.
>
> (Lachmann 1956: 62)

What are the ramifications of error in the model? In demonstrating them, Lachmann makes use of the concept of the 'ceiling', the maximum available quantity of a given resource or set of resources in a given time frame. Let us examine for a moment how rigid factor prices may lead the economy into widespread plan failure: Let us imagine a factor of production which is a complement in production plans economywide. As the use of this product brings us closer to exhaustion, or in our case to the ceiling, the price will normally be adjusted through bidding until agents either discontinue their plans utilising the factor at a lower expected return or otherwise economise on its use. Rigid prices, however, prevent agents from seeing the approach of the ceiling – suddenly it is reached, and the factor without which their plans cannot proceed becomes unavailable. Keeping in mind Lachmann's view of complementarity, we can see that shortages of complementary factors constrain final factor output; many of the factors whose output levels are constrained by the original factor shortage are complements in other production processes. The shortage spreads – if an agent had planned to bring to market a certain quantity of other (second-round) capital goods based upon the expectation of complementary resources, which expectation was disappointed because the ceiling was hit for those complementary resources, that agent might choose not to bring the second-round capital goods to market. Capital combinations to which those second-round resources not forthcoming are complementary may now be in peril. The scarcity need not even last for very long for widespread plan disco-ordination to occur – only an unexpected delay in the factor's availability is necessary:

> It might be said that raw material prices being more flexible than fixed capital goods prices, relative price figures tell us little about relative scarcity. It is true that a fixed capital goods ceiling will manifest itself, at least at first, in delayed delivery rather than in higher prices, so that absence of higher prices does not necessarily mean absence of excess demand. But the delay in delivery can only postpone, and not prevent, the emergence of excess capacity, unless of course the raw material shortage is merely temporary, not a '*ceiling*' but a 'bottleneck'. The mere fact that after both sub-ceilings have been reached the output of both, raw materials and fixed capital goods, will slow down, is irrelevant. It is relative scarcity of complementary factors which here causes excess capacity and upsets plans. For no factor can be used in isolation, complementarity is of the essence of all plans, and withdrawal of a factor, or its

failure to turn up at the appointed time, will equally endanger the success of the production plans.

(Lachmann 1956: 107, italics in original)

We can recognise here the added analytical value of heterogeneity – producers who had expected resources to be available which were to be needed at later dates (now the present) have organised their production processes and generated highly specific resources to be used in combination with the expected output of their suppliers. Many of these inventories of midstream products are useless without the complementary resources, and those capital combinations which generated them are not costlessly or instantaneously re-specified:

> Rates of interest which are too low, i.e. fail to establish *ex ante* equilibrium between savings and investment, are apt to convey such a misleading picture and thus lead to *wrong specifying decisions.* . . .
>
> The essence of the matter is that investment decisions are not merely irreversible in time, so that excessive investment in period 1 as a rule cannot be offset by disinvestment in period 2, but that they are also *irrevocable in kind*. Even if, at a later point during the boom, interest rates start to rise, the message comes too late for those who have made their irrevocable decision before.
>
> (Lachmann 1956: 118, italics added)

This phenomenon, born out of heterogeneity and multiple specificity, embeds plan failure in the system.

Lachmannian stabilisation policy

If we found ourselves as Lachmannian capital theorists 'on the morrow of the crisis', asked to formulate a policy to shepherd the economy back to its more normal degree of plan co-ordination, what would we do? The post-boom economy, as Lachmann tells us, is in crisis because the interest rate or price system has sent the wrong signals – projects have been undertaken and have drawn scarce resources away from other projects based upon false information on profitability, factor availability and the buying public's willingness to delay consumption. The landscape is littered with failed and failing projects, some of whose failure is based upon the lack of complementary resources, others failing because of the normal course of market activity. Bottlenecks have occurred and ceilings have been hit in crucial sectors of industry – say, primary materials. The main problem is one of malinvestment or mistaken allocation, and the *prima facie* solution would seem to be to reallocate the misallocated resources. This is what Lachmann suggests:

> The situation the economy faces on the morrow of the collapse of a strong boom clearly calls for capital regrouping on a large scale. . . . Plans have gone astray, hopes have been disappointed; capital combinations have to be dissolved and reshuffled. . .
>
> Some planned combinations cannot come into operation because of lack of complementary factors; these factors have to be created now. . . . Something might be done by shifting resources to where they are most needed. The critical sectors are those sub-ceilings which lie in the path of expansion. Here more investment is required in order to 'lift the ceiling'. To this end not merely must investment in other sectors be curtailed; additional factors able to help in lifting the ceiling must be recruited from wherever they happen to be, and this means as a rule that they must be withdrawn from those combinations of which they form part. Mobile resources from everywhere, even from the consumption goods industries, will have to be drawn to the critical sectors. . . . These mobile resources have to be detached from the specific and non-mobile resources with which so far they have co-operated, and this will lead to dissolution and reshuffling of existing combinations . . .
>
> In all probability mobile resources cannot be withdrawn and capital combinations will not be reshuffled without pressure being brought to bear on owners and managers of specific resources. In some cases it may not be possible at all without actual bankruptcy. To this end a 'severe' credit policy is required. But a credit policy sufficiently severe to 'crack open' the tougher kind of unsuccessful capital combinations may discourage investment in the critical sectors of the economy.
>
> . . . In such a situation there is much to be said for a 'selective' credit policy which need not be arbitrary if it merely reflects the degree of imperfection of the capital market which is the natural product of the past record of success and failure of individual firms.

... Suppose our critical sub-ceiling is in mineral mining. It is surely unnecessary to deprive existing coal mines of their mining equipment. Our purpose of moving mobile resources to the critical area may be as well served by the heavy engineering industries switching their plants from producing equipment for coal-using industries to producing mining (or 'mineral-economizing') machinery. In this way existing combinations may be moved bodily to 'another stage of production' without the painful need for disintegration.

(Lachmann 1956: 120–4)

These passages reflect an undeniably activist bent to Lachmann's analysis. The policy maker is charged with selecting which capital combinations must be dissolved and perhaps manipulating a 'selective' credit policy in order to break apart those capital combinations possessing resources useful to the 'critical sectors'. In a later passage on the dynamics of the post-'weak boom' economy, Lachmann states that the excess capacity generated by plan disco-ordination, even in the *absence* of ceilings, might be combated by means of a budget deficit combined with the aforementioned selective credit policy (Lachmann 1956: 125–6).

This is not the only occurrence of Lachmann's advocacy of government activism. In his 1935 Master's thesis at the London School of Economics, Lachmann advocates public works to arrest the process of cumulative depression:

But, once the cumulative process of destruction is swaying the economic system, what shall we do? For this case of emergency we propose a Public Works Programme somewhat on the following lines:
The great advantage a public works programme has over a mere stabilization policy of the kind just described consists in that it would affect both consumers good industries (via the purchases of the workmen now in employment) and producers goods industries (via the purchases of the necessary raw- and building-materials) at one and the same time: We are, so to say, arresting the cumulative process with hand-brake and foot-brake. Its main disadvantage, as has often been pointed out, lies in the necessity to invest capital for, at the existing rate of interest, unproductive purposes, i.e. in the net capital

consumption it implies. From this it follows that the object of such a policy has to be the stopping of the cumulative process with a minimum sacrifice of capital. *Hence, a public works programme has to be devised in such a way, the purchases of consumers goods and capital-goods have to be dosed so as to bring about reinvestment-equilibrium within the shortest time possible.*

(Lachmann 1935: 95–6, our italics)

Note the constructivist language. These are rather odd things for an Austrian economist to advocate, especially an Austrian who consistently emphasises the subjective nature of knowledge and the attendant unpredictability of economic systems. In fact, the second passage was preceded by a warning against inflationary policies, shored up by a lengthy discussion of the unpredictable character of dis-hoarding behaviour (Lachmann 1935: 89ff). And the most compelling subjectivist argument conceivable for government activism in times of massive plan disco-ordination, namely that such activism provides a signpost or strong signal for the re-co-ordination of individual means–ends frameworks, is nowhere to be found.

The description of the crisis referred to in these passages is certainly consistent with the Austrian theory of the structure of production, with Lachmann's view of complementarity, and with the Austrian Trade Cycle Theory, but what are we to make of the Lachmannian policy agenda?

In trying to make sense of Lachmann on policy, we return to the choices listed at the beginning of the chapter. The first of these is that Lachmann's economics are simply incorrect. Let us approach the argument: Is Lachmann's call for a reshuffling of capital combinations inconsistent with ending the crisis? *Given* that the critical sectors can be identified and the proper path for the economy can be divined, it is conceivable that a set of incentives can be formulated to redirect resources to their highest-valued use in the re-engineered structure of production, and that bankruptcy and sufficiently well-developed 'used capital' markets can be used to reorganise capital combinations economywide. We find, then, that as a matter of standard incentive-driven economic analysis, Lachmann's prescription fits the diagnosis.[10] We can reject the first alternative.

We now turn to issues arising out of the second and the third alternatives. These are that Lachmann either provided us with a coherent analysis or failed to shore up his economics with a firm epistemic footing. If we grant that Lachmann's economics are sound, and that his policy suggestions are valid in theory given the chain of events that has led us to the crisis, then we might conclude that the second alternative is satisfactory and our task is finished. Lachmann's policy activism results from sound economic reasoning and would be a reasonable response for an Austrian given the situation so described. But to take Lachmann's system seriously, it is insufficient to establish the validity of the theoretical mechanics and consider the problem of feasibility solved. Lachmann's book was as much or more a statement about economic knowledge as it was about the hard empirics of the trade cycle, and it is the problem of economic knowledge that will not let us rest with the second alternative.[11] Feasibility, it seems, is a more troubling problem than Lachmann appreciated. When we ask ourselves such questions as 'What rationale exists for the policy maker in deciding which sectors are critical to the recovery? What is the meaning of the *proper path* in an open-ended economy? How do we distinguish normal project failures from those brought about by the crisis?' we realise that the second alternative does not finish telling the story because it is not fully informed by Lachmann's view of 'who knows what' in the economy. The 'critical sectors' lie 'in the path of expansion' – but the economy is in crisis in the Lachmannian story *precisely because* agents' expectations about the time profile of productive activities are in disarray. Why is the theorist-as-policy-maker's position epistemically privileged?

Our third alternative suggests that the problem is one of internal inconsistency. Lachmann calls for a reshuffling of complementary resources to the 'critical sectors', which are supposedly simple to identify – this is a result of the use of what is undeniably a macro- or aggregate construct. It is an example of how Austrian economists sometimes find it meaningful to talk about broad categories, here surrounding capital goods' functional character in the structure of production. But because one can stylise the structure of production to understand individual acts of choice and specification does not mean one can understand well enough the *entire and concrete* economy on the operating table in order to diagnose the *concrete* problem and target specific policy – the two are potentially inconsistent acts of mind. One involves the theorist's understanding of the structure of production from within, from the point of view of the individual agents shaping its particulars, while the other involves a view of this structure from without – from the point of view no single agent or group of agents possesses. Lachmann's activism, as most interventionist arguments implicitly do, conflates the two perspectives. The categorical rejection of such a conflation represents one of the substantive implications of the Austrian criticism of aggregate macroeconomics.

Ironically, Lachmann's mistake in *Capital and Its Structure* (and elsewhere on this topic) is in being insufficiently subjectivist. On the one hand, capital combinations are outward manifestations of subjectively perceived relationships and objects, and on the other hand they are functionally categorised by the economist according to a view of their place within the structure of production. This second aspect is perfectly valid for understanding how a crisis might occur in theory, but its extension to diagnosis and economic policy in an actual crisis puts the economist in the grip of an epistemic contradiction. Lachmann's policy maker is being asked to 'bite off more than she can chew'. Lachmann forgot his own analysis in framing the policy maker's problem and in moving from generalised classes of strong and weak boom problems to an actual instance of the 'post-strong boom economy' type, with an objective knowledge requirement as large as that economy and a contextual knowledge requirement policy makers cannot begin to address from their standpoint. The problem of a radical subjectivist macroeconomics is this: The theorist has merely to think about *how* agents think; the policy maker must know *what* they think.

Conclusion

If the market process, as Lachmann has stressed, is best understood as 'a pattern of meaningful utterances of the human mind', then economists must focus their theoretical attention on problems of information acquisition and how institutions provide signals to guide our actions within the economic world (Lachmann 1986: 165). This also means that we can never drop the issue of knowledge from our attention for either modelling purposes or policy-making convenience. As he put it in another context:

> The market process is the outward manifestation of an unending stream of knowledge. This insight is *fundamental to Austrian economics*. The pattern of knowledge is continuously changing in society, a process hard to describe. *Knowledge defies all attempts to treat it as a 'datum' or an object in time and space.*
>
> (Lachmann 1976: 127)

Knowledge, to Lachmann, while essential to economic understanding is nevertheless elusive – a concept that simply cannot be
accounted for in the neoclassical model (or any determinate model
of economic affairs) because the very passage of time implies change
in the state of knowledge in society.

Lachmann's work stressed the extension of subjectivism from
preferences to expectations. In pursuing this radical subjectivist line
of research he offered important and deep insights into the dynamic
nature of market processes, the role of institutions as guideposts to
actions, the difficulty of signal interpretations, the role of time in
human perception, and the link in economic life between the -
dispersion of knowledge, the dispersion of expectations and the
dispersion of interpretations. These insights shook the foundation of
any deterministic rendering of the market process, including the
Austrian theory of entrepreneurial discovery. If Lachmann's insights
are valid, then the economic world is truly kaleidic.

The kaleidoscope, despite its indeterminacy, possesses a certain
pattern or order internal to its own operation. The market, from a
Lachmannian perspective, could be said to possess the same type of
patterned order – neither clockwork nor completely random. The
order of the market process has a logic of its own (see O'Driscoll and
Rizzo 1985: 71–91). Attempts to get outside of the system and
control it do not so much direct its operation as distort the
patterned order that characterises a market economy within a well-
established system of property rules.

In dealing with Lachmann's particular arguments for activism we
have suggested that he failed to consistently take his own subjectivist lessons to heart. If the world is truly kaleidic, then the policy
maker must face the same confusing array of signals as that of
market participants (with the same diversity of interpretation of the
signals). If private market actors do not face the incentives and lack
the ability to acquire the information to co-ordinate their behaviour
with others in the market due to the constantly changing conditions and diversity of interpretations of the signals these changes
produce, then why should we expect policy makers to be able to co-
ordinate economic affairs in a successful manner? The very
subjectivism that Lachmann championed undermines his Keynesian
proclivities. The analytical arguments that flow from subjectivism,
in other words, cannot sustain the Keynesian vision of policy
activism. It is not the determinism of New Classical economics that
defeats Keynesian policy, but the 'dark forces of time and ignorance'
that engulf us all.

Notes

1 Here we must be careful with our labels – the central issue of the paper is the juxtaposition of Lachmann's subjectivism with his *policy activism*. The fact that Keynes favoured activist policy (and in particular, public works) should not lead us to the (false) conclusion that all policy activism is somehow Keynesian. Lachmann's advocacy of public works programmes in his LSE thesis predates the *General Theory*, for example. Yet given the tendency of discussions of Lachmann to flow into discussions of Keynes, the policy comparisons to Keynes are an irresistible temptation and 'Keynesian' positions should here be narrowly interpreted as those 'adhered to most notably by Keynes'.

2 See, e.g., Garrison (1986 and 1994) where he carefully distinguishes his own Austrian approach from either the extreme subjectivism of Keynes, Shackle and Lachmann and the extreme determinism of Lucas and Sargent.

3 L. Lachmann, 'John Maynard Keynes: A view from an Austrian window', in D. Lavoie (ed.) *Expectations and the Meaning of Institutions*, London: Routledge, 1994.

4 D. Lavoie (ed.) 'Introduction', in *Expectations and the Meaning of Institutions*, London: Routledge, 1994.

5 Clearly there are 'varieties' of both subjectivisms and subjectivists – e.g. Keynes, Shackle, Lachmann, Hayek. To some extent, the propriety of subjectivist calls for policy activism is always (rightly) in question. This is particularly true, we think, for Lachmann. As Lavoie notes in his 'Introduction' to *Expectations and the Meaning of Institutions*, subjectivism was for Lachmann more than a minor point of methodology in value theory. Many economists can and do refer to themselves as 'subjectivists' and yet ultimately base their predictions (as they must) on objectivist or mechanical–intersubjectivist techniques that ultimately wring the subjectivism (and hence the fundamental unpredictability) out of human systems. Yet from Lachmann we would expect something different.

As for the obvious follow-up question about Keynes, our argument below to the effect that Lachmann bestows an unjustifiable epistemic privilege on the position of his policy maker can be extended to Keynes with no difficulty, despite the clear differences in the two economists' particular brands of subjectivism. Here we must leave the argument about Keynes so as to avoid getting too far afield of our focus, namely *Lachmann's* activist views. For more on Keynes's subjectivism, see Butos and Koppl, 'The varieties of subjectivism: Keynes and Hayek on expectations', *History of Political Economy*, 29 (2): 327–59 (1997).

6 This is true for both the assumption of homogeneity *and* for a world of unique specificity. The importance of economic calculation as a guide for the allocation within production plans of scarce capital goods is only highlighted in the world of heterogeneity and multiple specificity.

7 Though not always for the worse in terms of economic allocations. Lachmann notes in *Capital and Its Structure* that 'A number of invest-

ment opportunities actually owe their existence to the failure of past capital combinations to achieve the purposes for which they were designed' (1956: 9–10).

8 Kirzner (1966) provides an overview of the basic conceptual issues of concern in alternative formulations of capital theory. Also see Lewin (1994).

9 This, of course, is the theme of Hayek's Nobel Lecture, 'The pretense of knowledge' (Hayek 1974).

10 Of course, this analysis minimises or denies that the very subjectivism of expectations that makes speculative markets suspect as co-ordinating devices should be generalised to confront policy makers as well. In Austrian analysis it is often argued that questions of incentives cannot legitimately be separated from questions concerning knowledge acquisition. For the sake of argument, however, we assume that one can address these questions separately. Public choice theory, for example, often assumes perfect information on the part of government officials, but then asks the analyst to consider the incentive system. Austrians, on the other hand, typically assume benevolence on the part of policy makers, but then examine the difficulties of information acquisition. A full-blown theory of policy making would have to account for both information and incentives, but the usefulness of intellectually isolating these problems and examining the implications cannot be denied.

11 It is for precisely this reason that the principle of charitable interpretation is inapposite in this case – the policy conclusions in *Capital and Its Structure* (Lachmann 1956) and elsewhere run against the grain of *what we know* to be the knowledge-theoretic thrust of the Lachmannian research programme. There can be little question but that we are engaged in immanent criticism of Lachmann and find his conclusions wanting.

References

Garrison, R. (1986) 'From Lachmann to Lucas: on institutions, expectations, and equilibrating tendencies', in I. M. Kirzner (ed.) *Subjectivism, Intelligibility, and Economic Understanding: Essays in Honor of Ludwig M. Lachmann on His Eightieth Birthday*, New York: New York University Press, pp. 87–101.

—— (1994) 'Interview', in B. Snowdon, H. Vane and P. Wynarczyk *A Modern Guide to Macroeconomics: An Introduction to Competing Schools of Thought*, Aldershot, UK: Edward Elgar Publishing, pp. 383–97.

Hayek, F. A. (1974) 'The pretense of knowledge', in *New Studies in Philosophy, Politics, Economics and the History of Ideas*, Chicago: University of Chicago Press (1978), pp. 23–34.

Kirzner, I. M. (1966) *An Essay on Capital*, New York: Augustus M. Kelly.

Lachmann, L. M. (1935) 'Capital structure and depression', unpublished M. Sc.(Econ.) thesis, London University.

—— (1937) 'Uncertainty and liquidity-preference', in D. Lavoie (ed.) *Expectations and the Meaning of Institutions: Essays in Economics by Ludwig M. Lachmann*, London: Routledge (1994), pp. 29–41.

—— (1956) *Capital and Its Structure*, Menlo Park: Institute for Humane Studies (1978 edn).

—— (1976) 'On the central concept of Austrian economics: market process', in E. G. Dolan (ed.) *The Foundations of Modern Austrian Economics*, Menlo Park: Institute for Humane Studies, pp. 126–32.

—— (1986) *The Market as an Economic Process*, Oxford: Basil Blackwell.

—— (1988) 'Speculative markets and economic complexity', in D. Lavoie (ed.) *Expectations and the Meaning of Institutions: Essays in Economics by Ludwig M. Lachmann*, London: Routledge (1994), pp. 270–5.

Lavoie, D. (ed.) (1991) *Economics and Hermeneutics*, London: Routledge.

—— (ed.) (1994) *Expectations and the Meaning of Institutions: Essays in Economics by Ludwig M. Lachmann*, London: Routledge.

Lewin, P. (1994) 'Capital theory', in P. J. Boettke (ed.) *The Elgar Companion to Austrian Economics*, Aldershot, UK: Edward Elgar Publishing, pp. 209–15.

O'Driscoll, G. P. and Rizzo, M. J. (1985) *The Economics of Time and Ignorance*, Oxford: Basil Blackwell.

Vaughn, K. I. (1994) *Austrian Economics in America*, New York: Cambridge University Press.

10

EXPECTATIONS AND STOCK MARKET PRICES

Jochen Runde and Jörg Bibow

A familiar theme in Ludwig Lachmann's writings is the notion of 'divergent' expectations in stock markets. The following passage is fairly typical:

> The Stock Exchange consists of a series of markets for assets, i.e., future yield streams. In each market supply and demand are brought into equality every day. Demand and supply reflect the divergent expectations of buyers and sellers concerning future yields. Transactions take place between those whose expectations diverge from the current market price. Since as much must be bought as is sold, we may say that the equilibrium price in an asset market reflects the 'balance of expectations'. As without divergence of expectations there can be no market at all, we can say that this divergence provides the substrate upon which the market price rests.
>
> (Lachmann 1977: 161)

The many similar passages on the nature and role of expectations in stock markets that appear in Lachmann's writings are invariably insightful and instructive. His commitment to subjectivism, to analysing economic phenomena from the viewpoint of the interpreting economic actor, moreover, provides an important perspective that is denied on more conventional assumptions about expectations. Yet it seems to us that Lachmann is seldom particularly explicit about what he takes the term 'expectation' to refer to or express and, accordingly, that his distinctive and highly suggestive writings on expectations in stock markets invite both

183

interpretation and elaboration on this count. Our aim, then, is to outline Lachmann's conception of expectations and to use this to offer an account of his distinction between convergent and divergent expectations. We go on to raise some problems with explaining equity prices in terms of divergent expectations and, drawing on Miller (1977) and Keynes, attempt to resolve them.

Expectations

Lachmann offers various hints about his views on the nature of expectations and their emergence. Three themes recur consistently throughout his writings. The first is that expectations are incidental to the 'mental pictures' drawn to formulate the plans on which human conduct is based.[1] Expectations thus concern future events or states of affairs that exist only in the imagination of the actor at the time that the expectation is formed. The second theme is that expectations are not strictly determined by the 'data' of experience but are based on experience that is necessarily interpreted and that is, to this extent, subjective. Lachmann emphasises, in this connection, that the 'act' of interpretation is never wholly passive and, accordingly, that economic choice and action are never wholly determined by the actor's circumstances. Finally, Lachmann insists that it is not possible to have foreknowledge of future events and accordingly, that expectations tend to be subject to uncertainty.

Yet Lachmann's writings offer few direct statements about the nature and structure of the expectations he has in mind.[2] In his most explicit and extended discussion of the topic, Chapter 2 of his *Capital and Its Structure*, he begins by comparing what the businessman does in forming an expectation with what a scientist does in formulating a working hypothesis (Lachmann 1978: 23). Business expectations and scientific hypotheses serve the same purpose in that they both 'reflect an attempt at cognition and orientation in an imperfectly known world' and 'embody imperfect knowledge to be tested and improved by later experience'. Expectations are formed, according to Lachmann, by analysing one's situation in terms of the impact of possible 'forces' or tendencies believed to be operative in the situation.[3] The aim is to identify and separate dominant or 'major' tendencies from random or 'minor' tendencies. Expectations are then a reflection of the anticipated effects of the operation of the major tendencies identified. Lachmann seems to suggest that induction plays a major role in the formation of expectations:

in assessing the significance of price changes observed in the past for future changes we shall tend to neglect those we believe to have been due to random causes, and to confine our attention to those we believe due to more 'permanent' causes.

(ibid.: 24)

Expected values are then compared to realised values in order to infer whether initial assessments were correct.

But even here, it is only possible to infer his views on the possible structure of the expectations he has in mind from his application of Lange's (1944) theory of the 'Practical Range'.[4] In terms of this theory, price expectations are taken to consist of an imagined 'inner' interval of possible prices that the actor would consider 'normal' over some period or at some date, bounded on either side by an 'outer range' of prices considered 'possible'. This conception is consistent with Lachmann's views on expectations being subject to uncertainty: it appears to permit a rough gradation of possible prices in terms of a weak form of (comparative) epistemic probability, while avoiding the standard assumption about beliefs corresponding to numerically definite probabilities. From the actor's perspective, then, prices that lie within the inner price range are more probable than those lying in the outer ranges, and prices lying within the outer ranges are more probable than prices that fall beyond the outer ranges. Lachmann does not say anything about the time horizon of the expectations he has in mind.

Lachmann's advocacy of the 'Practical Range' conception is bound up with his views on how actors interpret the position and movement of actual prices within the ranges and, accordingly, how this influences the formation of expectations. There are three possibilities. First, actual prices may vary within the normal interval. In this case, Lachmann argues, their movement will be attributed to 'minor' random causes and, as such, will be interpreted as 'functionless' (meaningless). If a particular view of the normal range is widely held and firmly based, moreover, prices that move towards the limits of the inner range will tend to be brought back towards the centre by speculative pressure (speculators selling near the upper limit and buying towards the lower limit).

The second possibility is that prices may move into the outer range, perhaps as the consequence of the operation of 'major' (permanent) forces. Whether or not such price movements are interpreted as 'meaningful', according to Lachmann, depends on how long the new prices are sustained. If prices swing back into the inner range fairly quickly, this will confirm the conventional view of what is normal. However, if prices stay in the outer range, market participants will gradually come to revise their notion of the normal price.[5] This means that speculators will seek to buy at prices at which they would formerly have sold (and vice versa), suggesting that once the limits of the inner range have been breached, price movements may be carried further by the very speculative pressures that formerly resisted them. Finally, where prices move beyond the limits of the outer range they become 'unquestionably meaningful' and carry a definite message that cannot be disregarded. The market will have to revise its views on what is normal: 'It must now become clear to everybody that the hypothesis about the constellation of fundamental forces which formed the basis of our range structure has been tested and failed' (Lachmann 1978: 32). But while the negative message is clear enough, namely that the former hypothesis of what consisted as the normal is invalid, its positive content is less so. The message still requires interpretation, the soundness of which, according to Lachmann, will depend on the insight and intelligence of market participants.

Divergent expectations and equity prices

We are now in a position to say something about Lachmann's distinction between 'convergent' and 'divergent' expectations. If the expectations in question were the point predictions of asset prices at some future date held by different individuals acting in the context of a social group, the distinction would seem to be fairly straightforward. Convergent expectations would then be point predictions that have a significant tendency to converge (or have converged) on a unique value of the relevant variable over time, perhaps because its value has been stable in the past. Divergent expectations, in contrast, would refer to the case in which individual point predictions of the value of some variable are not convergent, or display a tendency to diverge over some time period.

But we have seen that Lachmann rejects the assumption of point expectations in favour of the interval-valued conception described above. Now it is possible to argue that the distinction between convergent and divergent expectations still applies. Convergent expectations might then be those the 'normal' intervals of which have a tendency to coincide more closely over time, or that do coincide. But things are not that simple. The trouble is that the wider the interval regarded as 'normal' by different individuals, the more likely it is that a significant portion of these normal intervals will overlap. In general, however, it seems that we would want to associate wider 'inner' intervals with more uncertainty, and hence, with *less* agreement about what the future price will be. So whether or not the interval-based price expectations of the members of some community qualify as convergent will always be relative to some prior judgement of how narrow intervals must be in order to be regarded as reflecting 'agreement' about future prices. This will clearly not be a hard-and-fast matter. But it does suggest a way of characterising the two cases: in what follows 'convergent' expectations or beliefs will refer to expectations held by the members of a social group, where (i) the associated normal intervals have a tendency to coincide more closely over time; and (ii) where this is not due to the intervals widening (in general, convergent expectations would be associated with relatively narrow normal intervals that narrow further over time). 'Divergent' expectations or beliefs, in contrast, will refer to expectations held by members of a social group that are not convergent, or where (i) the degree of overlap between the associated normal intervals has a tendency to reduce over time; and (ii) where this is not due primarily to such intervals narrowing (in general, divergent expectations would be associated with relatively wide normal intervals that may widen further over time).

As we have already noted, the notion of divergent expectations comes to the fore in Lachmann's writings on equity prices. The key theme is that such prices reflect a balance of the heterogeneous beliefs of market participants.[6] At a very general level, of course, this is true enough. But the notion of a 'bulls–bears' equilibrium of opposing expectations is more complex than it at first appears, and not only because of the difficulties in arriving at a precise categorisation of divergent expectations. In the first place, as we shall show, share prices reflect the ratio of holders of the share to potential holders in the market and generally do not correspond to the 'average expectation' of the market. Second, expectations of future prices and/or prospective yields are only one of the things that determine the value of a share to individual investors, and which thereby influence its market price. As Lachmann himself points out, share values depend on how prevailing prices are interpreted. Other important considerations include risk,[7] ambiguity,[8] and how actors respond to these. Finally, there is the impact of all manner of uncertainties that need have no particular bearing on the prospects of the particular share itself, and which introduce the more general considerations of 'market' confidence and liquidity.

These complexities suggest that the relation between divergent expectations and equity prices must be qualified and extended. We propose to do so by focusing on what we shall call the *diversity of opinion* between market participants, not about future prices, yields, etc., but about the value they attach to any particular share. In particular we would like to focus on the fact that, at any point in time, there are likely to be marked differences between market participants about what a share is currently worth to them in money terms *whatever the source of these differences*. The key distinction in what follows, then, is between the diversity of opinion on the one hand, and divergent expectations or beliefs (about future prices, for example) on the other. The former term, to repeat, will refer to the money value that investors, potential or otherwise, attach to a share at some point in time, the latter to expectations about the future value of variables. Clearly, as investors' valuations of a share are usually informed by their expectations, divergent expectations will tend to lead to increases in the diversity of opinion about that share. However, and as we shall see below, this need not always be the case.

Diverse opinion and equity prices

Although the prices of shares traded on the Stock Exchange appear to be 'continuously' on the move, definite prices are determined at discrete points in time. We shall call these 'equilibrium' prices, equilibrium in the sense that, at these points, market participants (both holders and non-holders of the share in question) do not want to change their position (Lachmann, 1976: 60). In equilibrium, then, all existing shares are willingly held at the prevailing price. In what follows the term 'average evaluation' will refer to the average of the values the individual market participants attach to a particular share at some point in time, be they holders or non-holders.[9] As will become clearer below, this average evaluation will generally *not* correspond to the market price of the share. Optimists will be defined as those individual market participants who value the share at more than the average evaluation, pessimists as those who value it at less. Not all optimists need be holders of the share.

According to Miller (1977: 1151) 'the very concept of uncertainty implies that reasonable men may differ in their forecasts'. It then follows that uncertainty will tend to lead to a diversity of opinion about equity values. Two important features of his analysis are that it applies to a share with severely restricted short-selling opportunities and that the number of potential holders of the share substantially outnumber the shares offered by the company. Miller's central result is as follows: only in the special case of the absence of any diversity of opinion about the value of the share will its market price correspond to the average evaluation. In all other cases the share will tend to be held by that proportion of potential investors who hold particularly optimistic views about its value.[10] He derives this result from elementary demand and supply analysis. The vertical axis measures the 'estimates of value' per share made by heterogeneous investors, the horizontal axis the number of shares demanded and supplied at each estimate of value.[11] The equilibrium price is given as usual by the intersection of the demand and supply schedules. With restricted short selling, the supply curve is vertical at the number of shares outstanding. Furthermore, in the absence of diversity of opinion, the demand curve is horizontal. In this case, and in this case only, will the equilibrium price reflect the average of the investors' evaluations. A diversity of opinion, in contrast, will be reflected in a downward sloping demand schedule, that is, the number of investors willing to hold the share will rise as the price falls. Here the price of the share will be higher than in the former case, reflecting the views of the more optimistic segment of the market rather than the average evaluation. The point is that the slope of the demand curve depends on the diversity of opinion. The greater the prevailing uncertainty, and hence the greater the diversity of opinion about the value of the share (and the steeper the demand curve), the higher its price will be.

What can be said about the impact of changes in the diversity of opinion on the price of a share? First, we must stress that the conception of an 'equilibrium' share price implies nothing about its stability. In the present setting the price of the share will alter whenever its supply, the demand for it, or both, change.[12] A change in supply (a shift of the vertical supply curve) will occur as the result of the company issuing new shares or buying back existing ones, and the effect on the price of such activity will be greater the greater the diversity of opinion in the market.[13] But this is probably the less important case and we shall concentrate on the demand for the share, taking its supply as given. We have already seen that the share will tend to be more 'overpriced' relative to the average evaluation the higher the diversity of opinion in the market. The question then is, starting from a given state of diversity of opinion in the market, what the impact of new information will be.

There are a number of possibilities. First, new information may reduce the diversity of opinion about its value.[14] The optimists become less optimistic and the pessimists less pessimistic, so that, in the aggregate, the share price comes closer to the average evaluation. In graphical terms, the demand curve would flatten out and the price of the share would fall. Since the share can only be held by a small proportion of the optimistic investors, it is the selling pressure of former optimists who have become less optimistic that leads the price to fall until it is again in line with their new opinions about what the share is worth (clearly this includes the possibility that some former non-holders change their minds sufficiently to become holders). Conversely, it is possible that new information may lead to an increase in the diversity of opinion in the market. In this case, by parallel reasoning, the demand schedule steepens and the price rises.

A second possibility is that the new information may lead optimists to become more (less) optimistic and pessimists to become less (more) pessimistic. In the limiting case individual investors' opinions about the value of the share would neither diverge from nor converge towards the average evaluation, but the average evaluation would itself shift. Recall that the price is always determined by the optimists in the market and will always exceed the average evaluation by a greater or lesser amount. A third possibility is that the new information may affect neither the slope nor the position of the demand schedule and hence leave the price unaffected, but that some trading nevertheless occurs. Such trading will either be between holders who want to change the amount of the share that they hold in their portfolio or between holders and non-holders who have changed camps. Clearly both sorts of trades may also occur in the cases already mentioned above.[15]

Miller mentions a fourth channel through which new information may impact on price by affecting the diversity of opinion, the possibility that new information may affect the number of potential investors who are paying attention to the relevant share. This possibility is related to the number of potential investors exceeding the number of shares available, and draws attention to the fact that information is not without cost. The new information may then affect the 'overhang' of investors over the number of shares, thereby possibly affecting the diversity of opinion and, accordingly, the share price.

Thus far we have said nothing about individual investors' attitudes towards risk. Miller makes the novel point that in the situation depicted above even risk-neutral investors have a reason to employ some kind of 'risk premium', or better, 'uncertainty premium'. For risk-neutral investors who understand the impact of the diversity of opinion on the price of shares would aim to discount the value of the share in order to avoid *ex post* disappointment. If all investors were risk neutral and acted in this way, share prices would be brought into line with the hypothetical average evaluation (and if the average evaluation were 'correct' then neither over- nor under-investment would occur). To be sure, the share would still be held by those who are most optimistic about its value. But given that individual investors do not know the average evaluation, they must all guess by how much they must discount the price of the share to compensate for the estimated bias in the price that results from their behaviour in the aggregate.

This brings us to the question of risk-averse behaviour. As Lachmann argues, in situations of uncertainty, expectations will generally not take the form of point predictions. We have already suggested that expectations with relatively wider inner intervals might be regarded as relatively more risky, from the perspective of the individual investor. Differences in riskiness will generally be reflected in differences in investors' valuations of shares, the normal case being that risk-averse actors discount projects that involve greater risk. What we have already said about the complexity of the relation between expectations and the price of a share, now seen to reflect rough judgement of and adjustment for risk, is given further force. The proportion of risk averters and risk lovers in market segments may also change, moreover, again leading to changes in the diversity of opinion.[16]

Yet the picture is still far from complete. In the first place, it is important to distinguish between what are generally regarded as 'blue chips' on the one hand, and 'non-blue chips' as covering the rest on the other. Miller's framework seems to be most relevant for the non-blue-chip category, since short selling opportunities do normally exist in the case of blue chips. Moreover, such shares are carefully watched by large numbers of financial analysts with vast financial resources at their command. This is not to suggest that the markets in such shares will not show a diversity in opinion, but that the possible impact of new information on the number of investors analysing the share relative to the number of shares outstanding appears to be much less relevant in the case of blue chips, in particular when the possibility of short selling is taken into account. It appears, then, that Miller's framework provides a possible explanation of the relative pricing of non-blue chips on the one hand, and blue chips and bonds on the other (bonds serve as a benchmark in Miller's portfolio investment decision).

This brings us to the temporal features of Miller's analysis and, in particular, that his share-issuing company has a very short life with a definite terminal date at which assets are liquidated. In practice, of course, equity investment differs from this in two important ways. In the first place, shares have an indefinite life-expectation. And second, shares are traded on liquid securities markets, institutions that serve to provide liquidity to the (portfolio) investor. These institutional factors have wide-ranging implications. First off, they permit the investment horizon of the individual portfolio investor to depart from the life span of the particular company involved. The type of commitment that the portfolio investor enters into when buying shares is therefore very different from the range of commitments that the management of the firm is setting up in order to generate the cash flows that represent what the portfolio investor is ultimately interested in. Whereas the firm is to some extent stuck with its physical capital once this has been acquired and/or produced (and has many other commitments that cannot be easily dissolved), investment in equities is *liquid* from the viewpoint of the investor and may be dissolved at any time. It follows that the portfolio investor is generally not concerned with the proceeds of liquidating the company, but with the possible proceeds of selling his or her stake in the company as an ongoing concern. And this in turn means that the investor also has to take into account what the likely price of the share will be in the future.

An important consequence of all this is that market participants may rationally show little concern with attempting to assess the 'real' prospects of the share. Instead they might try to anticipate how new information may affect other investors' evaluations of the share, and what the likely effect on the price will be. It is of course Keynes, more than anyone else, who stresses that securities markets organised to provide liquidity provide an incentive – undesirable from the social point of view – for investors to focus less on the factors that govern the yield of the real investment over its whole life, than on anticipating changes in the share price before the market. Keynes's famous beauty contest parable describes the outcome of behaviour directed at anticipating 'what average opinion expects the average opinion to be'. The notion of the 'average evaluation', far from reflecting the wisdom of the market, then takes on an entirely different hue. Keynes refers to securities prices so determined as the 'conventional valuation'. In situations in which everyone is trying to anticipate the anticipations of others, new information, which might have precious little to do with the real prospects of the investment, may cause violent changes in the conventional valuation.

We have taken Miller's framework as a general starting point in our discussion. How does what we have said so far relate to Lachmann's notion of equity prices emerging out of a balance of divergent (bulls' and bears') expectations? Clearly we cannot do much more than scratch the surface of the issue in the space available. Accordingly, we shall simply remark on some of the relevant issues, drawing on Keynes's analysis of the 'two views' or 'bull–bear' position in his *Treatise on Money* (1971) and his concepts of the own rate of interest and 'liquidity premium' in the *General Theory* (1973). We begin with investors' beliefs about future price movements, keeping questions about the diversity of opinion in the background. We then briefly return to the diversity of opinion in the section on own rates of interest.

The bull–bear position

Keynes defines a 'bear' as one 'who prefers at the moment to avoid securities and lend cash, and correspondingly a "bull" [as] one who prefers to hold securities and to borrow cash – the former anticipating that securities will fall in cash value and the latter that they will rise' (Keynes 1971: 224). In his *Treatise on Money*, the portfolio decision is simplified to a choice between bank deposits (or more precisely, 'savings deposits') and securities (where no further distinction is made between shares and bonds). As in the later *General Theory* (Keynes 1973), the portfolio decision is not an 'all or nothing' choice. Rather, investors tend to hold a proportion of their wealth in the form of 'savings deposits A', which are not highly unstable over the short period. The bear position shows up in the form of the proportion of wealth held in 'savings deposits B', which are unstable. However, as Keynes points out, bearish beliefs do not necessarily have to be expressed through the banking system, but may be expressed outside it (through direct lending to the money market or the Stock Exchange, for instance, or through short selling). The point to note here is that Keynes allows bearish beliefs to be reflected in changes in the size and possibly the composition of the banking system's balance sheet. (In the *General Theory*, in contrast, all institutional detail is suppressed and the whole effect of changes in beliefs is necessarily on security prices, given that the stock of money, that is the size of the banking system's balance sheet, is constant by assumption.)

To begin with, in the *Treatise on Money* bearish views on the part of the public may have *no* effect on securities prices where these views are compensated by the banking system taking the opposite view and buying the securities. An alternative possible case of divergent beliefs mentioned by Keynes occurs when 'two views' develop within the public. Whilst in the former case the banking system and the public hold opposing views, and the effect of a change in beliefs about future prices may be reflected partly in security prices and partly in changes in the size of the banking system's balance sheet, in the latter case changes in the size of the banking system's balance sheet do not necessarily require the banking system to take a particular view. Rather it may simply provide additional short-term advances to the 'bulls' who buy securities from the 'bears' who end up holding more 'savings deposits B'. Keynes finds that *both* 'bull' and 'bear' markets may occur with either convergent or divergent expectations about future prices. For instance, in the case of a bull market with convergent expectations, bears are closing their positions on a rising market and the volume of savings deposits B falls. In a bull market with divergent expectations, in contrast, bears may be increasing their positions on a rising market. To repeat, the size of the banking system's balance sheet (and the amount of savings deposits B provided) may change either because the banking system itself is taking a view on securities prices or because it decides to facilitate the changing degree of divergence of beliefs within the public, where the public may also take recourse to channels outside the banking system.

Keynes (1971: 225) ventures that both the volume of financial transactions and the size of bear positions are 'likely to be phenomena of rapidly *changing* prices rather than of an absolutely high or low level'. The volatility of prices, for instance, may reflect contradictory information that becomes available and increases the diversity of beliefs about future prices. In addition, Keynes mentions the possibility of speculative excesses leading to what we would now call 'bubbles'. He finds that such a development may be related in its final stage to beliefs about future prices that have diverged widely, with abrupt falls in security prices resolving the tension between opposing views.

Keynes's 'bull–bear' analysis goes beyond Miller's in that it permits short selling[17] and takes into account the 'conventional' behaviour of investors on markets that have been organised to provide liquidity. Furthermore, whereas Miller focuses on a single (non-blue chip) share, Keynes's general equilibrium analysis is meant to explain the core of interest rates in general. In its simplified form in the *General Theory*, the amount of liquidity is taken as given and securities prices alone (bonds and blue chip shares) have to adjust to bring forth a bear position of equal and unchanged size. The point to note is that although these prices represent a crucial segment of the structure of demand prices for existing assets, they do not reveal anything in particular about the different considerations and beliefs that affect investors' individual valuations. Keynes's notion of 'own rates of interest' sheds some light on these matters, and it is to this which we now turn.

Own rates of interest and the liquidity premium

Keynes defines the total return on any asset measured in terms of itself as the sum of $q - c + l$, where q is the risk-adjusted yield, c the carrying cost and l the liquidity premium. The liquidity premium on an asset is not a pecuniary return, but a reflection of the potential convenience or security that the power of disposal over that asset during some period offers (Keynes 1973: 226). To compare the returns of different assets, changes in their relative values a over some period must also be considered, and, expressed in some common measure, the total return on an asset is then the sum of $q - c + l + a$. An overall portfolio equilibrium requires, first, that all existing assets are held by someone and, second, that every portfolio investor is happy with the composition of his or her portfolio at the current structure of asset prices. Clearly, such an equilibrium is compatible with investors holding different beliefs about the structure of relative returns and their components on different kinds of assets.

According to Keynes, the crucial point is that money, being liquid *par excellence*, bears the highest liquidity premium and consequently stands at the core of the structure of own rates. The difference between the liquidity premium attaching to any particular asset relative to money must be compensated by either an excess in the net yield $q - c$ over money, by its expected rate of appreciation a, or both. Again, investors may differ in their estimates of both these terms, as they may differ in terms of their

assessments of the risk attaching to those estimates and their attitudes towards risk. This means that heterogeneous investors may
attach the same monetary value to an asset on the basis of quite
different combinations (and values) of the terms that enter into
their calculations. As before, no general statement can be made
about how new information might affect asset prices. Take the
special case of trading at unchanged prices, for instance, which may
occur when investors assess new information differently. These
differences may impact on any of the values of the terms entering
into the own rates calculus, and beliefs (and attitudes) may be
diverging in one respect and converging in another. In the extreme
case, prices may change without any transactions taking place at all
(which does not imply that beliefs about any of the relevant terms
remain unchanged).

But an additional complexity has now entered. Keynes relates the
liquidity premium to the notion of *confidence*, uncertainty or doubt
about the general economic climate at the systemic level that may
have no particular connection with the prospects of any particular
asset concerned. Changes in the state of confidence will, he argues,
be reflected in the size of the liquidity premium attaching to money
and other relatively liquid assets (Bibow 1998). While investors
may have very different views on the relative liquidity premia on
different types of assets, and may change their views in different
ways in the light of new information in this respect as well, what he
calls a 'crisis of confidence' will be characterised by a general 'flight
into liquidity'. Again, changes in the state of confidence, with their
associated impact on the relative liquidity premiums attaching to
different kinds of assets, may occur with or without changes in
beliefs in respect of any of the other elements entering into the own
rates of interest calculus.

Conclusion

We have attempted to provide an interpretation of Lachmann's
distinction between convergent and divergent expectations,
building on his conception of expectations as imagined price intervals. This interpretation was then used in a discussion of the idea
that equity prices emerge out of a 'balance' of divergent expectations. Two principal complications were introduced, the impact on
the price of equities of their effective supply relative to the number
of market participants (holders and non-holders) valuing them, and
that the value that market participants attach to equities generally

depends on considerations over and above anticipated future prices and/or yields.

These factors make it difficult to say much that is definite about the relation between expectations and the course of equity prices. In fact, on the argument we have been developing, it is possible that divergent expectations about the future price of a share may lead to a corresponding *reduction* in the diversity of opinion about its 'correct' value (if, for example, the impact of such expectations on equity valuations are offset by changes in perceptions of, and attitudes towards, risk and ambiguity, liquidity, confidence and so on). We have accordingly proposed that attention be directed at how heterogeneous market partici- pants value a share, beginning with the situation in which both holders and non-holders are content with their current position on that share. This provides a sensible point of entry for the explana- tion of equity prices, that is, for an analysis that proceeds by beginning with existing equity prices and spelling out the possible factors that give rise to and govern them.[18] One of these factors, clearly an important and often dominant one, is the divergence of expectations in Lachmann's sense. We have merely taken the opportunity to draw attention to a few more.

Notes

1 Lachmann (1977: 72). Clearly the definiteness, scope and detail of the 'mental pictures' he has in mind will depend on the situation in which they are arrived at, the relative importance of the 'plan' in the actor's scheme of things, as well as the information available to and the powers of imagination of the actor concerned. In the context of stock market transactions, and as the passage quoted in the introduction suggests, the focus of attention will generally be on the return on equi- ties, which depend on estimates and assessments of the possible factors that may affect the future flow of dividends and future prices.

2 Lachmann is curiously reticent as regards the nature and structure of the expectations he has in mind even in his important essay on 'The role of expectations in economics as a social science' (reprinted in Lachmann 1977).

3 Lachmann does not specify what he means by 'forces'. We shall substi- tute the term 'tendency' where this will be understood as a causal power that would bring about some specified phenomenon under certain conditions (Lawson 1994a).

4 Lachmann considers and rejects the main alternatives then available: Shackle's (1949) theory of 'potential surprise' and the practice of reducing well-defined probability distributions to certainty equiva- lents. He would therefore presumably also reject the modern version of

the certainty equivalent assumption: the practice of reducing expectations to the expected value of some utility function, where the beliefs about future 'states of the world' are represented by a conditional probability measure that corresponds either to an objective probability law (rational expectations) or to a subjective probability measure.

5 Lachmann points out that prices that move into the outer range will attract the attention of the 'more thoughtful' market operators:

> The mere fact that in spite of heavy 'speculative' pressure encountered near the limits of the inner range, and engendered by inelastic expectations and the sense of the 'normality' of the inner range, price could pass these limits at all is a pointer of the strength of the forces which must have carried it past such formidable obstacles. Such a move can hardly be due to random causes.
>
> (Lachmann 1978: 31)

6 For example:

> To coordinate bullish and bearish expectations is, as Keynes showed, the economic function of the Stock Exchange and of asset markets in general. This is achieved because in such markets the price will move until the whole market is divided into equal halves of bulls and bears. In this way divergent expectations are cast into a coherent pattern and a measure of coordination is accomplished.
>
> (Lachmann 1976: 59)

7 Lachmann does not say anything about how the actor may respond to differences in the width of the imagined price intervals (the analogue, in the present context, to the actor's attitude towards risk in expected utility theory). In general it seems that shares that are perceived as more risky in the present sense will be discounted relative to those that are perceived as less risky, that is, that actors are generally risk averse.

8 The boundary between the inner and outer intervals is seldom likely to be a hard-and-fast one, for example, and is likely to be more or less vague at different times. As in the case of differences in perceived risk and risk aversion, differences in ambiguity and attitudes to ambiguity may affect the value investors attach to shares. It is interesting to note in this context that Shackle's theory of potential surprise may be regarded as a generalisation of the Practical Range approach. The difference is that on Shackle's theory there is a continuous gradation of intervals, the outer limits of each bearing some degree of 'potential surprise'.

9 The average evaluation need not be the 'correct' evaluation in the sense of being that which corresponds to the 'fundamentals' of the economy (if such things as fundamentals exist).

10 This is no more than the familiar 'winner's curse', an informal discussion of which appears in Kreps (1990: 83–7).

11 Putting it another way, the share will always be held by a small fraction of the potential investors in the market. Miller simplifies the

analysis by limiting each investor to one share, thereby avoiding questions about the relative size of each individual investor's holding of the share. This assumption does not substantially affect the argument.

12 Save for a few special cases discussed below.

13 Short selling would of course also shift the supply curve to the right by increasing the effective supply of the share.

14 This may often, but not necessarily, be the consequence of expectations about future prices or yields converging in Lachmann's sense (see the section on own rates of interest below).

15 In fact this is a limiting case in which trade occurs at an unchanged price and the diversity of opinion, though changing at the individual level, is neither decreasing nor increasing in the aggregate. More generally, trading at an unchanged price could also occur in all cases in which the slope and the position of the demand curve change in an exactly offsetting way. This includes cases where opinion is either converging (the demand curve flattening out while shifting upwards) or diverging (the demand curve steepening while shifting downwards).

16 Much of what we have said about risk and risk aversion applies in the same way in the case of ambiguity.

17 Modern futures and options exchanges can be subsumed without much difficulty.

18 Readers familiar with the emerging literature on Critical Realism will recognise this as an example of the retroductive mode of argument that it advocates (see Lawson 1994b).

References

Bibow, J. (1998) 'On Keynesian theories of liquidity preference', *The Manchester School*, 66: 238–73.

Keynes, J. M. (1971) *Treatise on Money*, vol. 1. *The Collected Writings of John Maynard Keynes*, vol. V, London: Macmillan.

——(1973) *The General Theory. The Collected Writings of John Maynard Keynes*, vol. VII, London: Macmillan.

Kreps, D. M. (1990) *Game Theory and Economic Modelling*, Oxford: The Clarendon Press.

Lachmann, L. M. (1976) 'From Mises to Shackle: an essay on Austrian economics and the Kaleidic Society', *Journal of Economic Literature*, 14: 54–62.

—— (1977) *Capital, Expectations, and the Market Process*, Kansas City: Sheed Andrews and McMeel, Inc.

—— (1978) *Capital and Its Structure*, 2nd edn, Kansas City: Sheed Andrews and McMeel, Inc. (1st edn 1956).

Lange, O. (1944) *Price Flexibility and Employment*, Bloomington: Principia Press.

Lawson, T. (1994a) 'Tendencies', unpublished manuscript, Cambridge: Cambridge University.

—— (1994b) 'A realist theory for economics', in R. E. Backhouse (ed.) *New Directions in Economic Methodology*, London: Routledge, pp. 257–85.

Miller, E. M. (1977) 'Risk, uncertainty and divergence of opinion', *The Journal of Finance*, 32: 1151–68.

Shackle, G. L. S. (1949) *Expectations in Economics*, Cambridge: Cambridge University Press.

INDEX